D0991218

NEITHER PEACE NOR HONOR

Studies in International Affairs Number 24

Studies in International Affairs Number 24

NEITHER PEACE NOR HONOR

The Politics of American Military Policy in Viet-Nam

by
Robert L. Gallucci

The Washington Center of Foreign Policy Research
School of Advanced International Studies

The Johns Hopkins University Press
Baltimore and London

Manufactured in the United States of America.

The Johns Hopkins University Press, Baltimore, Maryland 21218
The Johns Hopkins University Press Ltd., London

Library of Congress Catalog Card Number 74-24949
ISBN 0-8018-1682-3 (clothbound edition)
ISBN 0-8018-1714-5 (paperbound edition)

Library of Congress Cataloging in Publication data will be found on the last page of this book.

In memory of
Ashley L. Schiff

CONTENTS

ACKNOWLEDGMENTS

Since this book grew out of a Ph.D. dissertation that was completed at Brandeis University, I owe much to that institution and the teachers who taught me. I am especially grateful to two, Robert Art and Kenneth Waltz, both of whom suffered through early drafts of this manuscript and offered most useful criticism as well as encouragement.

A Brookings Institution Research Fellowship supported me in my early research in Washington, D.C., and Leslie Gelb, then a Senior Fellow of the Institution, was particularly helpful in guiding me toward the most fruitful sources for my research. A Rockefeller Foundation Fellowship granted through the Washington Center of Foreign Policy Research gave me the opportunity to revise and prepare the final manuscript.

Of those who read the manuscript in one form or another, I want especially to thank Mac Destler, Robert Jervis, George Kelly, and Morton Halperin, all of whom provided detailed and substantial criticisms of the text. The burden of responsibility for the final product, however, rests entirely with the author.

Writing a book can be a painful undertaking at times. When it is, those who are close to the one doing the writing inevitably share fully in the pain of the thing, but much less so in whatever rewards may follow. I want to thank and acknowledge the help of Adele King who did indeed share the pain, and without whom I never would have finished.

* * *

Although the author is currently assigned to the Arms Control and Disarmament Agency, the views expressed in this book are his own and do not necessarily represent those of any agency of the United States government.

LIST OF ABBREVIATIONS

ARVN	Army of the Republic of [South] Viet-Nam
BLT	Battalion Landing Team
CAP	Combined Action Companies and Platoons
CHICOM	Chinese Communist
CIA	Central Intelligence Agency
CINCPAC	Commander in Chief, Pacific
CIP	Counter-Insurgency Plan
COIN	Counterinsurgency
COMUSMACV	Commander, U.S. Military Assistance Command, Viet-Nam
CTZ	Corps Tactical Zone
DIA	Defense Intelligence Agency
DPM	Draft Presidential Memorandum
DRV	Democratic Republic of [North] Viet-Nam
GVN	Government of [South] Viet-Nam
IDA	Institute for Defense Analysis
INR	Bureau of Intelligence and Research in the State Department
ISA	Office of International Security Affairs in the Defense Department
JCS	Joint Chiefs of Staff
JCSM	Joint Chiefs of Staff Memorandum
LOC	Lines of communications
MAF	Marine Amphibious Force
MAAG	Military Assistance Advisory Group
MEB	Marine Expeditionary Brigade
NIE	National Intelligence Estimate
NSA	National Security Agency
NSAM	National Security Action Memorandum
NSC	National Security Council
NVA	North Vietnamese Army
OSD	Office of the Secretary of Defense
PAVN	People's Army of [North] Viet-Nam
POL	Petroleum, oil, lubricants
ROK	Republic of South Korea
RT	Rolling Thunder Program

SAC	Strategic Air Command
SACSA	Special Assistant [to the JCS] for Counter insurgency and Special Activities
SEA	Southeast Asia
SNIE	Special National Intelligence Estimate
SVN	South Viet-Nam
TAOR	Tactical Area of Responsibility
USIB	United States Intelligence Board
USSBS	United States Strategic Bombing Survey
VC	Viet Cong

I. INTRODUCTION

There used to be a conventional wisdom about how Viet-Nam happened. Until fairly recently it was argued by some observers, and accepted by most of the rest, that America had slipped into Viet-Nam or, perhaps more accurately, that it had sunk into Viet-Nam over a period of time. The United States was portrayed as a nation that had become entangled and enmeshed in a war in a small alien country while trying to save a friendly regime. The involvement seemed to increase slowly each time the previous effort proved to be inadequate. Policy makers were confounded but went ahead expecting the next increment of aid to be the last. An especially important part of the image was that America be understood as trying all along, and more vigorously as time went on, to extricate itself from involvement as soon as it could be done reasonably in a politically practical fashion. Unfortunately, the longer the United States stayed the harder it became to leave and the deeper it sank. The country's predicament seemed to be the result of ignorance, misperception, and misunderstanding, all of which in time contributed to an ill-founded and ill-fated optimism on the part of the leaders and their advisors. They led the country deeper into war because they were misled about the war. In a sense, the United States was seduced into Viet-Nam. There are many variations on the theme, but Arthur Schlesinger's *Bitter Heritage* may be taken as a representative account of this perspective.[1]

There is another and more recent interpretation of how Viet-Nam happened, and partly because of the credibility of its advocates, it might be thought of as the new conventional wisdom. According to this second interpretation the United States neither slipped nor sunk into Viet-Nam; it was not seduced, and it did not find itself deeply involved because it miscalculated or misjudged the chance of success. Rather, it is argued, the United States intervened in Viet-Nam in order that that country not be "lost," and although the United States increased its commitment as necessary to prevent the loss of Viet-Nam, it was never unrealistically optimistic about the effects of the next increment. American leaders were always deliberately choosing to pay the cost, and have others pay as well, in order to avoid a dreaded outcome and its expected consequences. This interpretation has been put forth most forcefully by Leslie H. Gelb and Daniel Ellsberg. Gelb was the director of the study task force that produced the Defense Department history of United States decision making in Viet-Nam, commonly known as the *Pentagon Papers*. Ellsberg was one of the authors and the person most responsible for their de facto declassification. Gelb and Ellsberg presumably reached their conclusions independently and at least partially from the documents and analysis of the *Pentagon Papers*.[2]

The Gelb-Ellsberg characterization of the course of American policy in Viet-Nam is intriguing because it seems at first to be paradoxical. That is, if decision makers were not optimistic but genuinely pessimistic about the chances of success, why did they continue with the policy, throwing good money after bad, American living after American dead? The answer appears to be that, as costly as the war was, successive administrations perceived the costs of losing as still greater and the risk of attempting clear military victory as unacceptable. The resulting policy was therefore one of doing what was "minimally necessary," as Gelb put it, to avoid losing. What makes the argument still more interesting is that neither analyst finds the expected international cost to the United States to have been the primary concern of the American presidents, or at least no more of a concern than the anticipated domestic cost. Just as surely as presidents perceived a communist threat to Viet-Nam in terms of the potential loss of influence in Southeast Asia, the possible precedent for future Soviet or Chinese advances, and the weakening of European confidence in the American commitment, they also saw a domestic threat to their party, their policies, and themselves which needed to be met.

The argument is a reasonable one; the point both authors make about the importance of domestic politics in this matter of international politics is especially well taken. Presidents Kennedy and Johnson saw grave electoral consequences ahead if the Viet-Nam conflict were resolved badly—in any way seeming like a defeat. As the conflict wore on and America increased its investment, the salience of the war as a national political issue also increased, heightening the costs and risks for the president. It is possible that Kennedy and Johnson misconstrued the extent to which they and their party would actually suffer from the outcome in Southeast Asia. They may therefore have felt themselves more restricted in the conduct of the war than was necessary. That is possible, but even if it were true, it would not have reduced the stakes of the game as they saw them, and it also would not have reduced the importance of domestic politics as a causal factor.

There is a considerable difference between the two interpretations: whether we sunk or jumped into Viet-Nam—and the difference makes a difference. Anyone interested in understanding and evaluating this tragic episode in American foreign policy, especially in order to learn from it, must choose carefully between these interpretations or among others that might be put forth. Daniel Ellsberg, for one, would like to show that policy makers neither stumbled blindly into Viet-Nam nor were they seduced at critical points of decision by misinformed advisors who promised quick success. He would like to show this at least in part in order to remove the comfortable image of "America-as-victim" in Southeast Asia. He believes the quagmire image removes, or at least diminishes, responsibility and culpability for decisions having to do with the war. He argues persuasively that the first interpretation of Viet-Nam prevailed to some extent because it was more comfortable to think of our activity in Southeast Asia as a mistake committed by well-meaning but ignorant policy makers, incapable of changing or seeing the necessity of changing the course of events. Embracing this interpretation becomes a morally self-serving act for all Americans.

Quite apart from the implications of this interpretation for the accountability of decision makers, it also has consequences for the kinds of lessons we learn and the prescription for future policy that we extract. If United States policy in Viet-Nam is judged in some degree to have been a failure, the characterization of the way we became involved is relevant to suggestions about how to avoid making similar mistakes in the future. It is this concern to which Leslie Gelb addresses himself in a section of his argument entitled "Where Do We Go from Here?"

> If Viet-Nam were a story of how the system failed, that is, if our leaders did not do what they wanted to do or if they did not realize what they were doing or what was happening it would be easy to package a large and assorted box of policy-making panaceas. For example: fix the method of reporting from the field. Fix the way progress is measured in a guerrilla war. Make sure the President sees all the alternatives. But these are all third-order issues, because the U.S. political-bureaucratic system did not fail, it worked.[3]

And that is the point for Gelb: the foreign policy system of the United States worked when it produced policy for Viet-Nam, that is, it did what policy-making systems are supposed to do. His prescription, appropriate for a malady that afflicts not the process by which policy is made but the premise from which it proceeds, is to suggest a change in the definition of what is vital to American security in the world and a change in the American public's image of the nature of the communist threat. Cold war-style thinking about international politics by presidents and their advisors and the projection of cold war values onto the American public to produce an expected negative response to disengagement were responsible for United States involvement in Viet-Nam. The problem was with the premises of policy and that is what must be corrected.

Looking for Another Interpretation

The analyses of Gelb and Ellsberg must be taken seriously, but they need not be taken as definitive. In fact, in some ways the interpretation they offer is quite unsatisfactory. They would have us believe that the foreign-policy-making system worked well, providing leaders with information, generating alternatives for consideration, and executing decisions with precision. If in retrospect we see policies as somehow inadequate, we are to assume that deficiencies were a function of the premises upon which presidents based their choice rather than, for example, the manner in which their choice was structured. In moving us away from an image of American presidents blindly slipping into a morass, Gelb and Ellsberg have brought us to another, of our leaders fatalistically marching themselves and their countrymen, like lemmings, into the sea.

In thinking about this it is difficult not to wonder how American presidents could have held to such an unsuccessful policy for such a very long time. That is, even if we join those who do not see American involvement in Viet-Nam as a case of misplaced optimism and who believe that the use of military force was at some point calculated to be a strategy to bring about the "least worst outcome," it is appropriate to question how that calculation, and the premises upon which it was based, could be sustained for so long in the face of such mounting costs. Did anyone question the policy of military intervention at the start? Were alternative definitions of the situation in Southeast Asia offered? Were military and political options continually examined and rejected for what most would agree were legitimate reasons? Or might the course of policy be better understood if a less "rational" pursuit of objectives were assumed, if policies were to some degree thought a function of processes of choice that undercut rationality? In other words, perhaps the specter of American policy makers behaving like lemmings would fade away if the context of decision making were understood, if one took into account such factors as the progressive narrowing of the range of options perceived as legitimate, the peculiar flow of advice and support around the president, and the bureaucratic and political momentum of policy once initiated. It is the question "How could Viet-Nam continue to happen?" that may lead us to a more complex interpretation of events.

If the persistence of policy appears to demand a more substantive explanation, so it would seem does the conduct of policy. The Viet-Nam war is not a single event to be accounted for but a series of events that happened one way rather than another. That the war was conducted as it was is a matter of intrinsic importance because of the consequences of success or failure of the policy. It is, beyond that, a matter relevant to a broader conception of "how it happened" because revealing the pressures on policy makers to choose among instruments of policy will inevitably expose more of their motivations for choosing among policies. And if we go a step further, the more incongruous and inappropriate the means chosen for achieving their stated objectives appear, the more complex and extraordinary we may expect the set of calculations confronting American leaders to have been. The means to our ends in Viet-Nam have of course been characterized as incongruous and inappropriate. So if we also ask the question "Why did Viet-Nam come to happen the way it did?" we will again have to look past the premises of the Gelb-Ellsberg interpretation to find more evidence for another interpretation of why it happened at all.

Another Interpretation: Looking to the System

The direction of the argument here is backward, toward "the system" that has previously been exonerated. The partial dissatisfaction with an explanation that focuses on the premises of decisions leads to a broader explanation that includes the process of decision making. The focus of the analysis that is to follow is on the link between the way the system worked and the outcomes that it produced. Evaluation of the system is not the objective, although implicit throughout will be the proposition that the system was not working. In the end we can and ought to address ourselves to the question of evaluation, since we will be able to be precise about what is meant by failure and so adjust prescriptions for future policy accordingly. A position in opposition to that of Gelb's may then seem most appropriate. Before doing that, we must clearly establish the way process and content were related in key decisions of the Viet-Nam years.

The foreign-policy-making system, like any system, includes entities that interact. A description of the functioning of a system amounts to the specification of how the entities are related to one another. The more precisely relations are specified and the better the descriptions of what is going on can be, the more accurately changes at one point may be deduced from changes at another, and the clearer our understanding of the process will be. The foreign-policy-making system includes just those entities one would expect it to include: the president and his White House advisors, the National Security Council and its staff, the heads and members on the Departments of Defense and State, the intelligence agencies, and members of Congress—as a body, as committee members, and as individuals. Others who are without government affiliation but who have associations with those who do have formal authority also act as participants in the system. In some instances, in order to explain outcomes, it will be useful to talk of organizations as acting, but often disaggregation will be necessary. The Office of the Secretary of Defense (OSD) will have to be separated from the military in the Department of Defense and the chief of one service from the chief of another. Specifying the entities in the system, or the foreign-policy actors, involves some ambiguity, but it is not nearly as difficult as trying to state how they relate to each other. Actors are motivated by much that they share with others and by much that is unique to their position. The system is understood by all to exist in order to produce and execute a foreign policy that is in the best interest of the nation, but individuals and organizations in the system have different responsibilities and incentives and therefore perceive and define the national interest in different ways. The president is one actor among many, though an exceptionally powerful one. Conflict is inherent in the system; so is compromise. Relations are political within and between bureaucracies in spite of formal lines of authority. The structure of relations changes over time and especially from one administration to another; within one administration the power and influence of one actor will vary from one issue to another. The way entities in the system relate is complex and therefore so is the process by which policy is made.

That is all that needs to be said about the system for now, and though it is not much, it must be taken to heart. If it is not, and if we focus only on the president, as it is common to do, what follows will make little sense and hardly be worth the effort. A useful, if somewhat extreme, starting assumption would be that the president makes foreign policy only in the sense that a customer in a restaurant makes dinner when he orders his food: he chooses from a limited menu prepared by the establishment and usually must accept the interpretation of his choice as it is reflected in the execution of his order. That is to say, he "makes" it hardly at all, though those dining with him are likely to hold him responsible for the choice if they are made to consume it also. Such is the nature of foreign policy and the burden of presidents. Much more needs to be said about the power of the presidency and the nature of the foreign-policy-making system, and both will be addressed in a more precise and analytical fashion in the concluding chapter.

The Viet-Nam Decisions

The decisions on which the analysis will focus and to which we will shortly turn are essentially those involving the increase of American military presence in Viet-Nam and the determination of how the military instrument should be used. We begin with the Kennedy administration since it was in the period between 1961 and 1963 that the United States embarked upon a new level of commitment in Viet-Nam—commitment, at least in the sense of physical presence—and did so in the midst of considerable internal debate. Because of the nature of the debate, the availability of the record, and the importance of the decisions, it is a good period in which to try to relate governmental interaction before decisions were taken to the substance of the decisions after they were made. The central issue at that time was the nature and level of assistance to be extended to South Viet-Nam and, by 1963, the role the United States should play in a coming coup d'état. The narration of events is designed to highlight the policy options made available to the president and the positions of actors who advocated them. In each case presidential choices during the period are related to the exchanges and debate in the system. This will constitute the first part of the argument about the way process is related to content.

The working of the foreign-policy-making system in the next two years, treated in chapter 3, contrasts sharply with the earlier period. Debate throughout 1964 appeared constricted and choice limited. There was ultimately a consensus to begin the bombing of North Viet-Nam in early 1965, but it was an illusory one. The reasons why it developed and how it was transformed into substantive decisions turn out to be linked to the diversity of interests and motivations of the actors in the policy system and their relations with the president and also to the special appeal of the air power option. By taking chapters 2 and 3 together, by juxtaposing the policy process and policies of one administration with another, the imprint of the system on the course of policy will begin to take shape.

The next two chapters deal with the sustained bombing of the north and the conduct of the ground strategy in the south. In these chapters the task is to account for the particular and peculiar nature of the military strategy and then to explain the tenacious commitment to the strategy over a period of time and in the face of solid, substantive criticism and mounting internal opposition. In both cases the explanation depends upon an understanding of the special interests and motives of the military organizations as actors in the system. If we can relate military and civilian overseers in the Defense Department, and both to the president, three years of military strategy in Viet-Nam that might otherwise defy comprehension becomes comprehensible within the limited rationality of the bureaucratic–political system.

The four chapters about Viet-Nam policy making provide the basis for the final chapter's analysis and conclusions. The wider issue of American involvement in the period between 1961 to 1965, together with the critical operational decisions considered from 1965 through 1967, produces some broadly based explanations. As a result it becomes possible in the conclusion to speak not only to the question with which we began the analysis—"How could Viet-Nam continue to happen?"—but also to the larger issue of the way the foreign-policy-making process is related to foreign policy in America. It is the larger issue that leads to a discussion of the theoretical framework underlying much of the analysis of the preceding chapters. The theory, or model, or paradigm, or set of suggestive propositions—depending upon one's enthusiasm and one's methodological propensities—is generally known as bureaucratic politics.[4] The discussion in the final chapter is intended to be a critical examination of this style of analysis in order to draw from it the most useful inferences for understanding the way policy is made.

There is no attempt in this book to provide a complete history of events for the seven-year period. The focus is on a number of decisions made in Washington for Viet-Nam military policy and on how those decisions were executed. Neither the place of Viet-Nam within the spectrum of post–World War II American foreign policy nor its significance in contemporary international politics is considered. The regional issues, the Vietnamese, Chinese, and Soviet perspectives on the war, are not mentioned. The whole subject of diplomatic negotiations conducted during the conflict is essentially ignored, and the critically important legal and moral questions raised by the Viet-Nam War are left outside the scope of the study.

To a large extent the analysis that follows will be about what went wrong with American policy in Viet-Nam. In trying to explain the causes of various inadequacies, however, there is a danger that the discussion will be misconstrued. It may appear that the analysis is aimed at proving that certain policies were failures, proving that the Viet-Nam involvement was actually unnecessary, or that the strategies of bombing and counterinsurgency do not work. That is not the object since this is neither a study of what are appropriate American security interests in the world nor a study of the effectiveness of strategic bombing or land warfare tactics. It would be more accurate to say that decisions that initially involved the United States in Viet-Nam militarily are *assumed* to have been unfortunate and explanations are sought for them, while specific military policies pursued in Viet-Nam are *demonstrated* not to have been consistent with stated objectives and an attempt is made to account for their continued implementation. In other words, the argument that Viet-Nam was an unwise entanglement for America is taken for granted, and it is the process of entanglement that is addressed. At the same time, arguments that all bombing campaigns are ineffective or that counterinsurgencies cannot be won are put aside, while the proposition is addressed that the particular air and ground strategies that were chosen were less consistent with the commonly understood objectives than they should have been, given the information available to all participants at the time.

There are reasons for defining the task this way. The larger argument about Viet-Nam and the national interest has been addressed extensively by others, and a reasonably strong case has been made, I think, that the involvement was an error. We proceed from that point to why the error was made. As for retreating from drawing conclusions about the effectiveness of bombing or counterinsurgency, we are limited in making inferences about other cases by the special circumstances of Viet-Nam. Conclusions certainly should be drawn from the experience. Indeed, one of the points to be made is that past experience was not the guide it should have been when Viet-Nam operations were conducted. We can say, for example, that the bombing of North Viet-Nam from 1965 through 1968 was a miserable, costly failure, but that is not to say that the later bombings of the north undertaken by the Nixon administration could not have substantially contributed to stated American objectives, at least in the short run. Circumstances changed. The argument some would like to make, that air power is an utterly ineffective instrument of war, is usually based on grounds that proponents of air power might consider legitimate: effectiveness rather than morality. Unfortunately, overstating or misstating the case against bombing does not help the legal-moral argument, but it does weaken the real political-military case that can be made. The point is that questions of effectiveness have to do with certain specific claims for air power's ability to act on an enemy's will and capabilities, and the experience of Viet-Nam and earlier wars can help provide evidence. We must be cautious, however, about what we learn and about the morals we find.

The most useful conclusions that can be drawn from Viet-Nam will be those that form the basis for prescription. The prescription may be of the kind that has to do with manipulating the way policy is made and executed in order to improve it, or it may be of the kind that has nothing to do with changing anything except expectations. In his study of coercive diplomacy Alexander George makes the following observation:

> . . . Efforts to impose the requirements of careful crisis management on the use of military force often exacerbate the latent tensions between competing political and military considerations in limited warfare. Crisis management requires novel concepts of military planning, operations, and control that strain the experience, imagination, and patience of military professionals. The civilians' effort to transform military force into a highly refined discriminating instrument suitable for effective management of crises eventually breaks down if pushed too far.[5]

When we have looked at the sources of foreign policy in the way we do in this study, the difficulties encountered in controlling policy should become even clearer than they might otherwise have been. At the very least we may find more evidence to support George's conclusion. But we may also go further and conclude that we should hold even lower expectations about the possibility of controlling such events—that real pessimism should condition the attitudes of those considering the limited use of force as an instrument of foreign policy.

II. CONFLICT, DISSENT, AND MODERATION: 1961–63

It was during the Kennedy administration that the United States established a significant military presence in Southeast Asia. To be sure most of the U.S. army personnel that were introduced were officially advisors to the South Vietnamese military, but just as surely whatever American commitment to South Viet-Nam existed before was undeniably given greater substance by the increase in American presence between 1961 and 1963. Under the next administration the nature of the United States involvement changed again. Under Lyndon B. Johnson the United States went to war in Viet-Nam. By some accounts, however, the policy did not change from one administration to the next simply because the level of involvement had increased. Rather, what was required to continue the policy had changed. The threat to the government of South Viet-Nam from the communists in the south and the north increased during the Johnson administration, and so, it is argued, to maintain the existing policy of not letting Viet-Nam "fall," a military response of new proportions was necessary—only the imperatives of policy were altered.[1]

This interpretation of events relies heavily on the firmness of presidents and advisors in their commitment to South Viet-Nam. It assumes that, had the events in South Viet-Nam occurred three years earlier, President Kennedy and his administration would have responded in a fashion similar to President Johnson and his administration. It assumes that policy was already "set" in 1961, the decision had already been taken to do whatever was necessary to save South Viet-Nam, and that John Kennedy should presumably have been taken at his word when he said in his inaugural speech that the nation would "bear any burden, pay any price."

This argument has been pursued before, for different purposes, and it has not yet been resolved. Those who want to clear Kennedy of responsibility for the tremendous costs of the war conducted after his death argue that he would have ended, or that he actually intended to end, American involvement far short of the levels it ultimately reached; those who want to depict Johnson as having inherited a commitment argue that Kennedy set the course in Viet-Nam and that he would not have, and Johnson could not have, significantly deviated from it.

What John Kennedy would have done cannot be known with certainty, but that, fortunately, is not at issue here. We may be properly concerned, however, with whether or not there was a change in policy from the Kennedy to the Johnson administration. We may ask if it is possible that Kennedy moved slowly and deliberately in Viet-Nam precisely because his policy was not set, and if it is likely that his choices were essentially compromises among options presented by his advisors. We may ask if it would be accurate to characterize one president as pursuing a moderate policy in an atmosphere of conflict and dissent among policy makers and another as setting a new, firm course, narrowly bounded, in an atmosphere nearly void of credible detractors. To answer these questions we need to know about the atmosphere in which the decisions relating to Viet-Nam were taken—whether there was a consensus or conflict among participants; whether their disagreement was profound (over the basic direction of policy) or technical (over the most efficient means to achieve agreed-upon ends); or whether alternative means really reflected a willingness to pursue alternative objectives. As for presidential choices, we cannot be sure of intentions, but we can relate the substance of the decisions to the substance of the interaction among the principal actors prior to decision making. The policy-making process can be linked to the policy. And what is at issue here is whether the differences in the way policy was made in successive administrations explain any of the real differences in policy.

Viet-Nam policy in the three years of the Kennedy administration was defined by decisions that prescribed the level and character of American assistance. Within those years there are three periods in which the interaction of policy makers on such decisions is well documented, the issues sharply drawn, and the flow of policy clear. The periods were the spring and fall of 1961 and the summer of 1963. In the first period National Security Action Memorandum (NSAM) 52 temporarily set the level of American commitment; during the second period, which included the Taylor-Rostow mission to South Viet-Nam, the level was reset by NSAM 111; and in the third period, the principal question became whether to support the South Vietnamese president or the coup to overthrow him.

Some policy makers obviously perceived the conflict in Southeast Asia differently from others, some seeing the root of the difficulty as political, others as essentially military. During the periods just mentioned the positions of various bureaucratic actors on operational matters reflected their divergent interpretations. The viability of counterinsurgency warfare, the proper objectives and potential for success of the pacification programs, and the best way of dealing with the government of South Viet-Nam were all interrelated and recurrent in policy debates. Understanding which policy-making actors took what position for what reasons gives one a better vantage point from which to view and understand subsequent presidential choices. At the same time, the way the actors went about advancing their separate causes is also important to any conclusions relating the policy process to the substance of those presidential choices.

Put more directly, the argument of this chapter is that the fundamental nature of the dissent of some State Department actors from the definition of the conflict provided by most others in the government supports the interpretation of Kennedy's compromise decisions as studied moderation rather than as simple reflex acceptance of gradual increments. Furthermore, and just as important, a moderate policy benefited from and perhaps was even made possible by those alternative interpretations and prescriptions that emerged from a relatively open policy process. In short, the policy was moderate between 1961 and 1963, and it was so at least in part because the process was open. Because the same cannot be said about policy and process after 1963, the argument begun in this chapter must run through to the next.

The Setting

The mood in the spring of 1961 was one of activism. The Kennedy administration really did look out at the world and see challenges. Several observers say that Kennedy interpreted a speech by Khrushchev in December 1960 as directing a special challenge at the United States to which he felt compelled to respond. The speech listed three kinds of war, eliminated the first two varieties of nuclear and conventional warfare as undesirable, and advocated the third, protracted subversion or guerrilla warfare—the war of national liberation. The new administration rapidly prepared for this "shift in tactics" with new programs or at least with new rhetoric. Counterinsurgency became the fashion, and eventually everyone was forced to put on the new garb. The military, diplomats, and aid administrators were all required to take a counterinsurgency course before they took up assignments in developing countries.[2]

Arthur Schlesinger assures us that Kennedy well understood that counterinsurgency "meant a good deal more than teaching soldiers to black their faces and strangle enemies in the night," that it meant "political warfare."[3] But neither the distinction nor the emphasis appear to have been very clear in 1961. To the army counterinsurgency warfare (COIN) did not mean a social action program but a challenge to conventional thinking on how to fight a war; so they resisted the change. In spite of statements to the contrary, the Army of the Republic of [South] Viet-Nam (ARVN) was trained and organized by United States Army advisors along conventional lines with all the inflexibility that implies. The American Green Beret Special Forces, widely known to have been of personal interest to President Kennedy, eventually suffered the same slow death as other small elite units within the army. No matter what some claimed for it, COIN was in large part intended to satisfy the demand for a new kind of military response to an old political-military problem, and the army most of all struggled with that demand. General William DePuy observed in retrospect:

> In the early 1960's, when counterinsurgency was a household word around here, it was not thought out by any of us. We thought we could do it, and Kennedy and McNamara backed us. But they didn't understand it, or its implications, either. Counterinsurgency really is a catch phrase, you know, a slogan. The Army spent its time trying to figure out what it meant.[4]

A few people thought they understood what it meant, but even fewer agreed. What is more important is that everyone rapidly came to understand that counterinsurgency warfare was an important concern of the president and his closest advisors. The Laotian crisis competed with Viet-Nam for attention and provided more evidence of a guerrilla threat. Oddly enough, the recommendations of Maxwell Taylor and some others, including the attorney general and the director of the Central Intelligence Agency (CIA), who were given the task of determining what went wrong with the Cuban invasion in April 1961, ultimately resulted in the establishment of the special group for counterinsurgency.[5] As early as February 1961 Walt Rostow, then a special assistant in the White House, had the new president read a report passed to him by Secretary of Defense McNamara which had been prepared by Brigadier General Edward Lansdale. Lansdale was a veteran of Ramon Magsaysay's campaign against the Huk insurgency in the Philippines and also of various clandestine adventures in Viet-Nam in the fifties. The report included a pessimistic appraisal of events in South Viet-Nam and a recommendation for action. Kennedy was impressed and instructed Rostow to follow up on the matter.[6] Communist insurgency was to be the challenge, counterinsurgency the response, and Viet-Nam the test case.

All the adjectives, now clichés, used to describe the Kennedy men and their approach (e.g., brash, self-confident, arrogant, aggressive) seem to accurately describe the manner in which COIN was embraced and thrust upon the rest of the bureaucracy. Skepticism over the doctrine, it was said, could cost one his career.[7] This was the mood in the spring of 1961, and though the glamour and the appeal of unconventional warfare faded, the sense of challenge remained. This was the framework into which information about instability in a Southeast Asian country would be placed, and this was the legitimate mold to which bureaucracies were expected to shape their proposals. It proved to be a burden for some.[8]

There was, even before the president became acquainted with the Lansdale report, a Counter-Insurgency Plan (CIP) for South Viet-Nam approved by the White House. The amount of aid to Viet-Nam under the plan was not large, and its approval by Kennedy in January was apparently routine.[9] The CIP, which was superseded in May, was less important for its substance than for its form: it was a contingency agreement. President Diem of South Viet-Nam was required to make certain specific changes, among them administrative and civil reforms included at the insistence of the United States ambassador, Eldridge Dubrow. For the Kennedy administration this was the beginning of the process of trying to influence the actions of the government of [South] Viet-Nam (GVN) by making economic and military aid contingent upon political reform. There were occasional successes, but more often there was utter failure. The attempts in the spring of 1961 failed. They were an indication of what was to come in terms of both bureaucratic division and the intransigence of our Asian ally. There were then and there continued to be those in the State Department, like Dubrow, who saw the absolute necessity of civil reform if the GVN was to survive. Others, like the American military in Viet-Nam—the Military Assistance Advisory Group (MAAG), and the military in Washington—the Joint Chiefs of Staff (JCS), were more interested in getting on with the war and resented efforts to set up political hurdles over which the GNV would be required to jump. The short-run outcome in the spring of 1961 was that the hurdles remained, but Diem was permitted to go around them, and Dubrow was replaced as ambassador. On May 3, his last cable suggesting that pressure continue to be applied to Diem was sent to Washington, where the larger issue of bureaucratic preeminence was being decided.

SPRING 1961

On April 12, Walt Rostow sent a memo to President Kennedy that began, "Now that the Viet-Nam election is over, I believe we must turn to gearing up the whole Viet-Nam operation." The first of nine suggestions for "gearing up" was "the appointment of a full time first-rate backstop man in Washington."[10] Soon afterward, General Lansdale sent a paper to Secretary of Defense Robert McNamara and Deputy Secretary Roswell Gilpatric recommending the formation of a special task force to produce a program to deal with the Viet-Nam situation. Lansdale did this with knowledge of the Rostow memorandum and with the expectation that he would run the new program. By April 20 McNamara had discussed Lansdale's paper and proposal with the president and directed his deputy, on behalf of the president, to prepare a report by April 27 on the conditions in South Viet-Nam, including recommendations for action. McNamara's memorandum further suggested that Gilpatric might consult with other principals: "During the course of your study, you should draw, to the extent you believe necessary, upon the views and resources of the State Department and CIA."[11] Gilpatric, however, chose to follow the recommendation contained in Lansdale's paper and organized a special task force which would meet in place of the ongoing interdepartmental working group which had been headed by the State Department's acting assistant secretary for Far Eastern affairs.

The task force met for the first time on April 24. The group, which included representation from both the State Department and the CIA, produced what might be called the first compromise report on April 27. After characterizing the situation as "critical but not hopeless," the report went on to recommend specific programs that would "use, and where appropriate extend, expedite or build upon the existing U.S. and Government of Viet-

Nam [GVN] programs already underway in South Vietnam."[12] The specific recommendations included United States support for an increase in the size of the South Vietnamese Army, an increase in the size of the MAAG mission, the initiation of CIA-aided covert actions against lines of communications (LOC) in North Viet-Nam and Laos, and the formation of a presidential task force to direct the program. The report was at odds with Lansdale's position as stated in his paper to the Secretary of Defense and in earlier documents insofar as he had argued that what was needed in Viet-Nam was a new, less restricted approach, not tied to past programs, and staffed and directed by dedicated, hand-picked men. (Lansdale expected to do the picking and at one point began to do so.) Nevertheless, the report did keep to the spirit of the Lansdale proposals in providing for a special presidential task force with an operations officer rather than the usual interdepartmental group separated from operational control. Of equal importance was the designation of Gilpatric as director of the task force and Lansdale as the operations officer in Viet-Nam.

The State Department was less fortunate in the report. Besides loss of control of the Washington-based interdepartmental effort, the State Department stood to lose in the even more important area of in-country operational control. The ambassador was supposed to have responsibility for and authority over the "Country Team." There had even been an ongoing, if not altogether successful, effort to bring about such an arrangement by the Executive around the entire globe. Although the task force report did say that the ambassador was to act as head of the country team in Viet-Nam, it also stipulated the route and advisory nature of the control he would exercise: "He is authorized to advise the Director of the Task Force in Washington of any changes which he believes should be made in the Program."[13] The State Department did not react favorably to the proposed arrangement.

Events moved swiftly. On April 27, the day the president received the Gilpatric report, a National Security Council (NSC) meeting was held. The main topic, however, was not Viet-Nam, but Laos, where the battlefield situation was critical. With intervention in Laos now a possibility, no action was taken on the Viet-Nam proposals and the task force went back to work to produce an annex of prescriptions for the Laotian crisis, which it submitted the following day. The final draft of the annex included a recommendation for a significant increase in the United States MAAG mission in Viet-Nam over that specified in the previous day's report. On April 29 President Kennedy, preoccupied with pressures to intervene in Laos, acted to approve only the limited military proposals for Viet-Nam of the April 27 report. On Monday, May 1, another draft report came from Gilpatric. This one incorporated the annex in the body of the previous report and was accompanied by a note from Lansdale requesting comments from the task force prior to a meeting on May 3 in preparation for a scheduled meeting of the NSC on May 4.

At this point, Under Secretary of State George Ball asked for a one-day postponement of the task force meeting and received it from Gilpatric over Lansdale's objections. On May 3 the State Department produced its own draft report, which would ultimately turn out to be the basis for the final task force report of May 6. The State Department draft struck at both the bureaucratic structure and content of the Defense Department proposals. The proposal for a presidential task force under the direction of a deputy secretary of defense with a brigadier general as its executive officer was replaced by a conventional interagency working group with a State Department director. Lansdale and his role were eliminated from the proposal. On the substantive point of United States commitment, the earlier Defense Department draft, which stated the American intention to unilaterally intervene in South Viet-Nam if it became necessary "to save the country from Communism," was changed to a recommendation that consideration be given a new bilateral treaty with South Viet-Nam to provide for its defense. The acknowledgment that a commitment already existed under the Southeast Asian Treaty Organization (SEATO) was thus avoided.[14] On the critical question of additional United States troops, the May 1 draft's recommendation of an increase of 3,200 men to train new South Vietnamese divisions was referred to in the State Department's draft as deserving of further study. Finally, on a point that had already caused disagreement and would continue to do so in the future, the State Department took the position that Diem was not to be supported at all costs but only if he performed in a satisfactory fashion:

> Thus in giving priority emphasis to the need for internal security, we must not relax in our efforts to persuade Diem of the need for political, social and economic progress. If his efforts are inadequate in the field our overall objective could be seriously endangered and we might once more find ourselves in the position of shoring a leader who had lost support of his people.[15]

There is little evidence to show how this May 3 draft became the basis for the final May 6 version of the task force report. It is clear that Lansdale opposed it. He was dissatisfied with the new interdepartmental organization and wrote McNamara and Gilpatric, "My strong recommendation is that Defense stay completely out of the Task Force directorship as now proposed by State." Lansdale, commenting to Gilpatric later on the final report's position on the Diem regime, also noted, "This will have the U.S. pitted against Diem as first priority, the communists as second."[16] These objections notwithstanding, the report went to the president.

Between the May 6 task force report and the May 11 NSC meeting, which produced NSAM 52, the military had an opportunity to add their input directly. Responding to Deputy Secretary Gilpatric's request for their views on increasing American troop strength in Viet-Nam, the JCS made its recommendations on May 10: "Assuming that the political decision is to hold Southeast Asia outside the Communist sphere, the Joint Chiefs of Staff are of the opinion that U.S. forces should be deployed immediately to South Vietnam."[17] At an NSC meeting the following day the president decided against that recommendation, that is, he decided not to send any more troops than he had already approved on April 29. But he did decide to proceed with covert activities and instructed the task force, now under the direction of a Foreign Service officer, to study the proposal for increasing American troop strength.

The president's May decision to increase American involvement was made reluctantly and while under significant pressures for a higher level of commitment. One way of interpreting the importance of the State Department's contribution in May 1961 is to credit it with providing the president with the necessary flexibility to resist the more activist elements in the Executive. This may have been the policy objective of the movers in the State Department. Alternately, those principals may have acted primarily out of concern over the attack on their organizational role, producing the policy outcome as a by-product of a competitive bureaucratic process. In either case, the State Department was in a position to have an impact on policy, to moderate it, only because the policy process was relatively open and competitive.

Fall 1961

Through the summer and into the fall of 1961, the situation in South Viet-Nam grew progressively worse. Immediately after

NSAM 52, Vice-President Johnson traveled to Asia and, after meeting with Diem, wrote a report emphasizing the importance of meeting "the challenge of Communist expansion" by supporting the South Vietnamese government with more economic and military aid and possibly a new defense treaty.[18] In June, Diem responded to an American invitation to specify his military needs by asking for United States support for a 100,000-man increase in the size of his army. This would have required a previously unanticipated increase in the size of the MAAG mission. Though the specific request went unanswered for some time and eventually only received partial approval, it served to spur ongoing Washington discussions of the possible introduction of American combat units. (At this point Diem was unwilling to accept American ground forces and only wanted more MAAG trainers for Vietnamese forces.) Between the middle of August and the end of September, several reports on the situation in Viet-Nam reached the White House that, combined with the pressure to introduce United States troops, prompted the decision in October to send Maxwell Taylor to Viet-Nam.

The reports on conditions in Viet-Nam varied from the rather optimistic account given by the MAAG chief who could see "a spirit of renewed confidence beginning to permeate the people, the GVN and the Armed Forces" to Theodore H. White's conclusion that "the situation gets worse almost week by week. . . ." In between there was the August National Intelligence Estimate (NIE) that weighed military improvement against possible grave difficulties ahead in the political sphere. The State Department's summary quotes from Ambassador to Viet-Nam Fritz Nolting's assessment that the situation had not changed much but goes on to offer its own view that the military situation was indeed deteriorating.[19]

On October 11 an NSC meeting was held at which the Taylor-Rostow mission to Viet-Nam was authorized. The principal purpose of the trip was to consider the political and military feasibility of various plans for putting troops in South Viet-Nam.[20] There had been division of opinion over where the troops should be put. The JCS had favored putting troops in Laos to protect Viet-Nam or, if that were politically unacceptable, in the central highlands of South Viet-Nam itself. Walt Rostow, on the other hand, had proposed stationing United States troops along a border, either the one between Laos and Viet-Nam or the one that separates the two Viet-Nams. Regardless of which plan was chosen, the initial troop investment was to be about 25,000 men.

Important support for American military action also came from civilians in the Defense Department, notably William Bundy, then deputy assistant secretary for international security affairs (ISA). In a memorandum to McNamara he discussed the odds on a successful outcome, found them acceptable, and concluded, "On a 70–30 basis, I would favor going in."[21]

The Taylor mission arrived in Saigon on October 18; by November 3 his twenty-five-page report and accompanying memorandum had been published and distributed in Washington. While still in Saigon Taylor had begun sending back recommendations, but it was from the Philippines on his return trip that he sent his two strongest cables on an "Eyes only for the President" basis. In the first of these cables Taylor called for the introduction of an American military task force that would "conduct such combat operations as are necessary for self-defense and for the security of the area in which they are stationed . . . [and] act as an advance party of such additional forces as may be introduced if CINCPAC or SEATO contingency plans are invoked."[22]

The Saigon and the Philippines communications also mentioned the use of American troops in logistic support of "flood relief operations." The reference was to the flooding in the Mekong delta area at the time and the possible role of United States soldiers in relief and reconstruction. What is interesting, however, is that in the message intended for the president the wording about the flood relief and logistic functions of the troops was nearly stripped away and the military value and the necessity for American presence were emphazised.

The critical decision to be made in Washington, of course, was whether to introduce troops and, if so, how many and under what conditional arrangements with Diem. From the body of the Taylor report it would appear that there was a clear consensus: "Perhaps the most striking aspect of this mission's effort is the unanimity of view—individually arrived at by the specialists involved—that what is now required is a shift from U.S. advice to limited partnership and working collaboration with the Vietnamese."[23]

Actually, there was a much greater difference in perspectives. On the question of the political situation, the main section, presumably written by Taylor and Rostow, noted Diem's "extraordinary ability, stubbornness and guts," while an annex contributed by William Jorden of the State Department referred to "intrigue, nepotism and even corruption," in Diem's regime. On the issue of the commitment of troops, advocates existed for a token 8,000-man force made up mostly of engineers and also for the JCS proposal of sending from 25,000 to 40,000 combat troops. Sterling Cottrell, the State Department chairman of the Viet-Nam task force, did not dissent from the recommendation of sending *some* troops, but he did offer a clear and singular warning in his appendix to the report: "Since it is an open question whether the GVN can succeed even with U.S. assistance, it would be a mistake for the U.S. to commit itself irrevocably to the defeat of the communists in SVN."[24]

Indirectly, Secretary of State Dean Rusk became involved in the debate over whether Diem should be required to "perform" in return for whatever new assistance he might receive. The Taylor report had not mentioned any GVN reciprocation and, in fact, was in keeping with Lansdale's approach of attempting to win Diem's confidence rather than trying to coerce him into reforms. Rusk apparently anticipated Taylor's position and in a November 1 cable argued that thought should be given to whether "Diem is prepared [to] take necessary measures to give us something worth supporting." In a statement that foreshadowed the fundamental ambivalence in United States policy during 1963, he went on to say, "While attaching greatest possible importance to security in SEA, I would be reluctant to see U.S. make major additional commitment [of] American prestige to a losing horse [Diem]."[25]

With these inputs registered, a November 8 memorandum was sent to the White House that should have weighed heavily in any presidential decision. The secretary of defense, his deputy, and the JCS jointly recommended that the United States commit itself "to the clear objective of preventing the fall of South Vietnam to Communism" and support that commitment "by the necessary military actions." The memorandum specifically excluded the "8,000-man flood relief context" declaring it ineffective and called instead for "the introduction of U.S. forces on a substantial scale."[26] In short, civilians and military in the Defense Department had come out in favor of the most extreme military response, barred compromise, and did not mention any demands to be made upon Diem. Three days later a curious thing happened: the secretary of defense joined with the secretary of state in a memorandum to the president reversing his recommendations of November 8. McNamara and Rusk did not recommend that any American combat troops be sent, not even the minimum engineer force. The increased economic aid, equipment, and training that were recommended were to be offered to Diem only on condition that "the Government of Viet-Nam is prepared to carry out an effective and total mobilization of its own resources, both material and human. . . ."[27]

On November 15, there was an NSC meeting and seven days later NSAM 111 was signed. Except for a recommendation contained in the McNamara-Rusk Memorandum that the United States commit itself to saving Viet-Nam, NSAM 111 was substantially the same as the November 11 communication to the president from his secretaries of state and defense. Increased aid but no United States combat troops were sent to Viet-Nam in 1961, and the policy of trying to coerce Diem into political and administrative reform was endorsed. Given the recommendations of the Taylor mission and the earlier Defense Department memorandum there is reason to question how this came about.

One explanation, offered in the *Pentagon Papers* narrative and by Daniel Ellsberg, is that Kennedy wanted to take this course of action, overruled Taylor, Rostow, and the military, and simply directed McNamara to change his written recommendation for bureaucratic reasons:

> . . . The apparent turnabout by the Secretary of Defense clearly represents a standard high-level bureaucratic device to prevent leaks that would burden the President with responsibility for rejecting certain proposals, or suggest that the measures actually adopted were regarded by some advisors as inadequate.[28]

An obvious alternate explanation would be that McNamara changed his mind after his first memorandum, joined Rusk, and together they convinced the president of the merits of their position. Whether one finds it more likely that the president acted against the dominant flow of counsel or weighed conflicting advice in a balance, it is critically important that there was some credible dissent from that dominant flow of policy in the first case or something to put on both sides of the scale in the second. As in the spring, it was useful to the president that the State Department actors, for whatever reason, interpreted conditions in Viet-Nam differently from other principals and advocated a different prescription. At no time would it be accurate to say that the State Department brought a totally different interpretation of the international system to decision making or even that the State Department had totally resisted embracing the military characterizations and responses that were the idiom at the time; rather, the State Department was more skeptical, more critical, tended to see the political side more clearly, and was generally more cautious in committing the United States to action. When this perspective was aired by Jorden, Cottrell, and Rusk, it could not help but temper other inputs and help provide the president with a reasonable base from which to resist the military and other members of the Taylor-Rostow mission. If the president did direct McNamara to submit a new memorandum, the action surely was more likely because of the State Department's input; if McNamara changed his mind, the State Department may have helped in his conversion and together he and Rusk may have tipped the balance against intervention in the mind of the president. The point, of course, is a simple one: in the fall of 1961 the State Department was a major bureaucratic entity offering diversity of perception and prescription in Southeast Asia, and the substance of policy appears to reflect the strain of contending advocates.

Pacification—Then Diem

In the fall of 1963 there was a coup in South Viet-Nam in which President Diem and Ngo Dinh Nhu, his brother and advisor, were murdered and replaced by members of the military. The extent of United States involvement in those events is still the subject of much debate. At the time, the extent to which the United States *should* have involved itself in Diem's removal was the subject of debate. Most of those who thought "Diem must go" and worked most actively toward that end were members of the State Department, while support for the president of South Viet-Nam came largely from within the Defense Department. The difference in perspectives on Diem can be traced directly to the advocates' perception of the situation in Viet-Nam. Those who believed the struggle in Viet-Nam was basically a political problem were unhappy with Diem's inept, despotic regime and welcomed a coup. Those who admitted that there was a political component to the conflict but considered the insurgency principally a military problem did not want to risk the instability and possible collapse that might follow from a coup. The bureaucratic struggle over this issue was manifest continually through 1962 in the administration of the pacification program; it matured just prior to Diem's assassination in 1963 in debate over support for the coup; and it was resolved immediately afterward in the accession of a new American president and a worsening of the situation in Viet-Nam.

From the very beginning the organized effort at pacification of the people of Viet-Nam involved some kind of enclosure of parts of the population or removal of population to enclosed areas. The areas were to be defended and were to offer security as well as improved government services. It was hoped that ultimately people would come to identify with and support the government of South Viet-Nam. They would no longer be the water in which the Viet Cong, like Mao's fish, could swim and survive. In the early nineteen fifties the French had tried their hand at working on the civilian population and Diem did likewise with the Agroville program in 1959. Neither attempt was successful. American plans for a population program did not begin to become clear until after the mission to Viet-Nam by the Stanford economist, Dr. Eugene Staley, in the summer of 1961. Staley recommended fortifying local areas in a system of strategic hamlets. Prior to the rediscovery of the idea of strategic hamlets, MAAG drew up a loosely defined plan, directed at the population, for the United States military. The two plans did not clash until Sir Robert Thompson, the British expert on guerrilla warfare, made a report to President Kennedy in October 1961 and in November submitted a plan for pacification.

The substantive disagreements between the American military and Thompson had to do with what they thought was the major threat from the Viet Cong, where they would institute the pacification program, and what they would try to do in the "target areas." MAAG was concerned about attacks from rural areas on the major cities and therefore considered these areas to be of high priority. The area around Saigon, for example, was so designated. Thompson thought the problem was losing the rural population to Viet Cong control and designated the delta as first priority. The British expert conceived of the primary mode of operation as "static defense" and characterized the undertaking as a policing action; MAAG favored mobile operations, "sweeps," and believed the problem to be a military one in the conventional sense. Aside from these and other substantive differences, the United States Army's organization, mission, and prerogatives were also at stake. In anticipation of the struggle, General Lemnitzer, then chairman of the JCS, sent a memorandum to General Taylor before the latter's visit to Viet-Nam in October. In it he attacked Thompson's application of Malayan experience to South Viet-Nam, his lack of appreciation for the military nature of the conflict, and his motives:

> . . . There is some concern the Thompson Mission may try to sell the Malayan concept of police control without making a sufficiently care-

ful evaluation of conditions in South Viet-Nam. Additionally, there are some indications that the British, for political reasons, wish to increase their influence in this area and are using the Thompson Mission as a vehicle.[29]

This would perhaps be less important if President Kennedy had not liked Thompson's recommendations, and if they had not been championed in Washington by Roger Hilsman of the Bureau of Intelligence and Research (INR) in the State Department. Hilsman adopted Thompson's analysis and approach and advocated that the thrust of the entire American involvement in Viet-Nam be along the lines of a population-directed political program rather than a military campaign to eliminate the Viet Cong. Nineteen sixty-two proved to be the year of pacification, not because the population was pacified, but because the importance of the population program in relation to military efforts was greater than at any time in the future.

In June of 1962 Hilsman sent a research memorandum to the assistant secretary of state, Averell Harriman, summing up the previous three months of the new counterinsurgency phase and cautiously but optimistically concluding that

a judgment on ultimate success in the campaign against the Communist "war of national liberation" in Vietnam is premature, but . . . we do think the chances are good, provided there is continuing progress by the Vietnamese government along the lines of its present strategy.[30]

A July report requested by McNamara from the CIA station chief in Viet-Nam and distributed to the principals in Washington said:

In sum, we believe strategic hamlet program definitely moving forward both as organizing principle around which whole GVN counterinsurgency program has fair chance of being sold to people and as specific tactic in preventing spread Viet Cong influence among people.[31]

As late as April of 1963 an NIE said in part, "We believe that Communist progress has been blunted and that the situation is improving."[32]

Actually, the strategic hamlet program, pacification, and the counterinsurgency effort generally were not succeeding in 1962, and by the summer of 1963 the failure of the Diem regime should have been obvious. The strategic hamlet program was too often administered coercively and corruptly and provided neither physical security nor social reform. The chief reasons cited for failure vary with the critic: Jean Lacouture argues that the Vietnamese government had a different goal, that Nhu was less concerned with social justice than social control; Sir Robert Thompson of course points out that his prescription of security for individuals through a police effort within the hamlets was never followed.[33] In fact, it is easy to argue that pacification failed because neither Thompson's plan nor Hilsman's adaptation was tried and because a program begun in the wrong place on too large a scale and with poor administration was undertaken instead. But given the greater perspective of the American experience since then, including the pacification efforts from 1965 through 1969, it would seem that there is the more basic question of whether a Western-dominated program that forces change with no regard for traditional Vietnamese culture and society can result in increased confidence in the local regime. Some say a definite answer is not yet possible, while others wonder at the patience of those still waiting for success.

In any event, Hilsman's INR had dissented from the military's plan for pacification, and it appears to have been one of the earliest skeptics of the implemented compromise program. In December, six months after Hilsman's cautious but optimistic appraisal, INR's five-part research memorandum was issued. It was written as a contribution to a forthcoming NIE, and it placed primary emphasis on the need for the Diem regime to do more to stress "non-military aspects of the counterinsurgency program," integrate "the strategic hamlet program with an expanded systematic pacification program," and modify "military tactics (particularly those relating to large-unit actions and tactical use of airpower and artillery).[34] Beyond this clear incursion by the State Department into military matters (ARVN tactics were MAAG's prescribed tactics), Hilsman went on to discuss the likely effects of a coup, characterizing them as less than disastrous. The previous April, John Kenneth Galbraith had written a memorandum to Kennedy noting the weakness of Diem, advocating that a political tack be taken in the United States policy, and warning of the dangers of American military action or even association with the new "concentration program."[35] By the time of the Buddhist crisis in May of 1963 the political situation in South Viet-Nam had grown considerably worse, and those few early high-level critics began to draw allies.

Joining Hilsman and Galbraith was Averell Harriman, assistant secretary of state for Far Eastern affairs and later under secretary of state, and Michael Forrestal of the White House staff. As in other bureaucratic alliances, those who joined did not necessarily share the same beliefs about American foreign policy or even about the best overall policy for Viet-Nam, but they did agree on a particular course of action independent of what goals they perceived it as serving. Documents indicate that Hilsman and Harriman were quite close on broader goals, while Forrestal became an opponent of the pro-Diem forces simply because he did not think Diem would succeed. Arrayed on the other side of the question of maintaining Diem were the JCS, MAAG, and Ambassador Nolting. Nolting was a key supporter and apologist for Diem and during his tenure he had attempted to influence the South Vietnamese president by persuasion rather than by the threats others would have liked to have seen communicated. As late as July the ambassador was still arguing that "when Diem gave his word, he followed through although sometimes it was handled in his own way."[36]

The personal touch was indeed evident when the South Vietnamese government raided the country's pagodas in an attempt to crush the Buddhist opposition on August 21, 1963. Harriman and Forrestal reacted immediately by drafting a statement condeming the Vietnamese government; just as quickly American military intelligence in Washington assured the secretary of defense that it was Saigon's generals, rather than the civilian regime, who were responsible.[37] Henry Cabot Lodge, the new American ambassador in Viet-Nam, promptly corrected the Defense Intelligence Agency (DIA) account and joined forces with those in the State Department who sought the removal of, at the very least, Diem's brother. From this point in August, until the assassination in late October, the debate over policy raged continually in Washington. A few illustrations should convey the scope and intensity of the debate.

On August 24 a telegram was sent to Lodge by Hilsman, Harriman, Forrestal, and George Ball, who was then acting secretary of state (Rusk was out of town). This message is often taken as a particularly daring attempt by the anti-Diem forces to make United States policy, since it came close to authorizing Lodge to give the potential coup leaders of the Vietnamese military American support and encouragement, and because clearances for the cable were obtained under extraordinary and questionable circumstances. Most of the other principals, Kennedy, McNamara, Taylor, Rusk, and John McCone of the CIA, were either out of town and gave hasty concurrence by telephone or concurred after the cable was sent.[38] The result was that these decision makers eventually modified their position on a coup and conveyed this to Lodge. In subsequent days, President Kennedy sought more information from Viet-Nam only to have MAAG chief General Harkins and Ambassador Lodge show the same division of opinion already expressed in the NSC between those who wanted to give Diem more time and those who were impatient. The narrator of the segment in the *Pentagon Papers* dealing with this period calls the NSC discussions at the time "heated and testy."[39] The coup did not come off in August partially because the Vietnamese generals thought they were receiving conflicting signals and doubted the commitment of the American government. They were of course quite correct.

Neither was consensus in the offing. In the series of NSC meetings that followed, the president repeatedly heard doubts expressed about the most basic assumptions of our policy in Viet-Nam—doubts that would not be expressed in the same context in the next administration. At a State Department meeting chaired by Rusk on August 31, Paul Kattenburg of the State Department argued that if the United States continued to support Diem we would find ourselves on the losing side in a war and within six months we could be asked to leave. He went on to say that "at this juncture it would be better for us to make the decision to get out honorably."[40] Kattenburg drew quick disagreement from Nolting, Rusk, and Vice-President Johnson.

Seven days later at an NSC meeting Attorney General Robert Kennedy observed that the basic question of whether any South Vietnamese government could resist the Communists had not been addressed adequately. He argued that discussions of how to influence Diem were of second order priority because if victory were impossible the United States should now act to extricate itself. The president, perhaps in response to his brother's observation, sent another special mission to Viet-Nam which resulted in another NSC meeting on September 10. The mission of General Krulak, special assistant for counterinsurgency and special activities (SACSA); Joseph Mendenhall, a State Department Foreign Service officer; John Mecklin, United States Information Service (USIS) director, and Rufus Phillips, a director of United States Operations Mission for economic assistance (USOM), produced additional differing interpretations.

In his report to the president, General Krulak found the political situation in Viet-Nam unfortunate but not critical to the military effort, which he thought would be successful. Mendenhall, Phillips, and Mecklin saw various degrees of disaster ahead if Diem were supported. Mecklin suggested that the United States resolve to send combat troops to Viet-Nam if necessary after it had brought about a change in government.

Shortly after this session, Kennedy sent his secretary of defense and the chairman of the JCS to Viet-Nam for yet another appraisal. Their mission finally produced a more coherent policy recommendation involving a change in military tactics in the field and the application of real pressure on Diem in the form of withheld aid. It also produced an unfortunate White House statement about the end of the war: "Secretary McNamara and General Taylor reported their judgment that the major part of the U.S. military task can be completed by the end of 1965, although there may be a continuing requirement for a limited number of U.S. training personnel."[41] Predictions aside, the McNamara-Taylor report seemed to be consistent with the pessimism and anti-Diem sentiment of several State Department policy makers, and thus Kennedy's adoption of it may suggest the importance of contributions from the various skeptics.

A Relatively Open Policy Process

The argument of this chapter has been that the State Department made a significant contribution to Viet-Nam policy during the Kennedy administration and that that contribution tended characteristically to counsel caution, restraint, and appreciation for political rather than military factors. It is not that State Department actors were "doves," for they issued prescriptions involving the use of American military troops, and they did not shrink from advocating violent means—none had reason to believe that a coup in South Viet-Nam could be bloodless. But the recommendations from the State Department were nonetheless distinguishable from those originating elsewhere in the bureaucracy, and more important, the absence of comparable input after 1963 is reflected in the substance of United States policy in later years.

Certain senior officials at the State Department were of course unique and not in any sense "of the Department." Walt Rostow, for one, enthusiastically endorsed military prescriptions for Viet-Nam, but he had come to the State Department from McGeorge Bundy's White House staff—reportedly after Rusk had initially refused to take him and only after Bundy could no longer take him.[42] Roger Hilsman, director of INR before he replaced Harriman as assistant secretary, was another and the kind of activist some critics have claimed the State Department needed. Although his advocacy seemed atypical of the organization and he used understatement when he admitted to not being a dove in the sense of the term as later applied. Until his departure in 1964, Hilsman's appreciation for the political side of the conflict contrasted sharply with White House, Office of International Security Affairs (ISA) in the Defense Department, and JCS perspectives.[43] An indicator that the new administration did perceive a difference between its approach and Hillsman's is provided by the 1964 decision to deprive his Far East bureau of responsibility for Viet-Nam and make it a mere conduit for information flows to an interagency task force. As soon as Hilsman was replaced by William Bundy, responsibility shifted back to the bureau and the assistant secretary again reported directly to Rusk.

The secretary of state is the key to understanding why the Department was not even more active during Kennedy's administration and completely faded to the periphery in Johnson's. Rusk's perspective—or the "intellectual baggage" he brought to the Viet-Nam conflict—helps explain his position. His public defenses of American policy, calling upon memories of past aggression and appeasement and the need to demonstrate resolve, were sincere. Two perceptive observers write:

> Rusk knew that there were profound differences between the Sudetenland and South Vietnam, between Hitler and Ho. "I am not the village idiot," he once exploded. But he profoundly believed aggression by any other name was aggression still and that it must be checked.[44]

Add to this perspective what Galbraith called Rusk's "high respect for military acumen," which easily translates into the willingness to put military means ahead of diplomatic, and the secretary's restraint in the face of Pentagon advocates is understandable. Evidence of Rusk's respect for bureaucratic boundaries and the sanctity of those things military is provided by his reaction to a research memorandum circulated by Thomas Hughes of INR in October 1963. The Hughes report was a lengthy, detailed, statistical evaluation of the military situation in Viet-Nam, which concluded that, contrary to MAAG reports, there had been a trend of deterioration over the previous three months. In spite of the relevance of the report, the criticalness of the period, and the suspicion with which the military's evaluations were regarded, Rusk sent a letter to the secretary of defense expressing regret for the report:

> It is not the policy of the State Department to issue military appraisals without seeking the views of the Defense Department. I have requested that any memoranda given inter-departmental circulation which include military appraisals be coordinated with your department.[45]

The influence of the secretary's position on the nature of the conflict and his views on the preeminence of the military extended deep into the department. For obvious reasons there is reluctance to suggest, much less "invest in" and forcefully advocate, positions that are doomed to failure because they are at odds with the prevailing policy in an organization. This is one of several reasons for conformity in bureaucracies, and according to one astute participant–observer, there was indeed little tolerance in the State Department for those who ventured to advocate revision in our Viet-Nam policy.[46] It would be incorrect to call Rusk an architect of the Viet-Nam policy—that distinction is more appropriately reserved for the civilians and the military in the Defense Department—but it is accurate to say that the secretary's failure to balance military input with diplomatic and political inputs undercut a competitive bureaucratic process prior to the Johnson presidency and doomed it afterward.

The evidence presented here was intended to illustrate the extent and the kind of influence the State Department had on policy from 1961 to 1963. The literature on the department during the Kennedy years, however, is almost without exception critical of the ineffectiveness and inefficiency of the bureaucracy at Foggy Bottom. The conclusion of these accounts is that it was therefore necessary to shift the locus of foreign policy making elsewhere.[47] As it turned out, "elsewhere" meant to McGeorge Bundy's and then to Walt Rostow's staff in the White House and to McNamara's civilians, most of whom were in ISA. There is a partial conflict in interpretation between such accounts and the argument of this chapter. First, although some of the State Department's critics were no doubt correct about its many ills, it is likely that displeasure with the department's output depended to some degree upon the substantive position espoused by State's analysts rather than the quality of thought that went into it or the swiftness with which it was produced. As one former Foreign Service officer observed about charges of conservatism and sloth, "It is just possible that some of the diplomatic professionals, true to their tradition, were advising prudence and suggesting, with deference, that the president might be misreading the situation."[48]

In other words, caution in policy substance may have suffered the criticism due an overly cautious policy process.

The second point is simply that there is a difference between the State Department's role before and after President Kennedy's death. It was because of the different policy premises and policy-making preferences of the two presidents, and also because of objective changes in the nature of the conflict in Viet-Nam by 1964, that the State Department's contribution diminished and the focus of policy making shifted further in the Johnson administration in the direction of Secretary of Defense McNamara and his staff and the advisor to the president for national security affairs and his staff. The change was reflected in one way by the new procedure of having a White House staffer attach a covering memorandum to all memoranda sent from the State Department to the president before forwarding them to Johnson. The State Department is said to have resented the screening of communication.[49] Possibly in response to this procedure, Under Secretary of State George Ball attempted to make use of a Foreign Service officer assigned to the White House staff. He used Lee T. Stull as a direct means of communicating with the president and cut down the State Department's cable traffic to McGeorge Bundy's office. When an aid to Bundy pointed out what was happening, Bundy had Stull transferred—first to Policy Planning in the State Department and then to Pakistan.[50] The State Department was gradually being "boxed out," to a much greater degree than in the previous administration.

The case has been made for the State Department's role prior to 1964. It remains to show how policy and process changed after 1964 and that is one of the tasks of the following chapters. It should be pointed out, however, that 1964 was the year in which senior actors began planning for a bombing campaign, the first public threats of massive bombing of North Viet-Nam were issued, covert activities were accelerated to a new level, and the DESOTO patrols led us into the Tonkin Gulf reprisals.

The policy process from 1961 to 1963 was a relatively open one. It can be shown that there were a good many bureaucratic battles and that policy reflected the division by its moderation. One could of course claim that the results in Viet-Nam by 1963 were hardly moderate, but the easy and appropriate answer is that they were moderate relative to the results in the following years.

III. THE 1965 CONSENSUS AND THE DECISION TO BOMB NORTH VIET-NAM

In March 1964 the secretary of defense addressed the James Forrestal Memorial Awards dinner and spoke of the threat to American interests in South Viet-Nam. Explaining the variety of interests and the recent deepening of the threat, he went on to announce that military action against North Viet-Nam was an option not to be ruled out. One year later the United States embarked upon a policy of sustained bombing of North Viet-Nam. There appears to be a certain continuity here in retrospect, a movement from verbal threat by the secretary to fulfillment by military action. As a case for the study of foreign policy decision making it may even appear uninteresting: there was broad agreement in the government that it was in the United States interest that the insurgency in South Viet-Nam fail; the source of support for the insurgents was in the north, and the means were available to exert direct pressure; the decision to exert the pressure was embraced by virtually all participants at the time. One might ask what there is to question or examine beyond the starting premises about national interest and international threat.

There is actually a great deal to question and examine. What appears to have been simply continuity between the first clear public warning and the initiation of a policy consistent with it is really an interesting story of policy momentum. There was not, in fact, an unambiguous commitment in 1964 to pursue the kind of policy adopted in 1965, although in 1964 there certainly were advocates of such a course or even a more extreme one. The administration arrived at the policy it did in the winter of 1965 in a progressive, seemingly inexorable fashion. The narrowing of the bounds of legitimate debate and the pressure from advocates of military solutions did much to create a momentum in the policy-making process that became increasingly difficult to break. And what finally appears to have been consensus in 1965 was really an extremely shallow and ultimately fragile bureaucratic alliance. The purpose of this chapter is to examine the nature of that alliance and the various sources of its support and to suggest some of the implications for policy born of a process like the one that prevailed—the policy of bombing North Viet-Nam. The pace of events in 1964 built the momentum and set the scene for the decisions of the winter and spring of 1965.

The situation in Viet-Nam in early 1964 looked bleak to everyone. There was disagreement only over exactly how bleak and exactly what should be done about it. The first coup since Diem's assassination the previous November occurred before the end of January, and before the end of the year there were six more changes in government. The GVN was not able to achieve stability in 1964. The situation in the countryside was also poor and steadily deteriorating. The Viet Cong engaged the ARVN directly in order to weaken what was seen as a potential source of stability for the government. They pursued a strategy used previously and which they would use again—concentrating efforts in the central portion of South Viet-Nam in an effort to cut the country in half.

The reaction in Washington was focused largely on North Viet-Nam. Although there was precedent for this approach in the covert activities during the Kennedy years, the emphasis in 1964 was of a higher order. In January Maxwell Taylor, then chairman of the JCS, sent a memorandum to McNamara that argued for an escalation in the American effort:

> The Joint Chiefs of Staff consider that the United States must make ready to conduct increasingly bolder actions in Southeast Asia.

Among the actions listed were:

> Arm, equip, advise, and support the Government of Viet-Nam in its conduct of aerial bombing of critical targets in North Viet-Nam and in mining the sea approaches to that country. Conduct aerial bombing of key North Viet-Nam targets, using U.S. resources under Vietnamese cover, and with the Vietnamese openly assuming responsibility for the actions.
>
> Commit U.S. forces as necessary in direct actions against North Viet-Nam.[1]

The narrative of the *Pentagon Papers* makes a point of the programmatic nature of activities actually begun against the north the following month.[2] Rather than setting the actions in an ad hoc framework, the February program was phased over a twelve-month period with operational control exercised by the Commander of the U.S. Military Command in Viet-Nam (COMUSMACV), coordination and support coming from CINCPAC and the CIA, and reports channeled to the JCS. Thus, at a very early stage, even though the administration signed on only for the four-month first stage, action against North Viet-Nam was becoming institutionalized, making escalation something more of an expectation.

Interagency activity on Viet-Nam at the time further structured thinking in the direction of the north in order to solve the problem of insurgency in the south. The president had explicitly directed his principal security policy decision makers to pay particular attention in contingency planning "to shaping such pressures so as to produce the maximum credible deterrent effect on Hanoi."[3] When McNamara made a trip to Viet-Nam in March, he took with him the summary of an interagency study group's report on pressures against the north. The secretary's own report no doubt drew upon the study's conclusions and itself became NSAM 288 on March 17, the day following its submission to the president. Setting forth the goal and the threat in Viet-Nam, it said in part,

> We seek an independent non-Communist South Vietnam. . . . Unless we can achieve this objective in South Vietnam, almost all of Southeast Asia will probably fall under Communist domination (all of Vietnam, Laos, and Cambodia). . . . Even the Philippines would become shaky and the threat to the West, Australia and New Zealand to the South, and Taiwan, Korea, and Japan to the North and East would be greatly increased.[4]

It is important that in the months that followed NSAM 288 would serve not only to set the tone of policy but also to limit the scope of debate. Not only would the emphasis on action against North Viet-Nam spur policy in that direction but the section on "U.S. Objectives in South Vietnam" set forth the extent of American interest in Viet-Nam and seemed to preclude reconsideration of that basic issue in future policy reviews.

NSAM 288 was not without dissent. The military were unhappy with what they saw as an inadequate commitment to act against the source of the insurgency (i.e., North Viet-Nam), and Assistant Secretary of State Roger Hilsman thought emphasis should more properly be placed on the insurgency itself (i.e., in South Viet-Nam). In a memorandum for the secretary of defense commenting on a draft of NSAM 288, Maxwell Taylor conveyed the reservations of the JCS on the proposed military activity:

"The JCS do not believe that the recommended program in itself will be sufficient to turn the trick against the Viet Cong in SVN without positive action being taken against the Hanoi government at an early date."[5] The opposite view was registered by Hilsman in a memorandum to the secretary of state on March 14, three days prior to the NSC meeting:

> In my judgment, significant action against North Vietnam that is taken before we have demonstrated success in our counterinsurgency program will be interpreted by the Communists as an act of desperation, and will, therefore, not be effective in persuading the North Vietnamese to cease and desist.[6]

In the months that followed policy drifted in the direction of the JCS position with ISA and the Far Eastern Bureau of the State Department acting to temper, slow, and lay the political groundwork for the military moves against the north. Hilsman left the administration.

The military were out in front of the civilians on the question of action against the north in their interpretation of the prescription of NSAM 288 and in their position on the proper response to the Laos crisis. This was evident later in the policy review at the Honolulu conference in June. The JCS were united in recommendations on Viet-Nam and stood against the secretary of defense and ISA and, until his departure, their own chairman, Maxwell Taylor. They did not extend their many parochial mission and budgetary battles to Viet-Nam policy but agreed on a tack that would, if adopted, bring policy to depend even more on their capabilities.[7] That they should have combined against the OSD is not surprising. Ever since the abortive Bay of Pigs there had been a special mistrust of the military by civilians and, in turn, McNamara's efforts at gaining control of military budgets and programs led the military to resent and mistrust the secretary. This background of ill feeling underlay the 1964 JCS-OSD differences over how and when pressure should be exerted on North Viet-Nam and foreshadowed the more severe civil–military tensions of the next three years. It is interesting that in the summer of 1964 the JCS perceived a wide gap between their military proposals and the "political-military" approach which the administration seemed to be following. When General Earl Wheeler took over as chairman of the JCS he made his position clear: "It is fashionable in some quarters to say that the problems in Southeast Asia are primarily political and economic rather than military. I do not agree. The essence of the problem in Vietnam is military."[8] Presumably had Wheeler been present at the Honolulu conference instead of Taylor, the recommendation of the JCS for "positive, prompt, and meaningful military action" would have been endorsed rather than dissented from.[9]

Looking back, it is clear that the military were out in front—doing the hauling on Viet-Nam policy—but it is also clear that the differences between civilians and military were not of the kind that had marked debate in the earlier period. The policy recommendations of the JCS were more extreme than those favored by civilian principals involved in planning policy, but the premises of both about the nature of the conflict in Southeast Asia and the kind of solution that was required were becoming strikingly similar.

The various kinds of pressures applied against the north during this period need not be recounted here, nor is it necessary to take up the question of whether the Tonkin Gulf incidents in August were orchestrated by the United States or even fabricated.[10] It is sufficient to note that, given administration thinking that it would be desirable to further impress Hanoi with American commitment, the occasion to bomb North Viet-Nam in overt reprisal was not an unwelcome opportunity. A lull in activity followed the raids, perhaps in order not to muddy the public's perception of Hanoi as provocateur, but also presumably to preserve the president's image in the election campaign. That image as peacemaker, contrasted with his opponent's image as warmonger, may well have confused the North Vietnamese if they were as signal conscious as Washington decision makers always assumed they were. At one point in the campaign the president assured the country and anyone else who might have been listening, "Sometimes our folks get a little impatient. Sometimes they rattle their rockets some, and they bluff about their bombs."[11] It was just a such a signal that the military and the new ambassador to South Viet-Nam, Maxwell Taylor, hoped to avoid. In stressing the need to continue to impress Hanoi with United States commitment in unambiguous ways, CINCPAC said that our August 5 reprisal strikes "created a momentum which can lead to the attainment of our objectives in S.E. Asia" and therefore should be maintained. The JCS warned that "failure to resume and maintain a program of pressure through military actions . . . could signal a lack of resolve."[12] Events would indicate that the military need not have been concerned about momentum, for neither the temporary pause in government action nor the softening of rhetoric revealed the degree to which the policy of pressuring the north had taken hold of the bureaucracy.

In late August and September intelligence reports showed that conditions in South Viet-Nam were alternating between "no improvement" and "deteriorating." Even a study produced within the State Department tentatively recommended that escalating military activity begin immediately with such actions as harassment of North Viet-Nam's coast and borders by South Vietnamese (34A operations), United States destroyer cruises along the North Vietnamese coast (DESOTO patrols), and tit-for-tat reactions to any special Viet Cong "dirty tricks." Ultimately these actions were to lead to "systematic military action against DRV" (Democratic Republic of [North] Vietnam) should the deterioration become sufficiently critical and especially if there were "clear evidence of greatly increased infiltration from the North."[13] In a September policy review the JCS recommended the beginning of a rapidly intensifying bombing campaign against a list developed earlier in the year of some ninety-four targets in North Viet-Nam. Although the military were not alone in advocating such action against the north, others like McNamara, McCone, and Rusk thought the government of South Viet-Nam too weak a political base to sustain the move at that time. (Later such a move was thought necessary *because* the GVN was so weak.) There was agreement among those principals as well as John McNaughton, assistant secretary of defense for ISA William Bundy, assistant secretary of state for Far Eastern affairs, and Walt Rostow, counselor for the State Department, that negotiations should be shunned until after pressure could be applied to North Viet-Nam and that the use of United States ground troops was to be avoided. The actual military actions undertaken during the fall of 1964 closely resembled those recommended by the State Department and differed most from those advocated by the Joint Chiefs.[14]

One point should be clear about this period in the decision-making process and that is that the participants were planning for actions they expected the United States government to undertake. Perhaps that seems too obvious to mention, given available evidence, but much has been made of the contingency nature of plans in 1964 with the implication that having ninety-four targets all picked out in North Viet-Nam was like having one hundred and ninety-four picked out in the Soviet Union—we had to have them in the unlikely event of a catastrophic occurrence like a nuclear attack. This point is related to the game of trying to figure out when President Lyndon Johnson really decided to bomb North Viet-Nam.[15] That particular moment of truth will be left for others to ferret out, but as for the prevailing mood, atmosphere, and expectations of the national security bureaucracy, it is here asserted that all believed in the fall of 1964 that the United States would very likely be acting directly against North Viet-Nam and probably by January of 1965. Presumably a nuclear attack was not perceived to be nearly as imminent. This is important not so that we can establish that the president and his administration were guilty of duplicity in not informing the American people of their plans (though it appears that they were), but because these plans and expectations tended to severely limit the scope of a major review of Viet-Nam policy engaged in during the month of November.

The formation of the special NSC working group in November 1964 followed directly from a meeting to consider the appropriate American response to a Viet Cong attack on Bien Hoa Air Base that killed four Americans and destroyed a number of B-57's. Since the attack took place on November 1 immediately prior to the presidential elections, no American response was forthcoming, but it was agreed that an interagency working group would meet "to study 'immediately and intensively' the future courses of action and alternatives open to the United States in Southeast Asia and to report as appropriate to a 'Principal Group' of NSC members."[16] This was to have been, and certainly at the time appeared to be, an exhaustive and thorough review of the situation and the choices available. In fact it began from exceedingly questionable assumptions, proceeded to narrow to three only marginally distinguishable options, and finally resulted in a policy best described as a blend of those options that could be supported by none of the individual rationales.

From the start of the review attention was focused not on South Viet-Nam but on the north because, as McNaughton noted, "progress inside SVN is important, but it is unlikely despite our best ideas and efforts."[17] If McNaughton was correct about the unlikelihood of influencing the course of events in the south, and if something were going to be done anyway, that did indeed leave only the north in which to do it. Unfortunately the initial assessment from the intelligence community was clearly pessimistic. The chances of damaging North Viet-Nam severely enough to prevent it from supplying, or to convince it not to supply, the minimal amount of aid required by the Viet Cong to continue the insurgency in the south were small. But before some dramatic conclusion could be drawn from the combination of McNaughton's observation and the intelligence assessment, the JCS representative to the working group objected to such "negativism" and apparently prevailed on the critical question of whether the war in the south could be won by applying pressure to the north. The group apparently then proceeded to the next logical question of the kind of pressure that ought to be applied.[18]

William Bundy, the group's director, and John McNaughton generated only three options for study and recommendation to the NSC: Option A, "Continue present policies," called for assisting the GVN with actions in Laos and covert activity in North Viet-Nam with the United States role in the north limited to controlled reprisals when necessary; Option B, "Fast/full squeeze" was a systematic, rapidly escalating program of pressure on the north by the United States; and Option C, "Progressive squeeze-and-talk," involved a slow, deliberate increase in pressure against North Viet-Nam by the United States along with open communication with Hanoi.[19] In the first two options negotiations were to be avoided for some initial period until Hanoi's position had been weakened.

What is particularly striking about these options and the November review generally is the degree to which they appear to have been predetermined by prior interpretations of the events in Southeast Asia. For example, the options did not include seeking a political settlement without further military involvement, as George Ball had recommended in October. Ball's recommendation was itself part of a lengthy memorandum by the under secretary analyzing four broad options open to the United States. Although it was discussed by Rusk, McNamara, and McGeorge Bundy in October, it did not get before the president until January after the course of action had been set by the November review.[20] Why was it then, that a well-staffed interagency study uncritically presumed so much and failed to take a perspective even as broad as that of Ball's unstaffed memo—failed to go beyond the analysis presented eight months previously in NSAM 288?

An answer that is at once inadequate and suggestive is that Lyndon Johnson may have simply told his subordinates he did not want analysis of options that could involve "losing" South Viet-Nam. The participants in the policy review may then be assumed to have either shared the president's views or declined to differ with him. Alone it is an inadequate explanation for the content of the November review because there is no evidence that the mandate for the "NSC Working Group on SVN/SEA" was that narrow, nor is it likely that there was an explicit directive to so limit the policy if only because, no matter how phrased, it would appear an irrational boundary on the "search process" for future policy. Nonetheless it is likely that the president and others felt just that way and that common perceptions about the significance of the loss of Viet-Nam pervaded the bureaucracy in more subtle ways. One way is by shared images. Two such images are revealed by Johnson's oft quoted comment to Cabot Lodge, "I am not going to be the President who saw Southeast Asia go the way China went."[21] There is here the cold war image of the world as divided into two camps with those areas as yet unspoken for serving as the spoils of the competition between the superpowers. There is also the second image of a curse on the Democratic party following from the charge that the Democrats had been soft on Communism. Holding these images or coming to policy making with this "intellectual baggage" limits the number of options and actions the decision maker will seriously consider. Commonly held images act to constrain policy choice. The first image of the world provided the bounds of the national interest; the second image of public opinion provided the bounds of personal and party interests through fear of electoral punishment.[22]

The narrow scope of the policy review in November 1964 is at least partially explained by recognizing the degree to which the flow of policy discussions throughout the year had created and reinforced images of the conflict in Southeast Asia that precluded analysis proceeding from other premises consistent with other images. The monopoly on legitimacy was reflected in the language of the debate by easy references to the American commitment and the consequences for our Asian allies if South Viet-Nam were to go Communist. That language was allowed to stand without consideration of whether the American commitment really extended from one administration to another, or whether our influence in Asian countries would not have been increased by withdrawing and demonstrating independence from our South Vietnamese ally, or even whether anyone knew or agreed on what happens when a country "goes."[23]

Another reason for the policy process to be so unimaginative in November 1964 was that the same people who had been responsible for policy for the previous three years were asked to review it. In some ways this was as unfortunate as it would be to ask the Navy to judge the relative merits of carrier versus land-based tactical air power: vested interest could be expected to produce bias. Although organizational subunits such as ISA in the Defense Department and Policy Planning in the State Department are free from the normal bureaucratic biases of organizations that have missions and budgets to protect, it is still likely that key actors such as William and McGeorge Bundy, John McNaughton, and Walt Rostow all had an important stake in policy. None may have had organizational interests to protect, as is usually the case in the politics of bureaucracies, but all of them had "invested" in Viet-Nam policy over the years and a reversal of their stand would have been as difficult as are all decisions to "cut bait." Using the phrase, "protecting our commitment," to explain American presence in Viet-Nam may be as pertinent in its application to individual actors as it is to the nation as a whole.

The record at the end of the Viet-Nam policy review in November is not altogether clear. The working group made recommendations to the principals of the NSC and they in turn met with and advised the president at a December 1 meeting.[24] Available evidence indicates that Option A, continuing the present course, was the recommended immediate action, with the expectation that after a period of thirty days Option C, a gradual "Squeeze-and-talk," would begin—only without the "talk." The president apparently accepted the two phase recommendation but actually approved only the immediate program of continuing pressure. So American policy would continue as it had for a time until some unusual act of provocation by the Viet Cong in the south occurred that might serve to justify the beginning of overt pressures on the north. The pressure would then be gradually increased. This was the conclusion in spite of much agreement that conditions would only worsen if present policy were continued, in spite of the military's position that the "slow squeeze" would not produce results, and in spite of the reluctance to engage in negotiations when talks were initially an integral part of the "slow squeeze" option.

Although the chosen tack did not represent the clear victory of one actor over another it did combine the caution some advised with the promise of the more aggressive strategy advocated by others. It was the kind of choice that would characterize decisions in Viet-Nam—achieving the support of an apparent consensus at a very high cost to the content of policy. The possibility of real differences over Viet-Nam surfacing at that point was small and the differences in objectives that did exist were smoothed by a policy sufficiently compromising to satisfy the principal decision makers. The policy was a collection of actions that could be agreed upon even if there was underlying disagreement over what would be accomplished by particular acts. This strategy of decision making would have far-reaching consequences for the content of Viet-Nam policy, consequences that were felt almost immediately after the initiation of the bombing of North Viet-Nam the following February.

Choosing to Bomb North Viet-Nam

During the first month of 1965 the situation in South Viet-Nam worsened, and no one expected any improvement to result from current American policy. There was considerable pressure on the president to begin "Phase II" of the program deferred in November, air attacks on the north. Much precise planning had been undertaken in preparation for a bombing strike, with three packages of attack options, each with a different number of targets, readied for immediate use. Aircraft from carriers like the Coral Sea had been practicing in the Pacific for months to improve their capability in various operations against North Viet-Nam, including an operation called MINEX in the event the port of Haiphong was to be mined.[25] The resumption of the DESOTO patrols off the coast of Viet-Nam by American destroyers was scheduled for February 3 with the expectation that the North Vietnamese would be provoked into some unusual action to which the United States could then "justifiably" respond. It appears clear that by the end of January a decision had been made by the president to launch FLAMING DART, limited air reprisals against the north, as soon as an opportunity was presented.

As it happened it was not the DESOTO patrol that provided the opportunity but a Viet Cong attack on the American position at Pleiku. The destroyer patrols had never begun because of concern over Soviet Premier Kosygin's visit to Hanoi, but even if events were not proceeding exactly as planned, the attacks in the central highlands did not totally surprise Washington planners. The State Department had predicted that Pleiku or a similar target would be hit, and McGeorge Bundy, who was in Viet-Nam at the time, was told to carry his contingency plans with him.[26] Apparently CINCPAC was not similarly informed, for the high state of readiness of its carriers in the Gulf of Tonkin was relaxed after the DESOTO patrol was cancelled. Two of the three carriers were leaving the area and one, the *Coral Sea*, was steaming to Subic Bay for "Rest and Relaxation." When word came to launch the strikes, aircraft had to hold until the carriers could return and all were "on the line."[27]

The decision to strike following word of Pleiku had been made in Washington after a hastily called cabinet meeting produced the support President Johnson required—including the support of his country team in South Viet-Nam. Bundy, who had gone to Pleiku and is said to have been emotionally moved by the destruction, concurred with Taylor and Westmoreland in recommending the strike. He later coldly but aptly characterized the incident when he told a newsman, "Pleikus are streetcars"—meaning that the United States had been waiting for such an incident and planned to make use of it.[28] Another streetcar came along three days later on February 10 when more Americans were killed in an attack at Qui Nhon, and FLAMING DART II was launched against targets in the North Vietnamese panhandle. The second United States strike was, like the first, linked to activity in the south; but unlike the first it was not designated a reprisal for a specific act, but an air operation in response to events in the south. By February 13 the president had decided to terminate FLAMING DART operations and begin ROLLING THUNDER (RT), a continuing program of air raids on the north. A cable from the White House to Ambassador Taylor signaled the change.

> We will execute a program of measured and limited air action jointly with GVN against selected military targets in DRV remaining south of 19th parallel until further notice.
>
> FYI Our current expectation is that these attacks might come about once or twice a week and involve two or three targets on each day of operation.[29]

The first ROLLING THUNDER strike, launched March 2, was numbered V, the first four in the series having been cancelled because of yet another coup in South Viet-Nam, diplomatic moves involving the Russians and weather difficulties. RT VI followed on March 15 and was another "one-day fixed target" strike.

The same day that RT VI was launched President Johnson again changed the character of the bombing program by setting forth new guidelines loosening his control over the strikes and regularizing their operation.[30] The change followed considerable pressure from Ambassador Taylor and the Joint Chiefs to move in this direction and to step up the program. The bombing campaign continued through April, the month in which the president came closest to extending the olive branch of peace in his speech at Johns Hopkins University, and was only interrupted in May for five days while diplomatic moves were undertaken. The controversy over the character of the air campaign also continued through the spring, it being interrupted only by the diversion of attention at critical points in making the decision to introduce American ground troops into South Viet-Nam.

The decision makers who endorsed the policy of bombing North Viet-Nam did so, as we shall see, for different reasons. They differed over what, specifically, they hoped the policy would accomplish, and they differed over the costs and risks they were willing to run to pursue the policy. Because of these differences it is not surprising that they also had individual perspectives on how the bombing should be conducted to achieve their separate goals. So although it is roughly true that the policy consensus was really an alliance over means rather than ends, bombing was an acceptable means to all only so long as the specifics of the action were not spelled out. The specifics were not, in fact, spelled out in advance and one of the reasons they were not was to avoid eroding the base of support for the policy. This failure to define the content of the program and the impossibility of maintaining a consistent objective for it are among the consequences of policy supported by the alliance in 1964–65. There are others.

As the bombing policy in 1965 came to be defined by the pattern made by the strikes themselves, disagreements erupted among the decision makers who did not think the policy being pursued was serving their ends. Controversy led to further compromise in the conduct of the policy to avoid alienating support. Compromise in the pursuit of objectives, however, contributed to failure to achieve any objective. Failure, finally, produced a displacement or redefinition of goals to accommodate real results, as well as more controversy and the beginning of the withering of support for the policy. The evidence for this argument begins with the principal participants in the alliance of 1965 and what each saw in choosing to bomb North Viet-Nam.

The military are often described as advocating the use of or display of force as the solution to whatever problem might be put before them. This is undoubtedly an unfair characterization as well as an oversimplified one. It is accurate, however, to attribute to the military services the tendency to perceive problems with all the distortions and biases common to any large organization with its own mission and interests to protect. In the most understanding terms, Alain C. Enthoven and K. Wayne Smith describe the motivation of the military to take organizationally determined stands:

While senior officers attempt to rise above the narrow parochialisms of their particular areas within a Service, and indeed above their Service itself, it is a psychologically difficult thing for any man to do. We are all most at ease in familiar surroundings, and the military man has the greatest confidence in the forces he understands and knows best. This tendency is reflected in recommendations as to the priority of military objectives as well as to the best kinds of forces for achieving them.[31]

The air force was no exception in this respect and not surprisingly its officers were among the first and most active supporters of a bombing policy. What is interesting is that the air force has been more zealous than other services in its claims for the capabilities of its forces, not only in Viet-Nam but throughout its history and prehistory as a separate service. Immediately after World War I air advocates in the belligerent countries began campaigns to convince political leaders of the future importance of air power and of the necessity of investing in it. During the interwar period and World War II itself, the campaign in this country was waged principally for the prize of autonomy as a separate service. The air force's special need to demonstrate the legitimacy of its capability produced a highly politically conscious leadership who went to unusual lengths to make their case. When Wendell Willkie promised autonomy if elected in 1940, the Air Officer Corps made the very unique gesture in return of openly supporting him for the presidency. Perhaps even more unusual was the service's attempt to set the record straight on its role in the allied victory in World War II by sneaking one of its own volumes into the collection of 316 other volumes of the United States Strategic Bombing Survey (USSBS) authored by an independent civilian agency.[32]

The air force, like no other advocate, was fighting for the credibility of a part of its organizational identity and the preservation of primary missions by arguing that bombing would "work" in Viet-Nam before it was begun, maintaining that it was effective after it was started, and protesting that it could not produce victory unless it was conducted with more vigor after it appeared to fail. The record on the effectiveness of conventional air power had not been set straight by the USSBS nor by the Korean experience, and so it was again at stake in Viet-Nam.[33] One could argue that Viet-Nam was a poor place for the air force to seek to demonstrate the effectiveness of its capability, that is, in a limited war against a nonindustrial state engaged in modified guerrilla activities in jungle terrain. However, as one observer noted, the air force was well aware of the risks in seeking to demonstrate its capability for short-range organizational goals.[34] The risk, of course, was that the conclusion reached in the St. Louis Post-Dispatch editorial entitled "Air Power Fails Again" would be shared by some future appropriations committee:

> One fact that emerges clearly from the latest enlargement of the Indo China War is the total failure of the United States Air Force, or rather, air power in general. American planes, with virtually uncontested command of the skies, have been conducting history's heaviest bombings, with zero effect on the course of the war.[35]

The position of the other services on the bombing differed from that of the air force. They had no reason to share the air force's faith in its own ability to replace land armies, and so the Joint Chiefs opposed an air force proposal in the fall of 1964 to reduce the number of ground troops to be provided in favor of greater reliance on tactical air power should the Chinese enter the war.[36] But on the question of bombing the north the other services would be less concerned about its effectiveness and more interested in the degree to which it committed the United States to Southeast Asia and ultimately involved their services' capability. It is important, therefore, that while they advocated extensive bombing of the north, the principal military leaders did not think it would work in ending the engagement and fully expected both bombing and involvement to continue.[37] In short, at least for some at an early stage, and for others by the spring of 1965, bombing was a means to their own participation in the war. Generals Westmoreland and Wheeler might well have been skeptics about air power and still joined in advocating it, because its use increased the likelihood of a larger American military commitment, which, in turn, made it more likely that they would receive what they thought was needed to win the war on the ground. The navy, of course, shared the air force's interest in demonstrating air power's capability, since any action against the north would involve its carrier based aircraft. Admiral Sharp, head of the Pacific Command, was a natural supporter of the bombing and was only slightly less aggressive than Air Force Chief of Staff McConnell.[38] The military perceived the bombing policy from their own organizational perspective and, in each case, found it desirable to support it.

Maxwell Taylor, ambassador to South Viet-Nam, and McGeorge Bundy, the president's special advisor on national security affairs, advocated the bombing of the north but emphasized different objectives. In a February cable advocating a program of gradual reprisal, Taylor listed the objectives as weakening the will of Hanoi's leadership, improving the morale of the GVN, and reducing the north's ability to support insurgency and added, "Of these three, the first appears to us by far the most important, since our effectiveness in influencing Hanoi leadership will, in the long run, determine the success or failure of our efforts in both North and South Vietnam."[39]

Although advocating a policy of sustained reprisal, Bundy's influential memorandum of February singled out a different objective as primary:

> We emphasize that our primary target in advocating a reprisal policy is the improvement of the situation in *South* Vietnam. Action against the North is usually urged as a means of affecting the will of Hanoi to direct and support the V. C. We consider this an important but long-range purpose. The immediate and critical targets are in the South—in the minds of the South Vietnamese and in the minds of the Viet Cong cadres. (Emphasis in the original.)[40]

The requirements for the fulfillment of their respective objectives eventually led to a divergence in recommendations, but in the beginning of the bombing program both were strong supporters.

Walt Rostow was perhaps the earliest and most aggressive civilian advocate of a policy of pressure against the north. During the September policy review in 1964 principal actors received copies of the "Rostow thesis" on the necessity of countering aggression by striking at its source, and copies of a critique principally authored in ISA. At that time Rostow was not so far different from those in State, OSD, and the White House in the actions he advocated as he was in his position that the United States was sufficiently justified in bombing North Viet-Nam to overtly engage in it as a declatory policy. The ISA critique charged that "the Rostow approach risks domestic and international opposition ranging from anxiety and protest to condemnation. . . ." The charge was repeated later, since a similar scorn for such concerns characterized Rostow's attitudes when he became Lyndon Johnson's closest advisor on the subject.[41] Rostow's view, expressed repeatedly in the spring of 1965, was that the north could and should be coerced into ending its support for the insurgency and that the means to do this lay in heavier bombardment, specifically of certain key industrial targets in the north. It is clear that he had a well-developed idea of how the bombing program should be conducted and worked tirelessly to move policy in the appropriate direction. Rostow had invested heavily in bombing stock and remained, throughout, uniquely optimistic.

In sharp contrast to Rostow's genuine faith in the efficacy of the bombing was Ball's skepticism and hostility to the policy. In his lengthy memorandum of October 1964 referred to earlier, Ball systematically attacked the arguments favoring air action and prepared a thorough analysis of the risks it entailed. Yet in 1965, in spite of his well-known objections to the pursuit of the policy of pressuring the north with bombs, Ball went along for two reasons. First, since he was not prepared to resign over the issue and still hoped to influence the direction of policy, concern for the continuation of his own credibility required that he not alienate himself too far from the mainstream of policy. To be effective, dissent would have to be legitimate—it would have to come from one still thought of as sharing the same values and objectives as the other principals.[42]

The second reason is that Ball wanted to avoid the use of ground troops even more than the use of bombs and hoped that the latter would serve as a substitute for the former.[43] If some action was going to be taken in the early part of 1965, it was far better that involvement be limited to air action on the chance that further commitment could be avoided. Ball need not have expected the bombing to "work" in the sense of winning the war, only that it satisfy the principals' need to act until their views about Southeast Asia and what the United States was required to do there could be changed. Ball would bomb to avoid a war and so joined Rostow and other strange bedfellows.

For the most senior actors like Rusk, McNamara, and Johnson, the appeal of bombing in the beginning may have been more complex and involved larger political calculations than it did for their assistants at the various lower levels. It is most likely that all three hoped the bombing would be effective in saving South Viet-Nam, expected that it would not, but felt obliged to do it anyway. The hope was based at least partly on the experience of the Cuban missile crisis and generally on confidence in the American ability to put overwhelming pressure on an adversary. It did not matter to them that the parallels were absent and the analogy grossly faulty—ISA had described the steps on the ladder of escalation, and if followed, it seemed reasonable that a third-rate Asian power would capitulate in the same way as a super power had been forced to do.[44]

Bombing also appealed to these men for the same reason it

appealed to Ball and appeals to decision makers still, that is, compared to using troops, it is a lower level action, involving less risk and less cost—therefore it is a cheaper policy. Harry Howe Ransom described the debate in Britain in 1917 over how best to fight World War I and found that "political leaders sought an alternative to sending the flower of British manhood 'to chew barbed wire in Flanders,'" and "amidst a profound struggle between soldiers and politicians in England over the war's conduct, many eyes turned to the air for a panacea."[45] It is understandable that the president, motivated by a similar concern for the loss of lives and the domestic political consequences, would also look hopefully to the air where he thought he could achieve, as he later said, "maximum deterrence at minimum expense."[46]

In spite of their hopes these principals could not have expected the bombing to obviate the need to go further. As early as April 1964, Rusk was taking the position that if we destroyed the north's industrial capability it would not have a serious impact, and we would have "forfeited the hostage."[47] As secretary of state, Rusk was further restrained in his enthusiasm by concern over the effect the strikes would have on Soviet and Chinese calculations—a concern shared by the secretary of defense. McNamara probably at no time believed that bombing alone would suffice, although he did have certain expectations about its effectiveness that ultimately led to serious consequences when they were not fulfilled. As someone who questioned McNamara extensively on the subject put it, "He didn't think it could 'win it,' never did, but he did think it would help with the infiltration."[48]

Finally, we turn to the president who had made the decisions ordering FLAMING DART and ROLLING THUNDER. His choices may appear to have been the result of the "resolution of forces" exerted by those around him, but beneath that there were those biases and concerns peculiar to his position. He revealed his feelings about air power in a little noted message to Maxwell Taylor on December 30, 1964, when it was all but certain that strikes would be forthcoming: "I have never felt that this war will be won from the air and it seems to me that what is much more needed and would be more effective is a larger and stronger use of Rangers and Special Forces and Marines and other appropriate military strength on the ground."[49] Even with this attitude Lyndon Johnson thought the bombing was a necessary course, not to obtain political-military objectives, but for domestic reasons clearest to one holding the elected office of the presidency.

He might not have believed it true that he would have been impeached if he had not responded to Pleiku with bombs (though he said he did), but he was very much concerned with popular expectations that he respond to attacks on the United States, that he not repeat the mistake of another Democratic president and appear to be soft on communism.[50]

But that is only part of what the bombing decision accomplished for the president and, left at that, it is a misleading characterization of events. Support for the decision to drop bombs did not follow from a perception of direct domestic pressure, but from the perceived link between the use of air power and the use of American troops; bombs were dropped as a necessary political prerequisite to the engagement of American troops. The distinction is important. Daniel Ellsberg is incorrect when he asserts that bombing made sense if "one noted that 'doing something' to hurt Communist opponents, no matter how costly and uncompromising, is strong protection against domestic charges of criminal underestimation of a Communist threat. . . ."[51] Actually it did not make sense because the president and his advisors had no intention of simply making a face-saving gesture in South Viet-Nam, since they did not believe face could be saved by mere gestures followed by defeat. Instead they expected to introduce troops that spring and had to begin bombing to demonstrate the necessity of going beyond it to a higher level of commitment. In short, for those who had to concern themselves with the bounds of public opinion, the function of air power was to fail openly so that large scale losses of American lives on the ground in Asia could be justified.[52] In fact, a large part of the story of the ongoing air war to be explored in the next chapter turns on the necessity for the civilian leadership to demonstrate that air power was being used to the maximum desirable degree and, that its failure to end the war justified the constant increase in troop commitments.

The continuing air force propaganda and lingering air power mythology made bombing a political necessity. From the start the air force argued, and implicitly threatened to publicly argue, that if restrictions were lifted air power could break Hanoi's will, and then the insurgency in the south would wither away without adding more American troops and suffering more American deaths. Because the air force had support in Congress and generals had credibility with the public, the civilian leaders, especially the president, had to deal seriously with them. The consensus on Viet-

Nam in 1965 was a complex one, and in the spring of that year all the complexity seemed to be reflected in the conduct of the bombing of North Viet-Nam.

If we look back over the multiplicity of objectives and interests of the actors involved in the bombing decision, the controversy over what to bomb, how often, how intensely, and with what communications to the opponents and the public can come as no surprise. What is interesting and important for policy making is how the conflict affected the content of policy. Conflict at this level, it turned out, resulted in a compromise policy: a policy that compromised among the different strategies recommended by the participants, and a policy that compromised the objectives they sought as well.[53]

There is a tendency among some observers to see the gradual increase in the intensity of the bombing as an indicator that a carefully thought out, controlled plan of escalation was being pursued as restrictions on the bombing were removed. It looked not like compromise but like "compellence" in the Schelling tradition. Some of the earlier memoranda of John McNaughton add even more of this flavor. A closer look at the spring of 1965, however, reveals an incrementalism brought about by the tugging and hauling of many actors rather than a preprogrammed policy of pressure. The tugging is documented by the stream of recommendations, each different, from Taylor, CINCPAC, the air force, and the JCS to pursue a more aggressive policy and by the resistance of the president and his secretaries of state and defense. In an analysis of the administration's failure to consistently pursue a policy of pressure because of competing objectives the author concludes, "Washington's bluff about an upward escalation of air attacks against highly valued industrial targets was called in mid-April by both Hanoi and Moscow, and the Administration's response was to back away from implementing a strong variant of coercive strategy."[54] In fact some were bluffing, others were not, but they could not sway policy, and still others never intended the threat.

Just as some actors wanted to break Hanoi's will but failed to bring policy around to their position, others wanted negotiations and met with just as little success in controlling policy. It is likely, for instance, that those in the State Department and elsewhere who prevailed in early February and had the resumption of the DESOTO patrols postponed in order not to interfere with whatever positive developments might come from Soviet Premier

Kosygin's impending visit to Hanoi were not enthusiastic about the decision to launch FLAMING DART while the premier was still in the city.[55] The May bombing pause and "peace initiative" is another example. The Soviets refused to transmit to the North Vietnamese an American message giving its position on negotiations. Foy Kohler, the American ambassador in Moscow who received the Russian refusal, thought the message to be "rather strenuous" and recommended that in future efforts to send the message it be shorter and revised: "If cast in present form, I think we are simply inviting rebuff. . . ." The message was not revised, was recommunicated, and was rebuffed.[56]

In both cases the chances of diplomatic maneuvers producing a resolution to the crisis were reduced considerably by some actors who opposed negotiations from a position of weakness and by others who were concerned about the danger of conveying to the opposition something other than a firm American commitment in Southeast Asia. The tack of coercive diplomacy had been similarly undercut by the fears of those actors unwilling to run the risks involved in a continuing pursuit of such a strategy. The mix of motives of the participants discussed earlier produced a conflict that precluded an alliance adequate to support a consistent course of action. At the same time, it is in the nature of a policy process that demands broad support for action and thrives on consensus to resolve conflict by compromise. That is what happened in 1965, though the participants at the time may have thought that their policy was uncompromising and thus unambiguous. Ultimately a compromise policy may be a successful solution to a domestic political-bureaucratic conflict, but because a foreign policy must also be evaluated on the results it achieves in the international arena, such policy may be handicapped by its failure to achieve external coherence. As Alexander George observes, "Even if inconsistent approaches taken to different objectives can be compatibly rationalized from the standpoint of a government's internal relations, their intended meanings may not be readily differentiated by opponents and other outside observers."[57]

The failure of the bombing policy to achieve its original overt objective was partly the result of the compromised fashion in which it was pursued and partly, no doubt, due to the limits of the policy under the best of circumstances. In 1965 the failure of the policy to achieve stated objectives resulted not only in some alteration of policy, as might be expected, but it also produced a significant change in objectives. Specifically, the principal rationale of using bombs to apply pressure to Hanoi to halt its support of the insurgency was changed to using bombs to actually restrict the flow of material to the south in support of the insurgency. The change in policy occurred at least partly because the original plan had proved inadequate. On February 17 after 267 sorties had been flown against North Viet-Nam, Secretary of Defense McNamara sent a memorandum to the chairman of the JCS indicating his unhappiness. In customary backhanded bureaucratic language, McNamara warned that

> although the four missions left the operations at the targets relatively unimpaired, I am quite satisfied with the results. Our primary objective, of course, was to communicate our political resolve. This I believe we did. Future communications of resolve, however, will carry a hollow ring unless we accomplish more military damage than we have to date.[58]

In early April a new targeting program was begun with RT IX designated primarily to interdict the lines of communication from north to south. It represented at least the temporary abandonment of one objective, changing North Vietnamese minds by the threat of greater destruction, and the adoption of another objective, reducing the substantive capabilities of the opponent in the south. Bombing as a tactic was not abandoned but redirected and assigned a new mission by which to measure its effectiveness. By the end of April more of the participants had come to accept the new objective for air power. Demands for programs of "systematic pressure" against the north at the Honolulu conference were more isolated as the limitations of bombing became recognized. At an April 26 news conference McNamara made the change public: "The basic objective of the strikes has been to inhibit, to reduce, to deflect the movement of men and material."[59] A change in ends to accommodate means is not unique in public policy, but the critical question always remains as to whether the new ends are being served, or whether the means, in this case the dropping of bombs, are sustained by unstated interests and only rationalized by changing the overt ends.[60] The questions will be addressed in the next chapter.

Conclusion

The argument of the previous chapter was that policy was significantly influenced and moderated by the openness of the policy-making process during the Kennedy years. Legitimate dissent emanating from the Department of State effected the course of events. The argument here has been that very early in the Johnson administration the bounds of legitimate debate over Viet-Nam were set rather narrowly, and fundamental dissent over policy ceased to emerge. The exception was George Ball who dissented and did so for some time before joining others who left or were asked to leave the administration. In the absence of real dissent, the military pushed policy along, the civilians, sometimes more, sometimes less reluctantly, followed, and the president chose from among the options presented him.

So again the argument is that the process and structuring of decision making influenced decisions—the system was becoming closed and there were, and would be, policy consequences. If one asks if the president, to a very large degree determined whether the process would be more or less open to dissent, the answer is clearly, "yes." Just as clearly, however, though presidents may structure their foreign-policy-making apparatus and set its tone, they cannot control the consequences of their creations. In fact, a credible argument could be made that by not accommodating views markedly different from those put forth by his military advisors, President Johnson gradually put himself in the position of a leader without significant options—not a position he or any other president is likely to have contrived to attain. John Kennedy, it is recalled, had done otherwise. The process, then, dependent to some extent upon presidential prerogative, is an independent variable in explaining presidential decision.

Roger Hilsman described foreign-policy-making in America as a process of consensus building. "Getting a variety of people who hold different values to sit down and decide on how to rank those values would be next to impossible; but getting people to agree on a particular policy that serves a mix of values is done all the time."[61] It is as if policy making were a matter of engineering, of designing a policy sufficiently broad in appeal to attract the critical mass necessary to make it politically and bureaucratically viable. The bombing of the north was, in these terms, a ready-made policy option of that kind, one around which a consensus could form. But the measure of policy is whether it is likely to produce desirable outcomes for the nation in foreign affairs while it satisfies the diverse interests of the governmental participants, and the momentum of events and past policy in 1964 appears to have unfortunately narrowed the range of bureaucratically and politically viable options. In identifying policy with action and

avoiding the examination of underlying assumptions about the international system during the November review, decision makers may have successfully postponed bureaucratic conflict at the cost of embracing a poorly integrated series of actions ill fitting the international environment in which they were to be taken.

IV. EXPLAINING THE BOMBING: 1965–67

There was a consensus of sorts among policy makes to begin the bombing of North Viet-Nam in February 1965, and another one to stop the bombing for a period of time in March of 1968. To characterize the consensus in both cases would be to term them shallow—agreement at neither time extended much beyond the general action to be taken. Objectives, expectations, and premises were not widely shared. Nor, for that matter, were the specifics of the conduct of the action—bombs do not simply fall or not fall, but fall in greater or lesser numbers, more or less frequently, either here or there. Between 1965 and 1968 the bombing of North Viet-Nam continued and with it continued the disagreements among the decision makers over nearly every aspect of the policy. For three years the shape of the bombing policy reflected the conflicts from which it emerged. To account for the content of the policy is to first explain something about the sources of conflict and disagreement among the principal actors.

Air war policy was determined and defined by a variety of inter- and intra-organizational interactions. The intelligence community, the Office of the Secretary of Defense, the secretary of state, the president and his White House advisors, the JCS, elements of Congressional opinion, and perceptions of domestic public opinion all interacted to produce the bombing decisions. The interactions were often visible in conflicts over the issues of military effectiveness, the appropriate targets, the calculation of international risks, and the desirability of bombing pauses. Rarely, however, did the rhetoric of the contending actors on these issues reflect the underlying interests and objectives served by their respective positions on the issues. It falls to the observer to make that link.

The observer also has another connection to make in accounting for policy, and he must look within organizations to do it. Subunits of organizations responsible for executing policy often have interests of their own. These interests are created by the structure of rewards and distribution of functions in the organization. Subunit behavior may therefore be irrational in terms of national objectives but quite understandable when put into the narrower perspective of the internal goals of an organization. Making the link between these interests and the substance of policy is another contribution to the explanation.

In order to explain that set of decisions known as the bombing policy, the complex sources of those decisions in the conflict among principal actors and the shape the decisions took in the hands of the implementing organizations must be explored. With this in mind we will consider the contribution of the intelligence community to the decision-making process, the built-in political incentives to the services to support the bombing, the mechanisms used by the military to prevail over policy at critical points, and finally the overall flow of policy as it responded to the conflict among the actors around the president.

Looking back upon the bombing of North Viet-Nam from 1965 through 1968 an obvious trend of intensification is revealed, both in a quantitative and a qualitative sense. From 1965 to 1966, for example, the number of sorties flown tripled to 148,000 and the amount of bombs dropped quadrupled to 128,000 tons.[1] During the whole three-year period those targets released for strike not only greatly increased in number, but appeared further and further north, nearer the Chinese border and then closer to the heart of the population centers of Hanoi and Haiphong. The character of the fixed targets changed from munition dumps, barracks, and radar installations, to the strategic objectives of POL (petroleum, oil, and lubricants), rail, and power centers. Civilian operational control, still tight by comparison to the war in the south, was gradually loosened, giving the military greater discretion in timing, targets, ordnance, and restrike. All this happened slowly and incrementally. As with the early decisions to begin the bombing, this policy did not develop on schedule according to any overall plan of escalating pressure. Rather, the decisions represented responses to the push and pull of the principal actors over the three-year period. The trend was toward greater intensity but at least some of those creating the trend were only responding to mounting pressure with less and less success. Since it often happened that contention among decision makers centered on the question of the effectiveness of bombing and so raised the issue of intelligence and evaluation, it would be appropriate to begin the discussion on that issue.

The Contribution and Distortion of Intelligence

During a speech in March of 1967 President Lyndon Johnson made the following claim:

> Since February, 1965, our military operations have included selective bombing of military targets in North Vietnam. Our purposes are three: To back our fighting men by denying the enemy a sanctuary; To exact a penalty against North Vietnam for her flagrant violations of the Geneva Accords of 1954 and 1962; To limit the flow, or to substantially increase the cost of infiltration of men and material from North Vietnam. Our intelligence confirms that we have been successful.[2]

No one could deny that bombing had backed our men, or exacted a penalty, or increased the cost, principally because of the nebulous nature of such claims. But the implication that available intelligence unambiguously supported the bombing as it was being conducted was inaccurate. Beginning in August 1965, at the request of the secretary of defense, the CIA and the defense Intelligence Agency (DIA) produced the monthly "Appraisal of the Bombing of North Viet-Nam." Although these evaluations stressed the damage done to North Viet-Nam and enumerated the results in the various target categories (e.g., power plants, manufacturing, POL, etc.), the reports did not convey a sense of overall success. Finding that "the primarily rural nature of the area permits continued functioning of the subsistence economy," and that "economic deterioration so far has not affected the capabilities of North Viet-Nam's armed forces, which place little direct reliance on the domestic economy for material," one monthly report concluded that "the air strikes do not appear to have altered Hanoi's determination to continue supporting the war in South Vietnam."[3] That was a relatively early evaluation. At the end of 1966 the CIA summary was not any more positive in spite of the increased tempo of attacks: "The evidence available does not suggest that Rolling Thunder to date has contributed materially to the achievement of the two primary objectives of air attack—reduction of the flow of supplies to VC/NVA forces in the South or weakening the will of North Vietnamese to continue the insurgency."[4]

A little more than a year later the CIA again supplied principal decision makers, who were then in the midst of reevaluating the bombing policy, with its appraisal of the program: "Twenty-seven months of US bombing of North Vietnam have had remarkably little effect on Hanoi's over-all strategy in prosecuting the war, on its confident view of long-term Communist prospects, and on its political tactics regarding negotiations."[5] Less than a month after that, in a personal response to an inquiry from Secretary of Defense McNamara regarding some proposals for redirecting the bombing, CIA Director Richard Helms replied, "In general, we do not believe that any of the programs presented in your memorandum is capable of reducing the flow of military and other essential goods sufficiently to affect the war in the South or to demean Hanoi's determination to persist in the war."[6]

Nor was the CIA alone in providing the principals with negative evaluations of the effectiveness of the bombing. Perhaps the most rigorous analyses of the air strategy were conducted through the JASON Division of the Institute for Defense Analysis (IDA). The first IDA study was done during the summer of 1966 after preparatory initial exchanges between scholars at Harvard University and the Massuchusetts Institute of Technology, and Adam Yarmolinsky, deputy assistant secretary of defense for international security affairs. The project involved some forty-seven scientists, mostly independent of the government, and twenty IDA experts. The purpose of the study was not simply, or even primarily to evaluate the bombing, but to consider the technical feasibility of the construction of an antiinfiltration barrier along the Demilitarized Zone in South Viet-Nam. It was the hope of the secretary of defense that were it possible to establish some such barrier a major rationale for the bombing would be eliminated, and one element in a future peace settlement would be provided simultaneously. McNamara probably had these and other objectives in mind when he approved the first study in the midst of a policy debate over the desirability of systematically attacking North Viet-Nam's petroleum supplies.[7]

The 1966 JASON study was completed by the end of the summer and included four reports, the first of which was entitled "The Effects of US Bombing in North Vietnam." Aside from the virtue of the study coming as it did from an independent and prestigious source, the analysis was sure to have an impact upon those who saw it because of the unambiguous expression of its conclusions. The more so because the same could not be said of the routine output of the government intelligence community. The summary and conclusions began by dismissing the most important argument of those proponents of the bombing who had to confront its apparent failure thus far:

Although the political constraints seem clearly to have reduced the effectiveness of the bombing program, its limited effect on Hanoi's ability to provide such support cannot be explained solely on that basis. The countermeasures introduced by Hanoi effectively reduced the impact of U.S. bombing. More fundamentally, however, North Vietnam has basically a subsistence agriculture economy that presents a difficult and unrewarding target system.[8]

Proceeding through each of the rationales for the bombing, the analysis enumerated the failures in sequential fashion:

Since the initiation of the ROLLING THUNDER program the damage to facilities and equipment in North Vietnam has been more than offset by the increased flow of military and economic aid, largely from the USSR and Communist China.

Our past experience also indicates that an intensified air campaign in NVN probably would not prevent Hanoi from infiltrating men into the South at the present or a higher rate, if it chooses.

. . . the ROLLING THUNDER program clearly tended to overestimate the persuasive and disruptive effects of the U.S. air strikes and, correspondingly, to underestimate the tenacity and recouperative capabilities of the North Vietnamese.[9]

A second JASON Division study of the bombing was done the following year and completed in December 1967. By this time the intensity of the bombing had been vastly increased and the positions of the principal decision makers had hardened. In fact, the debate was all but over by then with McNamara scheduled to leave office very shortly. Nevertheless, the vigor of the study and clarity of the evaluations it yielded force themselves upon anyone concerned with the input to decision makers on the question of the bombing policy:

As of October 1967, the *U.S. bombing of North Vietnam has had no measurable effect on Hanoi's ability to mount and support military operations in the South.*

The bombing campaign against NVN has not discernibly weakened the determination of the North Vietnamese leaders to continue to direct and support the insurgency in the South (emphasis in the original).

There was no indication that bombing could ever constitute a permanent support for South Vietnamese morale if the situation in the South itself was adverse.[10]

Once again the conclusion had been reached that the air war was a failure as an antiinfiltration measure, a pressure tactic on the north, and as a support for the regime in the south—the three rationales for continuation that survived until 1967. It should be added that the first study was not distributed beyond OSD, the chairman of the Joint Chiefs, and the national security advisor in the White House, and that in the distribution of the second only the secretary of state and commander in chief in the Pacific were added. In short, they were not used as political resources in the public debate, not even indirectly by McNamara in the August 1967 Senate hearings. Like the evaluations of effectiveness from the government intelligence community, they were available to the principals to guide policy. Why then was not policy so guided?

Part of the answer is that the degree of effectiveness of the bombing is only one element in any account of the air war policy. But even limiting consideration to effectiveness as assessed by intelligence sources, the picture is far from clear. Besides the CIA and JASON evaluations already noted, there were studies done by Systems Analysis in OSD and by RAND during this period which were equally negative in their conclusions.[11] At the same time that these negative evaluations and analyses were flowing from the intelligence community, however, some rather positive predictions about potential results were also being put out. In May of 1965 the new director of the CIA, Admiral William F. Raborn made the following prediction in a communication to Secretaries Rusk and McNamara: "The DRV is, in my view, unlikely to engage in meaningful discussions at any time in the coming months until U.S. air attacks have begun to damage or destroy its principal economic and military targets."[12] In December of the same year the acting director of the CIA Richard Helms, supplied McNamara with an optimistic appraisal of the likely impact of an expansion of the bombing to POL storage at Haiphong and elsewhere:

> Destruction of the storage tanks and bulk unloading equipment at Haiphong would substantially increase the Communists' logistic problems and force them to improvise alternative POL import and distribution channels. . . . The loss of stored POL and the dislocation of the distribution system would add appreciably to the DRV's difficulties in supplying the Communist forces in the South.[13]

The view from the other intelligence sources expressed about the same time in a Special National Intelligence Estimate

(SNIE) was also optimistic. Excluding the Department of State's input from its Bureau of Intelligence and Research (INR), the conclusion reached was that the proposed intensification of the air war "might impose significant limitations on the numbers of PAVN and VC main force units which could be actively supported in South Vietnam."[14] The Defense Intelligence Agency and the National Security Agency (NSA) even went as far as to suggest that the proposed expansion in the bombing, added to expected troop increases, might result in breaking Hanoi's will to continue the war.

In the early months of 1966 the debate over the utility of a systematic attack on North Viet-Nam's POL facilities again brought out positive assessments from intelligence sources. In January the DIA produced a report favoring the JCS proposal to strike at POL. McNamara resisted but the JCS and CINCPAC continued to press their case during the next month. In March the CIA provided the military with the support they needed in a report strongly endorsing a greatly intensified bombing campaign designed to break Hanoi's will. The CIA dismissed the past failure of the bombing policy in much the same way as the military always had, by blaming it on civilian-imposed constraints:

> Self-imposed restrictions have limited both choice of targets and the areas to be bombed. Consequently, almost 80 percent of North Vietnam's limited modern, industrial economy, 75 percent of the nation's population and the most lucrative military supply and LOC targets have been effectively insulated from air attack.[15]

The prescription that followed was to forget about interdiction of supplies as a goal and end the concentration of strikes on the trail system, or at what was called the bottom end of the "logistics funnel." Constraints on air attack were to be reduced in turn, and strikes directed at the top of the funnel—in the populated north where the disruptive effects would be greatest. All POL storage was to be destroyed immediately.

The 1966 POL strikes were launched but failed to achieve their objective. Although the DIA at first limited its evaluation to the amount of absolute destruction expressed in terms of the percentage of enemy storage capacity destroyed (i.e. 70%), it eventually joined the CIA in making a much more salient observation concerning the effectiveness of the strikes: "There is no evidence yet of any shortage of POL in North Vietnam and stocks on hand, with recent imports, have been adequate to sustain necessary operations."[16]

Several points can easily be ascertained from this evidence about the contribution of intelligence to air war policy making, and some others may be deduced as well. First, as one of the two most important sources of evaluation within the intelligence community, the CIA increasingly produced more negative assessments but did not do so without important exceptions. It did support the bombing at some critical points, and since some of those points came after McNamara had decided to try to limit the use of air power, the CIA was not the absolutely reliable source of support for the Secretary some have contended. Some of the variation in the CIA's position may be accounted for in terms of changes in the objective situation, but, no doubt, the difference in perspective among those in the agency responsible for Southeast Asia was also significant. George Carver, who directed the agency's Viet-Nam task force, was generally more positive in evaluation and optimistic in expectations about Viet-Nam than others directly beneath him in the same group. This division extended to the question of bombing effectiveness.[17]

The CIA nevertheless developed a reputation for relatively dispassionate, critical analysis in contrast with the other principal source of intelligence on the bombing, the Defense Intelligence Agency. The DIA was created in 1961 along with several other agencies in the Defense Department as part of a partial unification of functions formerly performed separately by the individual military services. The agency is largely staffed by military personnel at the upper levels, and the director reports to the JCS and to the Secretary of Defense through the JCS. Knowing this, one can begin to appreciate why the secretary found that he eventually had to go outside his department to obtain intelligence. He did so not because the CIA had better sources—the two agencies worked with virtually the same data—but because the organizational structure of DIA provided very special incentives to distort intelligence.[18]

DIA suffered from the usual dangers of distortion by "uncertainty absorption" common to any upward flow of information in an organization as subordinates at successive levels decided what was worth passing up to the next level. The decision in the DIA, as elsewhere, was influenced not only by judgments of merit—which depended upon the ability of the one deciding—but also by expectations about what a superior was capable of understanding, what he was likely to believe, and how he was likely to react, especially with respect to the career of the one transmitting the information.[19] But in the case of the DIA, where an individual's personal career advancement is linked to a single military service, while he temporarily occupies a role in an organization designed to serve two masters who are likely to be at odds (the JCS and OSD), and one which may be internally divided even further (the JCS), the incentives to compromise the substance of communications to satisfy multiple superiors are compelling. Even if a DIA analyst was only concerned with protecting his own position and cared nothing for larger goals, his dilemma, like that of other military on similar detached assignments, was a complex one:

> The individual military professional assigned to such duty, whether on the Joint Staff in the office of an assistant secretary, or in one of the agencies, found himself in a delicate situation. His service expected him to produce evidence that he had "influenced" certain decisions, but he found that he could best prove his objectivity by pointing out to his new superiors the flaws in arguments being advanced by his own service.[20]

The influence of the organizational arrangement on the substance of intelligence relating to the bombing was substantial. At the start of the air war, for example, there was a good deal of concentration on infiltration routes, especially as the interdiction role became a primary policy rationale. Not surprisingly, the air force sought information which would indicate that it was effective in this role. Concurrently the army was beginning its build-up of troops in South Viet-Nam, and as justification for continuing troop requests it sought information which would support its claim that the North Vietnamese were infiltrating more and more troops into the south. The DIA responded by satisfying the intelligence needs of both services, at the expense of the needs of civilian policy makers. The agency reported that the infiltration rate was indeed increasing, but that, thanks to the air force, the rate had not yet reached such a point that the enemy would be capable of launching a large offensive.[21] The DIA's position, consistent with the claims of the air force, continued to be that bombing made infiltration more difficult. Evaluations of this sort, which did not relate the bombing to the rate of infiltration required to sustain the insurgency in the south or to the capability of North Vietnamese to sustain an infiltration rate beyond any limit that could be imposed by air power, evaded the central questions confronting decision makers who had to weigh the costs of the policy against its benefits. The DIA's reluctance to go beyond characterizations of destruction and relate information to policy goals clearly limited its utility to the secretary of defense.

Besides providing broad judgments on the effects of the bombing, the DIA also worked in concert with the air force in the week-to-week selection of targets and after-strike evaluations. The release of targets in the north was a focal point of contention between the civilians and the military throughout the air war. It was, at the same time, a problem for DIA analysts who were responsible for "generating" the targets. As the intensity of the campaign increased and the number of unstruck targets initially listed by the Joint Chiefs dwindled, pressure was applied to the DIA to produce targets and very often to produce targets which would satisfy the special needs of available weapon systems. A former DIA staffer writes:

"Pick out a building for us to hit," they'd [Joint Staff] say. DIA could have told the JCS this was the wrong approach, but it played the game. It sent photo-interpreters scurrying to their scanners to find, say, a two or three story building in an area open to U.S. raids. If they saw no signs of military activity around the building they would dub it a "possible military storage area," a description that gave J-3 the right to go hunting.[22]

On one specific occasion the agency's unwillingness to disappoint air force operations and JCS personnel led to the targeting of a North Vietnamese leper colony. On May 6, 1966, the barbed wire enclosed colony at Quynh Loc was bombed after the military concluded the compound was an enemy division headquarters. The DIA supported that conclusion in spite of an earlier contrary evaluation which noted that ever since the air war had begun over a year ago the North Vietnamese had abandoned such garrison areas. The agency changed its earlier position that there was "no information to support the existence of a division headquarters at that location" after the JCS insisted that the DIA label the facility a "possible military headquarters site."[23] The North Vietnamese claimed over seventy casualties were suffered in the attack on the colony, including thirty dead.

The problem with the organizational arrangement was a relatively simple one. Although DIA personnel had responsibility for evaluating policy, they often were simultaneously located in the chain of command of an organization with operational responsibility for the execution of policy. When an air force officer assigned to the agency found his analysis to be at odds with the organizational interests of the parent service to which his career was tied, there was considerable incentive for him to alter the analysis. Most often the alteration did not take the form of complete reversal, as in the Quynh Loc incident, but rather appeared in the form of a compromise reflecting the demands of his dual role. Obviously the air force senior officers need not constantly have reminded their subordinates in the DIA of their position for the distortion and weakening of the intelligence function to occur, though when there were lapses the air force did not hesitate to point out the implications of the organizational arrangement in explicit terms.[24]

The DIA input accounts for some of the lack of clarity in the intelligence picture, that is, for some of the positive evaluations of effectiveness as against the generally much more negative assessments from CIA, RAND, Systems Analysis, and the JASON group. To account for more, those analysts in the air force and the navy, whose responsibility it was to evaluate strike effectiveness and plan future strikes, may also be included. Organizational incentives operated here too, among those in military intelligence very close to operations, and produced distortions which affected the execution of policy.

The desire on the part of military intelligence personnel to exaggerate successes stemmed not only from the obvious incentives in the reward structure to please superiors but also from a sense of loyalty to one's own service in its competition with other services for missions and budgets.[25] One way in which this was manifest was in the standard operating procedure that developed for reporting the effectiveness of air strikes. Although photographic evidence was available in most cases from post-strike reconnaissance flights, it became common practice for briefings and reports moving up the chain of command to draw heavily upon pilot reconnaissance and "play down" the photography. The result was the acceptance of an overly optimistic assessment of bomb damage even though a more accurate one was available. Pilots flying complicated jet aircraft, dodging antiaircraft fire, surface-to-air missiles (SAM's), and enemy aircraft may not have been in an ideal position to provide bomb damage assessment. The incentives for the fighter pilot to exaggerate his success, as well as the real difficulty of determining the amount of destruction, literally before the dust settled, suggest the likely unreliability of pilot reconnaissance.[26] Sometimes infrared photography was available to indicate the accuracy of strikes, as well as the regular high altitude photographs used afterward to determine their effectiveness. So photographic evidence could only be put aside with some effort.

What is perhaps even more interesting is that while the air

force sought to demonstrate the effectiveness of its strikes by emphasizing pilot assessments, it also had an incentive, because of its direct competition with naval air power over the total number of sorties flown and indirect competition with all the services, to fly as many re-strike sorties as it could justify. It was photographic reconnaissance that could provide the needed justification for re-strikes. Once civilian control over the air war loosened to allow re-strike of approved targets at the discretion of the field commander, the only one for whom some re-strike justification was necessary was the pilot. Apparently it was here that the air force chose to use the less optimistic photo analysis, for it was the fighter pilot's perception that *too much* emphasis was given to "photorecon" and not enough to his assessments. A former F-105 pilot complained:

> I have bombed, and seen my troops bomb, on specific targets where I have watched the bombs pour in and seen the target blow up . . . only to be fragged right back into the same place because the film didn't look like that to the Lieutenant who read it way back up the line.[27]

The incentives for selective use of photo and pilot reconnaissance reports were built into the structure of organizational relations as were the incentives for distortions by DIA analysts.

The contribution of intelligence to policy making extends beyond that of informing the participants in decision making. Intelligence assessments are also political resources to be used by actors to legitimize positions often taken for reasons independent of the substance of these expert evaluations of effectiveness. Just as the air force and the army needed evidence to support their policy prescriptions and claims on resources, so did civilians in Defense and elsewhere—although their need was usually for evidence to support a restriction on resource expenditure. Since some of the reasons for the air force's desire to bomb more and OSD's desire to bomb less would not have been considered legitimate in policy debates, expression of their respective positions was largely reduced to contention over the accepted legitimate issue of effectiveness. Intelligence reports reflected the debate. The military produced "in-house" studies showing how intensifying the use of air power would increase effectiveness, and McNamara's civilians in Systems Analysis produced other studies to support the opposite conclusion. Because of the nature of the sources, and regardless of merit, these analyses had limited credibility. The DIA had a similar problem, although its special interest was more ambiguous. The CIA was least susceptible to such doubts.

One method of attacking an opponent's position in the bombing debate was to undercut the legitimacy of his supporting evidence. Walt Rostow, a highly consistent proponent of air power, apparently did attempt to cut into the CIA's credibility after McNamara had come to rely upon its analyses. On one occasion a leak of selected material from one of George Carver's CIA reports to a nationally syndicated columnist by Rostow produced not only the desired "appeasement-minded" characterization of the agency in the press but also a personal visit from CIA Director Helms to Rostow's White House basement office. The outcome was that the incident remained isolated and the CIA credible.[28]

Although it has been demonstrated that intelligence assessments of air power's effectiveness were not uniformly negative, the weight of evaluations from the most credible sources increasingly pointed to the failure of the bombing of the north to achieve any of the objectives set for it. The IDA study best described the reasons for that failure. The argument here has been that the substance of intelligence often served the organizational needs of the suppliers and amounted to distortion. Since civilian decision makers sought other evaluations and came to rely upon them, we do not take the position that they were ultimately deceived by the distortions. In fact, it is precisely because the failure of the air war to achieve its political-military objectives eventually became so widely accepted among civilian policy makers that the continuation of the policy demands further explanation.

Bombing and Organizational Interests

A very large number of organizations were involved in the making and executing of Viet-Nam policy. Each had a stake in the policy in that their involvement could ultimately affect their future credibility, the definition of their roles, the size of their budgets, and their internally felt identity and morale.[29] How much of a stake different organizations had in the war varied depending on the extent and importance of their involvement. Among those organizations most broadly involved, and thus most severely tested in the performance of their most basic missions, were the armed services. Among the military services it was the marines and the air force that had most at stake and had most to prove.

The army could have shown itself to have been inefficient, even inept, but there is no alternative to a land army, and in the most basic sense, no organizational competition for the army. The army survived the most serious doctrinal attacks of the fifties and can be expected to survive those of the seventies. As for the navy, it had less at stake because it was not performing its basic mission. The sea lanes were not at issue in Viet-Nam. Although aircraft carriers were engaged and naval air was pitted against land-based air, the navy had a good deal less to lose than the air force. From the time of the Tonkin incident in 1964, the navy had demonstrated its mobility and had been "first on the scene with the most." Since the vulnerability of the carrier, the historically critical issue, was not being tested in Southeast Asia, interservice aerial competition was reduced to the question of relative efficiency, with the burden of proof resting on the service claiming the advantage—the air force.[30] The marines were an elite assault group and, like the army, performed a function that would continue to be needed. Unlike the army, however, there was an organizational alternative to the marines threatening their existence, that is, absorption into the larger organizational unit of the army.[31] The survival of the United States Air Force was not at stake in Viet-Nam. In contrast to the marines, the air force performed in many roles, including the strategic-nuclear one, which were not affected by the war. Nevertheless, it became the perception of the air force, and others who would evaluate its performance, that the viability of certain missions—those that were closest to the organization's "essence"—were at stake in the air war in Viet-Nam.[32]

Phill G. Goulding, former assistant secretary of defense for public affairs, makes the following observation:

> Within the Department of Defense emotion overcame logic on discussions of the role and importance of air power and the specific missions of air power in Vietnam. Somehow *the bombing of North Vietnam became the symbol of the importance of air power,* which was both tragic and illogical. Advocates of air power should have been the first to point out the fallacies in this line of reasoning, but instead were, in many cases, the persons espousing it most vehemently. Air power was playing a vital role in the war—in transport between theaters and within the theater, in search-and-rescue, in reconnaissance and intelligence gathering and in close air support of ground forces. Air power enthusiasts strangely said little of these impressive military achievements. (Emphasis added.)[33]

There was actually nothing "strange" about air power enthusiasts displaying apparent modesty over their many accomplishments, and Goulding, who clearly was not without a sense of irony, knew this well. What Goulding did was to list those missions which rank lowest in air force priority, receive the least attention in planning, budgeting and allocation of resources, and which are performed by those least likely to rise to the top ranks. He is crediting the air force with success where it least needs and wants it. The missions he does not mention are those which the service values and in which it sought to demonstrate success. The priority of missions in the air force begins with the direct combat roles, independently executed, and thus excludes those listed above—even the close air support function which is dependent on ground element coordination. The primary missions are, in fact, strategic bombing (nuclear and non-nuclear), including "deep" or strategic interdiction, tactical interdiction to a lesser degree, and air-to-air combat superiority. It is no mystery that the bombing of North Viet-Nam came to symbolize air power's effectiveness rather than the air transport of material to support the army. What is interesting is how the missions of strategic bombing and tactical interdiction were translated to Viet-Nam, why it was perceived as necessary to do so in order to preserve them, and the implications of the translation for policy. Lest there be any doubt about the stakes for which the services were playing in Southeast Asia, (the roles and missions at issue) consider the admonition of Senator Stuart Symington to Air Force Chief of Staff McConnell during an appropriations hearing in 1967:

> If you all don't get after some meaningful military targets in North Viet-Nam, Air Force and Naval airpower will go down the river. People are going to lose confidence in airpower. This country will be left in a position where the Navy will consist of submarines and sea lift, and the Air Force missiles in silos and air lift.[34]

The Air Force Stake: Strategic and Tactical Interdiction

Although the distinction between the strategic and tactical air roles is no clearer than that between the broad categories of strategy and tactics, the ambiguity in the former case at least need not present any great difficulty for the purposes of this analysis. There are an adequate number of indicators to separate the categories, to distinguish the strategic air mission in Viet-

Nam from the tactical, though the dividing line between the two may be blurred in the case of specific operations. We may consider as strategic those missions flown against fixed targets, such as industrial plants and power facilities, POL storage and transshipment points, transportation centers and "choke points." In terms of location those targets situated north of the nineteenth parallel, mostly in route packages 4, 5, 6A, and 6B (see figure 1), should be considered strategic. LOC interdiction bombing conducted this far north or this "deep" should be considered strategic interdiction. Tactical bombing in Viet-Nam may be thought of as including the interdiction campaign in route packages 1, 2, and part of 3, the bombing of enemy staging areas, military concentrations, and "rolling stock," as well as all strikes in the proximity of, or in direct support of, ground engagements.[35]

The objectives of strategic bombing in Viet-Nam were roughly the same as those conceived by air power proponents in the 1930s and pursued by air strategists in the 1960s: the destruction of the enemy's war-making capability, and the infliction of sufficient damage on the enemy homeland so as to weaken the morale of the population and the leadership in order to force the termination of hostile activity. The objectives were qualified in Viet-Nam as they had been in the past. Civilian morale was not taken as a primary target in Southeast Asia, nor had it been, at least by Americans, for a very long time. In describing the Douhetian origins of the United States air doctrine, Perry McCoy Smith observed that this principle of the Italian strategist had long been discarded: "The abandonment of the undermining of civilian morale as a useful aim of bombardment was a result of a 1939 lecture presented to the tactical school, which made the point that Chinese morale and will to resist increased as a result of Japanese bombardment."[36] Smith's observation is consistent with the separate paths taken by British and American bombing strategists in World War II, the English settling on area bombing and the Americans on "precision" bombing. British faith in the efficiency of attacking the German population had much to do with their lack of ability to do otherwise and their preference for nighttime raids, just as American emphasis on critical industrial targets followed from the perceived capability to hit such targets based on the development of a better bombsight.[37]

For the army air force (AAF) strategic bombing meant not only the selective destruction of critical economic systems as a means of bringing the enemy to its knees but also the gaining of

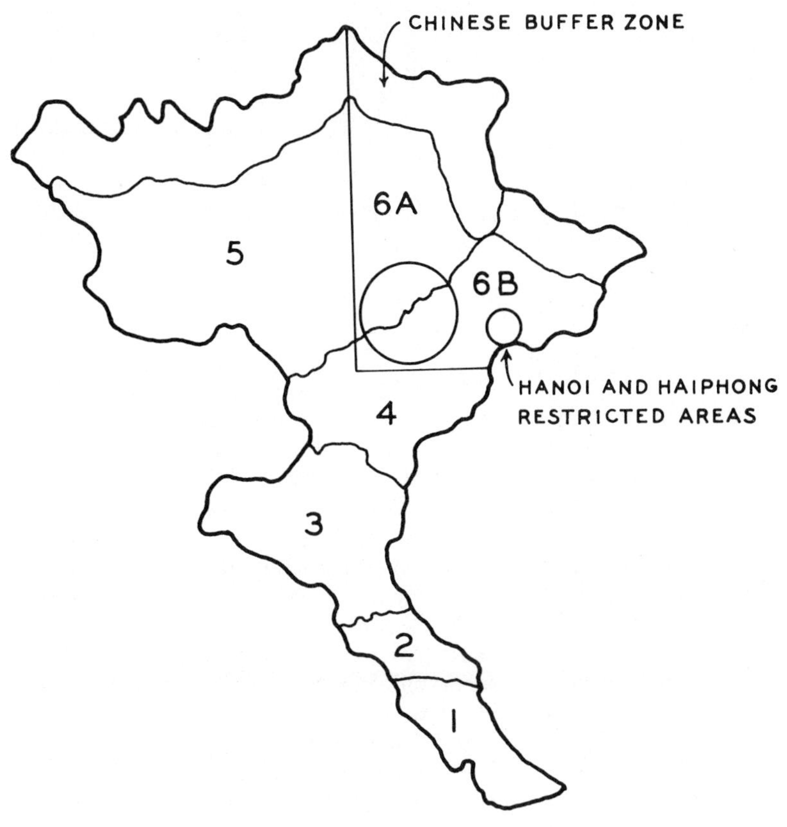

NORTH VIET-NAM
ROUTE PACKAGES

autonomy as a military service in postwar reorganization. Emerging from World War II, AAF leaders sought control of several peripheral air roles (e.g., tactical aviation, air defense, and transport), but they saw autonomy as the first priority and, in turn, saw "strategic bombardment inextricably tied to autonomy."[38] From the very beginning, air force thinking was conditioned by the rationalization for autonomy provided by the requirements for the performance of the strategic mission. The preeminence of this mission in the interwar debates and its importance in the success of postwar reorganization gave way to the dominance of the Strategic Air Command (SAC) through the fifties. If it is objected that the position of SAC can be accounted for exclusively in terms of the overall defense posture of the period and the development of nuclear weapons, the continued Air Force insistence on the viability of the manned bomber in the age of ICBM's should be recalled. The significance of the strategic mission as conventional and nuclear bombardment of selected target systems by manned aircraft remained the most basic one to the service.

The air force was denied the genuine strategic mission in the Korean War, but in Viet-Nam the way was gradually cleared for it to demonstrate its capability. The result was considerable destruction in the north but not the desired outcome. In World War II style, various target systems were developed by the military and most were eventually struck, including industrial plants, hydroelectric power sources, POL storage, and strategic LOC's in the populated northeast sector (6A and 6B). The reasoning supporting the strikes involved the usual expected impact on the enemy's capability and will to continue the war. The strategic interdiction campaign, designed to limit movement of supplies, was aimed at the former, while the strategic bombardment of industries and power sources was aimed at the latter—presuming to threaten the destruction of the limited and therefore highly valued industrial sector of this developing economy. In a memo to Rusk and McNamara in May of 1966 urging a coordinated attack on POL, Walt Rostow even drew support directly from what he saw as the success of such strikes in World War II.[39] But North Viet-Nam was not Germany, and even if it had been the industrial equivalent, the moral of strategic bombing from World War II was not the same for others as for Rostow. If there was a conventional wisdom emerging from the Strategic Bombing Survey it was that non-nuclear strategic bombing had not proved itself effective.

Although the lessons of bombing from World War II were not the same for everyone, it was at least evident to all that the results of attacks were severely limited by the degree to which the enemy actively adjusted to them. The costly allied attack on the German ball-bearings industry failed to produce the desired effect largely because the Germans responded by dispersing potential targets, using substitutions, and drawing upon back inventory.[40] In the support from the Chinese and Russians a quarter of a century later, the North Vietnamese had what amounted to an inexhaustible supply of material from food stuffs to trucks, from POL to arms. They responded at first as Germany had, by dispersing POL, but later fell back upon their allies. As long as this support continued, North Viet-Nam had the capacity to continue hostilities. Given the German experience and the North Vietnamese response, the logical question was, could the "top of the funnel" be closed and external support stopped? Even if mining harbors and concentrated bombing of rail links would have been effective, and there is every reason to believe it would not have been, given the redundancy of routes and the possibilities for coastal supply, the civilian decision makers refused to try to do it. They did not think it would work and were very anxious about Soviet and Chinese reaction. Nonetheless, in the face of this reality, the air force continued to push for the release of more strategic targets, gradually received almost all of them, and yet in the end had virtually no hope of success.

So whether it was due to civilian fears over the consequences of cutting North Viet-Nam off from its allies, or to the impossibility of doing so even if the risk was taken, the result was that strategic bombing as it was undertaken could not succeed by its impact on enemy capabilities. As for breaking Hanoi's will, the failure of the attack in the spring of 1967, first on the Thai Nguyen iron and steel complex, and then on power facilities in Hanoi and Haiphong, should have been evidence enough that the north's industry would not serve as a hostage in the conflict. Of course it was not evidence enough, even when supplemented by an intelligence picture that was more bleak by the summer of 1967 than it had ever been before. Interestingly, the ultimate futility of the strategic program had been predicted by JCS' own war games agency as early as 1964, when Sigma II showed that exhausting the proposed JCS target list, then numbering 96, would not prevent the north from maintaining or even increasing its support to the insurgency.[41] But neither war games nor war affected military recommendations. By the summer of 1967, 85 percent, or 302 of 354 JCS recommended targets had been struck; in the fall there was even further concentration on strategic targets after the military requests received congressional support.[42] As an essential air force mission, strategic bombardment had a *raison d'etre* quite apart from its impact upon the enemy.

The strategic missions could be abandoned by the air force in Viet-Nam only at the risk of jeopardizing the missions everywhere. The stakes were high just in terms of future aircraft procurement. Since the deep interdiction capability of fighter bombers was as vulnerable to civilian critics in the Defense Department as the strategic role for a heavy manned bomber, some of the running battles between the civilians and the air force over force structure were indirectly affected by events in Viet-Nam. During the 1960s, for example, the civilians found both the air force and the navy putting greater emphasis on deep interdiction, requiring quantities of large, complex, expensive aircraft. But as former Assistant Secretary of Defense Alain C. Enthoven, writes, "Systems Analysis studies suggested that there is reason to question the value of deep interdiction against industry and lines of communication, in both Europe and Asia."[43] The reasons for doubt were extensive, ranging from the difficulty in finding and hitting logistic targets, the redundancy of routes and the easy repair by the enemy, to the costs in the attrition of aircraft that must fly over heavily defended areas in the enemy heartland and carry complicated electronic equipment to aid in evasion. It was clear that tangible support for this argument could be drawn from Viet-Nam experience. What was being questioned was the need for a capability like that provided by the new F-111 fighter bomber and perhaps even for that of the newer long-range F-15 fighter. If it were to be concluded, based to some degree on Viet-Nam experience, that deep interdiction was not a viable mission, not only would the fighter bomber be vulnerable to cuts, but it would be considerably harder for the air force to justify the need for air-superiority fighters that also have the capability for carrying a heavy payload over a long range. The stakes were high.

The interdiction campaign against the LOCs in the lower route packages of North Viet-Nam's panhandle and against the trail system across the border in Laos also called into question an already questionable air force mission. Although this more tactical variety of interdiction was less essential than the strategic, and air advocates fought civilian efforts to concentrate sorties against these targets at the expense of others, it was an independently performed combat mission and thus one to be preserved. As with the strategic missions, the air force needed to demonstrate success—the viability of the mission had been established in neither World War II nor in Korea. The Korean experience was particularly relevant to Viet-Nam, and should have been considered so, for in both cases the United States attained nearly complete air superiority and engaged in extensive LOC interdiction against a technologically primitive, though imaginative, logistics system which was required to carry a very low volume of supplies to sustain hostilities.

In a position not unlike that more recently taken by some in Viet-Nam, the United States Air Force commander in the Far East during the Korean War, General Otto P. Weyland, put forth a qualified defense of air power's tactical interdiction capability during the Korean engagement:

> If one assumes that the objective of the road and railroad interdiction was to deny the enemy the long-term capability to launch limited objective attacks, or even more, to deny him the capability to conduct an obstinate defense, then it did not do the job. On the other hand, it was an unqualified success in achieving its stated purpose, which was *to deny the enemy the capability to launch and sustain a general offensive*. Moreover the attritive effects of the interdiction program directly supported the other parallel objective of punishing the enemy to the maximum extent possible. He suffered considerable losses in motor transport, rails, bridging materials, and rolling stock. When these losses are added to the destruction of airfields, supply centers, small manufacturing plants, and other facilities, and to the huge recuperative labor effort, we can better appreciate what the air offensive was costing the enemy. [Emphasis is added.][44]

If a moral is drawn, and the general's admission is translated to Viet-Nam, it may be observed that in Southeast Asia all that was required was the conduct of an "obstinate defense," since the Southern insurgents could be patient while the United States could not. But even if we acknowledge the claim of success for these Korean operations, it does not go unchallenged. General Matthew B. Ridgway, overall commander in Korea, found that, "It is impossible to interdict the supply routes of an Asian army by air power alone. [In Korea] we had complete air mastery. . . . We clobbered Chinese supply columns unmercifully. . . . But *we did not halt their offensive nor materially diminish its strength*" (emphasis added).[45]

The moral from Korea may not seem clear when drawn from

opposed partisans such as Weyland and Ridgway, but an analysis made by the RAND Corporation is probably as clear and objective as is likely to emerge.[46] An examination was made of Air Force tactics in general interdiction campaigns against road and rail and of the three special highly-concentrated operations, the first and second "Strangle" and "Saturate." The similarity in both Air Force techniques and enemy responses when compared to those found in Viet-Nam make the author's conclusion all the more pertinent: "The Air Force interdiction programs in Korea all seemed to follow the same cycle: initial success and then defeat by enemy countermeasures."[47] The point is that tactical LOC interdiction had not been notably successful in Korea, and thus, the capability of the air force to perform the mission was necessarily in question in Viet-Nam. As with the strategic missions in Viet-Nam, there was every reason to believe this mission could not be performed successfully.

If the Korean experience was bad, then the infinitely more deadly antiaircraft fire of the North Vietnamese and the greater redundancy of routes, density of cover, and the unfavorable weather in Southeast Asia should have forewarned of an even worse experience. This is especially so since aircraft capability for this mission had not improved in twenty-five years. Although the technology of the tactical air mission is complex, the defense strategy of the fifties, combined with the air force's preference for the strategic missions, more accurately explains the failure to develop an aircraft with adequate target acquisition capability which could be flown in the rain.[48] In sum, the air force embarked upon tactical interdiction, a secondary and often shunned mission, as it had upon its primary strategic mission in Viet-Nam. The evidence of failure provided by past experience and the obstacles provided by current circumstances only reinforced the need to engage its forces, demonstrate their viability, and preserve the mission, budget allocations, and organizational morale that were at stake.

Incentives for Competition and Some Implications

The air force was not the only service bombing North Viet-Nam, nor was it the only service with an interest in demonstrating the effectiveness of its tactical air capability. The navy also flew missions against the north and did so from its aircraft carriers stationed in the Gulf of Tonkin rather than from Thailand or from the south. With two services performing the same combat function, using different methods of operations (a land versus a sea base), it would not have been unreasonable to expect relations between them to have become competitive as each strove for larger portions of scarce resources.[49] Further, there was the opportunity for this competition to become dysfunctional to the national goal of the armed forces in Viet-Nam if the criteria to evaluate performance was not carefully established.

Under such circumstances when a secretary of defense wishes a military policy to serve certain political and military ends and informs the air force and the navy that decisions concerning the future of their air capability will depend upon their relative combat performance as measured by some quantitative indicators, he should be certain that behavior that results in high marks for the service by those indicators will be consistent with his larger policy ends in the war. More accurately, he should be certain that the services perceive the criteria for evaluation in a way that will not lead them to dysfunctional competition. In fact, sufficient care was not taken in Viet-Nam, and this was one reason why the bombing was not executed in the most rational fashion and why there was more bombing and pressure to bomb put upon the civilians by the military than there might otherwise have been. The incentives provided by OSD moved organizational behavior in this direction. In addition, the appropriations committees in Congress tended to compare the performance of the services in Viet-Nam in much the same way with the same effect—the air force and navy conducted operations with an eye to future evaluations which could be made at that point in the budgetary process as well as in OSD. The implications of these incentives were quite significant.

The Office of Systems Analysis, which was formerly the Office of the Comptroller, served Secretary of Defense McNamara by producing substantive evaluations of force recommendations emerging from the military. It is not surprising, given their role, that those in Systems Analysis would often find themselves at odds with the military, but even so, the degree of hostility and mistrust that ultimately developed between the two was extraordinary. The military fundamentally disagreed over the proper role of civilian management, believing firmly that at some point the expertise of those who fought wars must prevail.[50] They came to bitterly resent McNamara's attempts to prevent them from presenting their own judgments on defense requirements to Congress or the public once decisions had been made by the civilians. In turn, civilians in OSD, and particularly in Systems Analysis, claimed that the military were incapable of objective analysis, being motivated instead in their recommendations by parochial concerns. A former assistant secretary for Systems Analysis has charged, for example, that there was a lack of "career independence" in the services which bred conformity: "There have been loud complaints about civilians 'muzzling' the military; but anyone who is familiar with the system knows that most of the muzzling is done by the military themselves."[51]

Against this background Systems Analysis proceeded to evaluate air force and navy performance in the air war in Viet-Nam. Its evaluation was natural to its role of determining long-range force requirements on the basis of capabilities, as well as to its role of allocating resources to the services during the war itself. The evaluation process served not only to inform Systems Analysis, however, but also to influence the conduct of air operations in Viet-Nam.[52] The process began prior to the Viet-Nam engagement when Systems Analysis established expected flying capabilities or sortie rates for the various aircraft. At that time the services attempted to hold down the expectations of United States aircraft capability as much as possible since the lower the estimated sortie rate relative to the enemy's, the more aircraft would be justified in budget allocations. Once the air war began these established sortie rates were no longer important simply for planning purposes, but were perceived by the services as output measures that their individual interests required them to meet. This was true for several reasons. If, for example, the navy had argued for an expected rate for the F-4 aircraft of .95 sorties per day and Systems Analysis had estimated 1.35 sorties per day, then when in combat, the navy felt pressured to fly at the rate of at least .95 sorties lest Systems Analysis reduce the number of planes it would continue to supply to the navy, claiming that fewer planes were capable of the same total number of sorties.[53] Even monthly supplies of fuel and ammunition depended upon maintenance of the sortie rate. Ultimately the most serious concern of each service was that flying and bombing less than expected would damage its position in long-range planning of roles and missions. It is here that interservice competition intensified pressure, since comparisons between the efficiency and effectiveness of navy sea-based F-4 aircraft and air force land-based F-4 aircraft were inevitable. The shape of future tactical air capability was at issue.

The impact of Systems Analysis's evaluations was not limited to the pressure to fly more sorties nor was sortie competition a simple matter. For instance, if the services allowed the competitive situation to push the number of sorties flown much past their previously estimated rate, they would damage future rationalizations of need based upon comparisons with the rates of enemy systems. Thus the situation was structured so that they attempted to fly at least their estimated rate, but to do so no matter what other factors made the continuation of flights irrational in all but the narrow organizational sense. When a group of formerly restricted targets was released as part of a new ROLLING THUNDER series, there was an unhealthy eagerness to strike rapidly lest political considerations cause targets to be lost in any civilian reconsideration. An air force pilot complained:

> Common sense and in fact military sense, often fell by the wayside and the fact that Hanoi was not going to move during the next few days seemed lost to the decision-making view as did the fact that we had waited a long time for these targets and could afford to wait a few more minutes to do the job right.[54]

It was not only a matter of running unnecessary risk in the haste to hit new targets, but in addition there was continual re-strike of targets which did not need to be re-struck:

> Unfortunately, hit or miss, we often find ourselves repeatedly fragged against targets that have already been bombed into insignificance except for the defenses that are left, and reinforced, to capitalize on our pattern of beating regular paths to each new target released from the "Restricted" list.[55]

The way in which targets were released, that is, in groups or "packages" every two weeks also meant that before the military achieved the right to decide on re-strike itself, much strike and re-strike was done in adverse weather to guard against the loss of targets should authorization be revoked, as well as to keep up the sortie rate. This was admitted quite clearly by Major General Gilbert L. Meyers, former deputy commander of the 7th Air Force in Viet-Nam during Senate testimony in 1967:

> If the weather was bad, we were always concerned about the repercussions as a result of not flying the sorties that had been allocated to us.
>
> Obviously if you [the Air Force] do not fly them, you [OSD] can make a case that you [the Air Force] did not really need that many anyway. On that basis, sortie allocations could be reduced in the future.
>
> This is the kind of pressure that we operated under to meet these schedules.[56]

If bombing when the target could not be found was an unfortunate result of the incentive system, then flying over enemy targets and anti-aircraft fire without any bombs was probably even more distasteful to pilots. Although there is a good deal of disagreement over the exact nature of the munitions shortages in 1966 and over responsibility for the shortages, it is clear that there was some kind of shortage and that missions were continued as if there were none. It appears that in the spring and summer of 1966, an insufficient number of whole bombs of the desired variety were to be found at the necessary points—the body of the bomb, its fuse, and its tail turning up at different locations. In response to this situation, in the words of a special military study of logistics in Viet-Nam, "CINCPAC established monthly allocations of critical air munitions and specified maximum ordnance loads for air munitions."[57] In other words, the military continued to fly the same number of planes, cutting down not on sorties but on the effectiveness of each aircraft. There was more cost and more risk of pilot loss than necessary. Referring to this period an air force colonel said, "Our planes were flying with one-half a load, but bombs or no bombs, you've got to have more Air Force over the target than Navy."[58]

The insanity of the sortie-rate game was multiplied in the choice of aircraft as well. After the A-6 Intruder became available at Yankee Station in the Pacific, the navy had a plane capable of carrying up to a 15,000 pound load and delivering it at night. According to one reporter, on the subject of the air war, it was only concern for the total sortie number that led the navy to continue flying larger numbers of its less effective light, daylight-limited A-4 Skyhawks.[59]

The air force and navy did not limit their competition to the numbers of sorties allocated each, nor did they perceive their interests as served by dropping bombs without regard for the importance of the targets upon which they fell. The focus of controversy between the military and civilians ovér the air war, in fact, centered upon the particular targets released for strikes rather than the number of sorties permitted. In terms of interservice competition this meant that fairness required the air force and navy to share an equal number of the more desirable targets as well as absolute numbers of sorties. At the beginning of the air campaign problems of coordination and rivalry led to confusion over target responsibility and resulted in the division of North Viet-Nam into seven route packages (see figure 1). The concept of "fair share" that marked defense budgeting in the 1950s had become an integral part of air operations in Viet-Nam. Only in the most critical area with the most desirable targets, the northeast quadrants of 6A and 6B, did both services bomb simultaneously. The other route packages were assigned separately to the services and when one area became "exhausted" the next ROLLING THUNDER series would include a reassignment to redress inequities. The division of the Asian turf so as not to favor either service with an advantage in later evaluations made good organizational sense, if not always good operational sense. It was a means of keeping the services together by restricting their competition. A similar function was served by the equally arbitrary staffing guideline for the Pacific Command Headquarters which oversaw all air operations. Admiral Ulysses G. Sharp described his command team as follows: "This unified command is a perfect example of a unified command. My staff is exactly one-third Army, one-third Air Force, and one-third Navy-Marine, and all positions are allocated that way. This is the only staff other than the Joint Chiefs of Staff staff that is so divided."[60]

The obvious caution with which interservice rivalry was treated in the field was based on the inevitable competition between the services in Washington, before committees of Congress as well as before the Office of Secretary of Defense. The air force and navy have never agreed on the performance of the tactical air role. When the air force was striving for autonomy as a service in the middle 1940s it also sought control of virtually all air missions and so began very early to attack the vulnerability of aircraft carriers and laud the effectiveness of the submarine.[61] The debate was continued in the joint committee hearings in 1970 on the navy's CVAN 70 aircraft carrier.

In the navy's attempt to demonstrate the virtue of sea-based tactical air power, Admiral Thomas Moorer, chief of naval operations first testified that he would avoid comparison with air force performance: "I do not view this as a debate on the relative merits of land-based versus sea-based air." Nonetheless before long he went on to contrast naval performance in Viet-Nam with that of the air force, explaining, "I feel that the Navy is obligated to respond to comparisons which have been initiated by the critics of the Navy and the opponents of the carrier."[62] The point is simply that the navy had its prized nuclear powered carrier at stake, and a good part of the supporting argument for the desirability of, and need for, such a craft turned upon the viability of sea-based tactical air power. That argument, of course, rested in turn upon the navy's record of accomplishment in the bombing of North Viet-Nam compared to that of the air force. Assuming that the services plan ahead and given the generally-shared perception of a fixed-ceiling defense budget, interservice competition in the air war, with all its implications, becomes as understandable as it was regrettable.

The argument of this section has been that the criteria used to evaluate performance led to aberrations in the behavior of organizations seeking to protect their own interests. But since the navy and the air force have been taken as units, attention has been focused only on the motives of relatively high-echelon actors. It should be noted at least briefly, however, that organizations can respond to the grand incentives of missions and budgets only because upper-level concern for these issues is conveyed to the rest of the organization by the structure of rewards and punishments within it—the incentives internal to the organization. For instance, the squadron commander on an aircraft carrier will be considered for promotion on the basis of a fitness report which shows, among other things, the performance of his squadron in terms of sorties flown. He will thus have a stake in sortie allotment, and he will be sure that when there is a bridge to be destroyed at least some of the A-4's assigned will be from his squadron. Below him there will be a pilot, as yet without command responsibility, but nevertheless with a career and a fitness report of his own. If he seeks advancement he will want to win points toward as many air medals as he can collect during his tour; he will receive one point for each mission he flies—two points if it is a combat sortie. As always when discussing organizational incentives, neither the naval lieutenant, nor his captain, nor the admiral, nor their opposite numbers in the air force, is assumed to have been motivated simply by self-interest. Rather, the pilot and his superiors most certainly believed in the war, believed that bombing North Viet-Nam was the best way to win the war and, generally, believed that the more bombing the better. However, the incentives to a particular kind of behavior associated with a position in an organization do serve to reinforce and sometimes change prior perceptions; they will nearly always make it less likely that perceptions will develop or behavior occur which is inconsistent with organizational interest; and they will often produce behavior that is dysfunctional to larger policy ends and irrational in all but the most limited sense.

POLICY FROM CONFLICT

An overview of the course of the bombing policy reveals an increase in the intensity of the program paralleled by an increase in opposition and dissatisfaction with it among key civilian decision makers. The original consensus on the decision to begin bombing in 1965, tenuous and shallow from the start, gradually broke apart until open and bitter conflict between the Office on the Secretary of Defense and the Joint Chiefs became a routine part of the decision process. Yet the various phases of the air war from February 1965 through March 1968 are characterized by successive, qualitative escalations and decreasing civilian oversight.[63] From quantitatively escalating LOC interdiction attacks upon the lower route packages in 1965, the campaign changed in early summer of 1966 to a systematic bombardment of POL storage facilities; in the spring of 1967 attacks began against urban industrial and power facilities and eventually extended to targets within the cities of Hanoi and Haiphong and to the Chinese buffer zone. In the end the military had achieved considerable flexibility in total sortie allotment, choice of ordnance and restrike authority, as well as the release of virtually every target on the JCS list except the port facilities and harbor at Haiphong. They also witnessed the passing of the secretary of defense. A look at the conflict over the bombing tells much about civil-military relations in time of war and about the pressures exerted upon a president from the Congress as well as by the military.

DOD: JCS VERSUS OSD

The success in Washington of the Joint Chiefs' bombing campaign was achieved over a three-year period by a process of successive compromises. It should be noted at the outset that because the JCS prevailed in this way, that is, they were not able to pursue the air war with the vigor they wished from the very start, they have in this most significant failure their most important asset in postwar debates over the effectiveness of air power. By only gradually acquiescing to military demands, the civilians can now be held accountable for the failure of the bombing to have had the desired impact on infiltration and enemy will and capability. Therefore, drawing conclusions about the effectiveness of air power in Viet-Nam may be considerably easier than drawing conclusions about potential effectiveness. In Congress and in the press, air power advocates have referred to the crippling effect civilians had upon the war effort, so that though they finally achieved a near *carte blanche*, the argument that it was not given soon enough remains. There are those, like Arthur Schlesinger, who see this as a classic military maneuver to escape responsibility.[64] Indeed, it is in the nature of the logic of coercive diplomacy-by-bombs that as long as there is anyone left to coerce, the requirements of the strategy may be said to be unfulfilled. In an attempt to demonstrate that the strategy was fairly tested, one might point to the repeated failures of specific portions of the bombing program which were pursued according to military recommendations to achieve their advertised results—most notably the concentrated attacks on LOCs, POL storage, and hydroelectric power target complexes. In the end, however, it must be recognized that the bombing was increased slowly, that the JCS wanted to escalate more rapidly, and that the outcomes that might have followed from the acceptance of their recommendations cannot be stated with certainty.[65]

Putting aside their failure to escalate as rapidly as they would have liked, the simplest explanation for the general success of the military over the civilians in the Defense Department is that the battle was fought while there was a war in progress. In what may finally stand as an understatement, Alexander George refers to presidential-military relations as something other than simply superior-subordinate in nature:

> Military leaders have a strong advocate's role in determining policies, and once a diplomatic crisis erupts into warfare their bargaining position within the policy-making arena becomes even stronger. As a result, even though the president retains control over critical decisions of strategy and tactics, he may feel obliged to negotiate and bargain with his military advisors before making these decisions.[66]

The president was so obliged for good reason, and by virtue of that obligation so was his secretary of defense. The senior military carry the mantles of expertise, nonpartisanship, and patriotism. Since they also must be trusted to execute decisions, their support insures the effectiveness as well as the legitimacy of policy.[67] The value of gaining military support in peacetime defense policy is high because civilians have less standing with Congress and the public in such matters, although they do have the potential to directly oversee the execution of decisions; the value in wartime is many times higher because civilians have considerably less credibility in matters of strategy and tactics when it is the military who suffer the losses in lives, and because civilian oversight of a battle theater is at best indirect. In describing the pressure applied to General Matthew Ridgway to support Eisenhower defense budgets, Samuel Huntington makes an observation that applies with equal force to Lyndon Johnson's efforts with his military leaders: "The intensity of the pressure applied was a tribute to the value of the approval sought."[68]

The military were of course aware of their position and took care not to jeopardize it by disunity. If there were serious differences among the JCS over the conduct of the war, they did not emerge in public. The few exceptions were minor and had to do with traditional differences over roles and command authority. For example, General Westmoreland was known to have been unhappy about the loss of some close air support capability when the navy moved a carrier from "Dixie Station" in the South China Sea to "Yankee Station" in the Gulf of Tonkin so that it might join in the war against the north.[69] The marines were clearly upset in 1968 over command changes which cost them their independence in I Corps and the "organic" relation between their air and ground units; and the army intelligence representatives to the United States Intelligence Board found themselves joining the Department of State in opposition to the other services to dissent from a 1965 SNIE which seemed to imply that a proposed air campaign might singlehandedly be successful enough to prevent large scale Viet Cong activity in the south.[70] What is significant about these and other differences is that they were not of the same order as those that would divide the military on policy either in the eyes of the president or the public.

When critical decisions were to be made the JCS stood together, and with increasing frequency against McNamara. A good example of the character of their stand occurred in October 1966 when the secretary returned from a trip to Viet-Nam and made a series of recommendations to the president on the conduct of the war, including a change in the bombing policy: "At the proper time, . . . I believe we should consider terminating bombing in all of North Viet-Nam, or at least in the Northeast Zones, for an indefinite period in connection with covert moves toward peace."[71] The Chiefs' response came the same day in a memo to McNamara with the request that it be passed on to the president. The chairman of the JCS, General Earle G. Wheeler, first represented the Chiefs as being opposed to the secretary's recommendation and then, after explaining their opposition, recalled that past military recommendations had not been followed at the cost of a successful policy:

> The Joint Chiefs of Staff do not concur with your proposal that, as a carrot to induce negotiations, we should suspend or reduce our bombing campaign against NVN. . . . In JCSM-955-64, dated 14 November 1964, and in JCSM-962-64 dated 23 November 1964 the Joint Chiefs of Staff provided their views as to the military pressures which should be brought to bear on NVN. In summary, they recommended a "sharp knock" on NVN military assets and war-supporting facilities rather than the campaign of slowly increasing pressure which was adopted. Whatever the political merits of the latter course, we deprived ourselves of the military effects of early weight of effort and shock, and gave to the enemy time to adjust to our slow quantitative and qualitative increase of pressure. This is not to say that it is too late to derive military benefits from more effective and extensive use of our air and naval superiority.[72]

This communication to the president documented a united military position, shifted responsibility for past failure to a politically motivated civilian choice, and offered better results only if the full military program were adopted. A president could ignore such "advice" only at the peril of possible future political costs.

There is evidence that in 1967 the military even used the ultimate threat of resignation to insure that McNamara's proposals for a cutback in the bombing did not succeed. Assistant Secretary of Defense John McNaughton is reported by David Halberstam as having said that "at least two senior military resignations" would have followed had the president decided to limit the bombing to the lower route packages. A similar account is found in Townsend Hoopes's discussion of that period.[73] Resignations of any kind would have been costly to the president, but a defection of the military would surely have been thought intolerable. Even when the bombing pause of 1968 was announced (the pause that ultimately became a halt), and the military position was weakened by the Tet Offensive, the military had to be "brought along" by Secretary of Defense Clifford with assurances that sorties would be redistributed to the panhandle of North Viet-Nam and Laos.[74]

Between the confrontations over major changes in bombing policy, such as a new campaign against a particular "target system" or the initiation of a bombing pause or the termination of one, the civilians and the military regularly engaged one another over the standing JCS target list. The JCS list was not the standing list in the sense that it was the only one, because CINCPAC had one too, and it was longer; nor was it a standing list in the sense that it did not change, since it constantly changed by growing longer. Rather, the JCS list was the one standing list by virtue of its acceptance as the base from which the Chiefs drew the fixed targets that they wanted authorized as part of each two-week bombing package. The authorization process came to be a "routinization" of JCS-OSD conflict as well as a partly symbolic exercise in "civilian control of the military."

The JCS recommendations were generated from military intelligence sources and field commanders' requests, and then sharpened to increase their appeal to OSD. As one well acquainted with the process and sympathetic to the military put it, "If you look at the targets recommended you'll see that the Chiefs tailored their list, I mean, they went up that hill so many times they learned to submit what they thought they could get. Sharp [CINCPAC] didn't limit himself that way."[75]

Tailored, but still including more targets than there was any expectation of receiving, the JCS request went to Secretary of Defense McNamara, who in turn transmitted it to his assistant secretary for International Security Affairs. Within ISA a calculation was made about which targets could be successfully withheld, and the recommendation for target authorization was then sent to McNamara. The final decision on which targets were to be authorized did not come until the conclusion of the White House "Tuesday Lunch," at which time McNamara made his recommendations to the president. General Wheeler was an irregular participant in these affairs, at least until the August 1967 hearings, after which congressional interest in the military plight assured his presence more routinely.

There were others present at the White House meetings who may have contributed to the decisions, especially Walt Rostow and Dean Rusk. The secretary of state was in fact armed with an independent critique of the original JCS list, provided to him by Benjamin Read, special assistant to the secretary of state and executive secretary of the department, and Assistant Secretary William Bundy. According to Read, he, Bundy and State's Viet-Nam task force usually had twenty-four hours after receiving their copy of the JCS request in which to prepare a staff paper supporting recommended restrictions on JCS targets judged to be too sensitive for strikes. Then, just prior to the lunch, the secretary would be briefed on its contents so that he might use the material to eliminate more targets from the McNamara-JCS list —something he apparently did on occasion.[76]

Several observations about this procedure are in order. First, it provides the image of strict civilian oversight—at least triple oversight if the president is included. Indeed, most of the 515 pages of Senate hearings on the air war in August 1967 were devoted to OSD's unreasonably harsh restraints, applied largely by the restriction of targets allowed to the military. Yet, as of August 8, before the expected Senate hearings inflated the JCS recommended target list and increased the pressure to authorize them, 202 of the 213, or 95 percent of JCS recommended targets had been authorized in the course of the regular target approval procedure.[77] More tons of bombs had been dropped on North Viet-Nam by that time than had been dropped in the whole Pacific Theater during World War II. It had perhaps been a slow, painstaking, deliberative process, but given the growing disenchantment with the bombing within the OSD it was surely a process of submission to the military rather than an exercise in control over the military.

Second, the civilians had not only attempted to keep the military satisfied by gradual apportionment of fixed targets, but also by authorizing large numbers of sorties against LOCs. In fact, less than 10 percent of the 173,000 combat sorties flown in North Viet-Nam by August 1967 had been flown against fixed targets of the kind on the JCS list.[78] The arrangement permitted the air force and navy sortie rates to remain high, even if the "rolling stock" on the LOCs of the lower route packages were not nearly as desirable to the military as the hard targets in the northeast quadrant (6A and 6B). This tacit agreement fell apart, however, when sympathetic senators questioned JCS members and the CINCPAC commander in August 1967. The potential for them to improve the proportion of strikes against sensitive targets was clear, and they were quick to imply that OSD had led them to waste most of their ordnance on the LOCs and less important fixed targets, while the really worthwhile targets remained off-limits. They were not content with trying to get more targets but sought to shift total responsibility for past failure to the civilians. When McNamara was confronted with this charge during his appearance before the subcommittee he reacted sharply, revealing a sense of betrayal as well as anger:

Secretary McNamara: . . . If he [Admiral Sharp] says these aren't significant targets, why did he recommend them? And I am not suggesting that all targets he recommended were authorized. It is clear they weren't. But this implication that pilots are striking targets that aren't of value and they are striking them because somebody in Washington overrules the field commander just is not correct. No fixed targets have been authorized in Washington that I am aware of that haven't been recomended by the field commanders.[79]

The final point to be made here concerns the fundamental differences dividing civilians and military, OSD and JCS, on the issue of targets. Civilian caution in State, OSD, the White House, and segments of the intelligence community was based first on the fear that a massive bombing campaign would result in a more active response by China or the Soviet Union or both, in Viet-Nam or elsewhere. This accounts for the restrictions OSD attempted to maintain by creating the Chinese "buffer zone," in prohibiting the mining or striking of the port of Haiphong where foreign ships would be endangered, and until September 1967, in keeping Mig-capable airfields from destruction lest the North Vietnamese be forced to reliance on Chinese air support. A second concern of the civilians was that vast destruction in the north, especially civilian losses, would cause the administration to run unacceptable political costs internationally and domestically. This second concern may have been less the expression of a political value than a humanitarian one, though in recommendations and decisions the motivation for preventing collateral civilian damage and avoiding a strategy of purposeful population destruction is impossible to determine. What is clear, however, is that the military and civilians differed sharply on the willingness to run the risks of enlarging the war and on the value which they placed on the lives of North Vietnamese civilians. On the first point, although the JCS were more optimistic about Soviet and Chinese thresholds of tolerance, since no one could be certain of enemy response, the military's advocacy of the provocative attacks demonstrates their rather higher propensity to risk taking.

On the question of concern for enemy civilian deaths, one might argue that civilian decision makers were no more concerned than anyone else. Support for such an argument can be found in a January 1966 paper by John McNaughton, assistant secretary of defense for ISA and a chief architect of the air war until his death in 1967. Under the heading of "possible further efforts against the North" he wrote:

Strikes at population targets (per se) are likely not only to create a counterproductive wave of revulsion abroad and at home, but greatly to increase the risk of enlarging the war with China and the Soviet Union. Destruction of locks and dams, however—if handled right—might (perhaps after the *next* Pause) offer promise. It should be studied. Such destruction does not kill or drown people. By shallow-flooding the rice, it leads after time to widespread starvation (more than a million?) unless food is provided—which we could offer to do "at the conference table." (Emphasis in original)[80]

It is unlikely that McNaughton was the only civilian who made such a calculation (though he may have been the only one who committed it to paper) and so fairness requires its recording. However, the best evidence of the civilian position can be found at the points of actual operational recommendation and authorization. It is here that OSD repeatedly rejected or restricted JCS target requests on the basis of likely civilian casualties. It was in fact a routine consideration of those in ISA reviewing JCS requests.[81] A documented example of the secretary's concern occurred in June 1966, when approval had not yet been given for the POL strikes, and McNamara told CINCPAC explicitly that, "Final decision for or against [the strikes] will be influenced by the extent they can be carried out without civilian casualties."[82] The secretary went on to ask what would be done to limit casualties and the Pacific commander explained the various and special precautions that would be taken whereby he could project less than fifty casualties. The CIA projected two to three hundred.[83]

Over the three-year period the issue of civilian casualties remained a principal source of irritation between the military and their civilian overseers, reflecting in the most basic way one of the dilemmas of limited war. The civilian administration had not only to try to continually reconcile the restraint in the conduct of such a war with the population, but also with the military, for it was they who could most directly influence policy. The reconciliation was never accomplished. Neither the avoidance of actions that might widen the war nor the avoidance of actions that might cause significant death to North Vietnamese noncombatants were ever accepted by military leaders as legitimate rationales for bombing restrictions. As late as March 1968 the JCS were pushing for urban strikes, arguing, somewhat incredibly, that there were no longer any real civilians left in the cities of Hanoi and Haiphong, and "consequently, air strikes in and around these cities endanger personnel primarily engaged directly or indirectly in support of the war effort."[84] Perhaps the difference in values is most clearly reflected in the opinion of a former high ranking air force general who was important in operational control of the bombing as well as in recommendations on its conduct. He expressed disgust at, and disdain for, civilian timidity in Viet-Nam. He cited the experience of United States strikes against Japan in

World War II as an example of how prior warning before raids could limit civilian deaths to an acceptable number: "We gave them seventy-two hours in Tokyo, then we bombed the hell out of them. When the people came back their homes were burned down but we didn't kill very many civilians."[85] According to the United States Strategic Bombing Survey, of which the general was no doubt aware, the Tokyo raids killed 93,050 persons.

The bombing debate was of course not limited to OSD-JCS exchanges. Very early on Presidential Assistant Bill Moyers worked from his position in the White House to restrict the extent of the strikes and move the president towards a pause and negotiations. According to one account he and his assistant, Hayes Redmon, built a network of second level officials in the foreign affairs bureaucracy and used information from these sources to undermine the positions of their superiors in the Pentagon and State Department who favored an aggressive policy.[86] Under Secretary of State George Ball's opposition to the bombing from the start, and his efforts at bringing about a bombing pause, are also well known. Nevertheless, Moyers, Ball and many lesser known opponents of the policy eventually left the administration —and without making a public dissent from policy. The Office of the Secretary of Defense was left as the principal source of restraint and the principal source of support for any desire for restraint the president might have had.

The posture eventually taken by the secretary was not his initial one and came about only after a period of conversion. In the first draft of a memorandum to the president dated July 1, 1965, McNamara recommended an intensification of the air war, including the mining of Haiphong harbor and the destruction of rail and road links between China and North Viet-Nam. He revised his July recommendation after making a trip to South Viet-Nam and after receiving some negative intelligence reports, but still called for a gradual increase in strike sorties.[87] As McNamara continued to approve escalations of the bombing throughout 1965 and into 1966, his pessimism about their results deepened. His enthusiastic support in 1966 for the development of the barrier across South Viet-Nam as a substitute for the bombing was one indicator of his skepticism about air power's capacity to counter infiltration. The gross disappointment of the POL strikes later the same year undercut whatever efficacy the policy may have had on other grounds.[88] By 1967 McNamara had come to accept the position of several of his assistant secretaries and sought ways of severely limiting or totally halting the bombing. He did so, however, without attempting to bring allies to his position or even to confront the president directly. Even in preparation for his testimony before the Stennis subcommittee in August 1967, in which he went as far as he ever did in publicly splitting with the military over the bombing policy, he worked virtually alone.

Several of those close to the secretary in 1967 have described him as "torn" or ambivalent. His assistant secretary for public affairs, Phil Goulding, has written that "McNamara looked upon possible national acceptance of the hit-them-harder-and-win theory as catastrophic," and yet feared the results of any "overt conflict between the President and himself."[89] Townsend Hoopes describes staff meetings with McNamara in this period as "entirely barren affairs," never going beyond the technical questions to the basic cleavages dividing decision-makers.[90] His staff in the office of Systems Analysis had even begun to try to independently stimulate debate on several aspects of the war including the bombing. They published and distributed the monthly *Southeast Asia Analysis Report*, an unofficial piece carrying the relatively unrestrictive classification of "secret," in which the contributors often critically evaluated the techniques and conduct of ground and air operations in Viet-Nam. Although it did not cause the military to rethink its position, it did lead the chairman of the Joint Chiefs to recommend to McNamara that the report be limited to internal OSD distribution so as to "reduce the dissemination of incorrect and/or misleading information to senior officials or other governmental agencies, as well as our commanders in the field."[91]

Without the active support of McNamara the impact of such activity was limited. As it turned out, the fall of 1967 saw the strike authorization for even those few targets that had until then been withheld. The secretary of defense did not seek allies for his position and limited his own dissent rather than paying, and forcing the president to pay, the costs of its expression. The dissent of those beneath and around McNamara proved to be more productive only when he was replaced by a new secretary who made different calculations under different circumstances. While McNamara was under conflicting pressures, caught in a "loyalty trap," the man to whom he owed that loyalty had his own, quite separate, set of pressures. We must look at him next, because to focus upon OSD-JCS conflict as we have is to lose perspective on the office of the president, and only by refocusing will more of the important pressures on policy become visible.

View from the White House

The bombing of North Viet-Nam began only when Lyndon Johnson decided to initiate it, it was halted only on the occasions when he saw advantage in a pause, and it was resumed only when he thought resumption was required. Recognizing this does not diminish the importance of the conflict between bureaucratic actors or the importance of the sources of their conflict, but it does suggest that attention should be payed to the perspective from which the president is likely to have viewed the conflicts around him and the progress of the war. Appreciating that perspective means looking at the men who were closest to the president and most influential on this issue, and looking at that which would have been of unique concern to the president—congressional and public opinion.

In describing policy making in a different air war, A. J. P. Taylor wrote of the relations between Winston Churchill and his confidential advisor, Lord Cherwell. He characterized the latter less as one responsible for policy than as one contributing support for it: "He merely provided arguments to sustain a case which was already being strongly pressed by the air ministry and the chief of the bomber command."[92] A similar statement could be made about National Security Advisor Walt Rostow's position in the Johnson administration. Of those supporters of the war who were closest to the president, Rostow became notorious for his enthusiasm and irrepressible optimism over the war. That is not to say that he could have prevailed in the absense of others or that he was as important as others as a source of policy; the military, especially the chairman of the Joint Chiefs, Earl Wheeler, and the secretary of state were surely of more importance to Johnson, as was McNamara until he could no longer be counted upon. Nevertheless it was Rostow, perhaps because of his proximity, who is often singled out as reassuring the president in the face of dissent, as arguing that "staying the course" would eventually produce results. Several of those in OSD who were active in efforts to demonstrate the failure of the bombing and move the policy toward negotiations in 1967 have referred to Rostow as the one primarily responsible for having screened out such arguments and kept them from reaching the president. He has been described by the same frustrated officials as impervious to analysis and arguments and as perpetually advocating the next escalation as "the final turn of the screw." In the words of one observer, "The general feeling was that, military advisors aside,

Rostow was the man who most often assured Johnson that victory was just around the corner."[93] Without commenting on the justice of such characterizations, it will suffice to say that the image of Rostow at the president's ear was widespread and, since he is not among those who have found the war a mistake and have become opponents-in-retrospect, we can be fairly sure about the nature of his advice.

In naming a few of those who were close to the president and presumably influential, Clark Clifford and Abe Fortas deserve special note. Special, because prior to Clifford's replacement of McNamara as secretary of defense, their advice was based on personal relations with the president and not in any institutional arrangement. The result, as former White House Assistant Chester Cooper has pointed out, was that these man were themselves inaccessible and under no obligation to respond to the arguments of those inside the administration. Rostow, Wheeler, and even Rusk, on the other hand, could be forced to deal with the evidence presented by other governmental actors, or at least one could be certain they had such evidence. There was, furthermore, a pervasive and well-founded belief that Clifford and Fortas were hard-liners on Viet-Nam and that the president had a high regard for their opinion. They had after all been "right" in January 1966 in opposing the long bombing pause, and Johnson never forgot it—nor for that matter did those who argued for pauses after that. On an issue like the bombing where much of the maneuvering was done for the benefit of the president, it is easy to understand how the position of these personal advisors could have been demoralizing to others competing for the president's ear:

> Accurate or not, it was common gossip that whenever the President rejected suggestions for cutting back the bombing, more often than not it was after these two personal friends had dropped by the White House for an evening of chat and a night cap. For some of us the Clifford-Fortas relationship with the President was a source of frustration and despair.[94]

To say that the president was influenced by those close to him is not only unacceptionable but also uninteresting. To assert that the president became isolated from the arguments of others by those close to him, that as the support of his intimates stiffened his accessibility to those not offering support decreased, is to say something more important. This can be said of Lyndon Johnson on the Viet-Nam War issue. It was not that Johnson approached Viet-Nam without preconceptions and became a victim of his advisors, nor was it true that he was unaware of dissent from his policy. On the contrary, the president had a world view and a conception of national interest and international threats which provided a baseline for his decisions, and he certainly knew of the growing divisions in the country, as well as those within his own administration. What was happening, however, was that those who lost sympathy with the war policy also lost the confidence of the president and tended to move or be moved out of government and away from the president. George Ball, Bill Moyers, McGeorge Bundy, and Robert McNamara were the most notable.[95] By the middle of 1967, Lyndon Johnson was surrounded, or more accurately, surrounded himself with loyal advisors who supported him in what he thought he had to do for reasons domestic and international. This gradual isolation of the president was part of the reason for the president's failure to come to grips with the very substantial criticisms of air power emerging from the intelligence community and elsewhere.

Although this is a fairly common view of what was happening, it is not a universal one. John P. Roche, who served as special consultant to the president from 1966 to 1968, takes issue with it when he writes that

> . . . several chroniclers emphasize President Johnson's "isolation" and the extent to which his "courtiers" protected him from reality. Translated this means "Why didn't Lyndon talk to me?" Similarly, we are told that no one dared to challenge the President on his Vietnam policies, that he went up in smoke if anyone suggested a bombing halt. Translated, this means "I didn't dare argue because he might have fired me."[96]

It would seem, however, that Roche gives the argument away in attributing these concerns to advisors. If Lyndon did talk to them less, or if they came to believe, correctly or not, that dissent could be so costly, then isolation would still be the outcome. In citing his own frequent dissent from the bombing and its failure to produce presidential reprisal, Roche can prove little since his loyalty and support were broad and genuine, his dissent only technical. As he says, "I supported the defense of South Vietnam but opposed the whole notion of a cut-rate, air-power war."[97] In view of the deterioration of the president's relations with others who came to question the foundations of the policy, it would seem reasonable to expect remaining advisors to grow more and more cautious in dissent, especially as dissension in the administration increasingly became a political issue itself. So if they did not challenge the president because they feared that they might be fired, then perhaps one might want to translate that motivation further, for some at least, into a concern for the course of Viet-Nam policy if all opposition were eliminated or denied legitimacy.[98]

Domestic Opinion from the President's Vantage Point

All that has been written about the domestic sources of the Viet-Nam policy applies to the prosecution of the air war, only more so. Daniel Ellsberg, Leslie Gelb, and others are right in offering varieties of a "1950" thesis which emphasize Lyndon Johnson's concern that Viet-Nam not be "lost" as China had been. There was a fear that if this became a widespread perception, domestic reaction, like the one in the fifties, would be bad for American foreign policy, bad for the Democrats, and bad for the president who was held responsible. The Johnson administration did see itself as the last domino in this interpretation of the classical "theory."[99] But the bombing of North Viet-Nam was something more than just another aspect of the effort to prevent it all from happening. It had become a symbol of the effort, a rallying point for proponents and opponents, for hawks and doves. The fact that, for policy makers, opposition to bombing escalation or support for a pause was really a poor indicator of "dovishness" was less important than the image of it as essential to the Asian commitment.

The people and the Congress expected the north to be bombed if the war was going to be fought by Americans, and the war had to be fought by Americans. The implications of this logic forced themselves upon the president more than anyone else because of his accountability. He had to conduct an air war, independent of his own conception of its efficiency, for the same reason he had to initiate it before introducing American troops in 1965: because the American people would not accept the costs of the ground war unless the United States concurrently attempted to prevail by the less expensive route so strongly advocated by the professional military. In order to fight in the south, Johnson had to continue to escalate the bombing in the north, if for no other reason than to minimally demonstrate that this method was being tried and that it was failing. The more the military and other air war advocates complained about restrictions the more pressure there was on him to remove restrictions and show that he was not the cause of the policy's failure. In short, there were substantial limits on the extent to which the president could conduct a limited war.

The pressures on Lyndon Johnson were tangible. His secretary of defense accurately summed up this aspect of the impact of the air war when he reported to the president at the end of 1965 that "some critics, who advocated bombing, were silenced; others are now as vocal or more vocal because the program has been too limited for their taste."[100] One such critic was a prominent Republican, Richard Nixon, who castigated the "soft line" of those who favored an extension of the bombing pause in January 1966. At the same time there was the raw data of public opinion provided by a Harris poll which showed 61 percent in favor of a step-up in the bombing if the pause was fruitless.[101] A year later the same poll indicated 67 percent supporting the bombing.[102]

The logic of the popular support for the bombing of the north depended not only on the value it was presumed to have in applying pressure to the "real enemy" but also on the direct support it was thought to be to American men fighting in the south. The impression of such a support function was forcefully conveyed to the public by the military in the field and in Washington. A marine commander in Viet-Nam told the press, "There is a direct relationship between the number of American troops killed and the bombing—there is no argument about that. When the bombing stops, more Americans are killed."[103] No less explicitly, the chief of naval operations testified to the same effect before a Senate Appropriations Committee hearing in early 1967:

Senator Thurmond: . . . We have been doing only a limited amount of bombing, but the limited bombing we have done has been helpful, hasn't it?

Admiral McDonald: I think it has saved hundreds of lives of U.S. soldiers and U.S. Marines.

Senator Thurmond: If we were to discontinue that bombing, that means in your judgment, I presume, it would mean that there would be more American lives destroyed as the war goes on?

Admiral McDonald: That is correct.[104]

The degree to which the air war in North Viet-Nam was actually related to American casualties in South Viet-Nam was not, however, as clear to civilians in the Defense Department and elsewhere. Townsend Hoopes indicated as much in a memorandum to Secretary McNamara on the subject:

There appears to be, in military reality, only the most tenuous relationship between bombing in the North and U.S. casualties in the

South. This is the express or implied conclusion of each of the studies and statements cited herein (and of earlier CIA analyses as well). . . . Present U.S. casualty levels in the South are not a function of the bombing against the North. They are a function of the U.S. ground strategy in the South.[105]

Shortly after making this argument to one secretary of defense, Hoopes, then under secretary of the air force, reframed it for another, with a conclusion that indicated that he understood the position of Clifford and the president: "In my judgment we thus confront a linkage that is in large part a military fiction, but at the same time a palpable political fact."[106] That was exactly right, and as long as it remained so the bombing would be a prerequisite to the costly ground activity and, conversely, the prerequisite for a reduction in the bombing would be a shift to a less costly ground strategy. Appreciating this political linkage would prove helpful in understanding some of the events of 1968.

The force of public opinion influenced the president by virtue of the combination of his own indirect perception of that opinion and his expectations about the extent of public tolerance and the nature of public reactions. By contrast, the pressure and influence of Congress on the conduct of the Viet-Nam war was more direct. The influence was not all exerted in one direction, to be sure, but one group was easier to keep at bay than those on the other side. When Senator Vance Hartke drafted a letter to Johnson on January 27, 1966, urging him not to end the bombing pause and added the signatures of fourteen other senators to it, the president responded with only a two-paragraph note and the resumption of the bombing four days later. When Senator J. William Fulbright, another foe of Viet-Nam policy, sought to use public hearings before the Foreign Relations Committee to draw attention to his cause, the president chose exactly that time to suddenly announce a trip to Honolulu and preempted the broadcast of the Senate proceedings.[107] Generally, the dissent of the doves held less legitimacy in the country and thus could be isolated more easily by the administration with appeals for unity and support in the time of crisis. Eventually those in Congress who sought to deescalate the war did present a problem for the president, especially after Tet in 1968, but until then the most significant congressional pressure came from the advocates of a more aggressive policy.

The Senate hearings before the Preparedness Investigating Subcommittee of the Committee on Armed Services conducted during August 1967 were convincing evidence of the ability of these congressional forces to push the president on the air war. The subcommittee membership consisted of Senators Symington, Jackson, Cannon, Byrd, Smith, Thurmond, and Miller, and its chairman, Senator Stennis. Without exception, though with varying degrees of enthusiasm, the members were sympathetic to the military's charges of civilian interference and believed the bombing should have been escalated in accordance with JCS and CINCPAC requests. There was acknowledged and prior communication between the subcommittee staff and members of the senior military in preparation for the hearings. The military had made clear in advance what they wanted changed and how civilian decisions had hampered operations up to that point.[108] The record of the testimony runs some 515 pages and documents the military's case for expansion of the air war and Secretary McNamara's defense of civilian imposed restrictions on its conduct.

The effect of the hearings began to be felt as soon as it was known that they would be held. In the month preceding their initiation, the JCS increased its target list by 75 percent and the civilians significantly expanded their authorization. On August 8, the night before the first day of testimony, sixteen new previously unauthorized targets were released for strike. This was noted in the hearings and prompted Senator Henry Jackson to quip that the authorization was "timed very well."[109] The impact of the hearings continued to be felt throughout the fall of 1967 as more and more targets that had been unauthorized for more than two years were released. Some, like the port of Cam Phu, were targets McNamara had explicitly testified should not be struck. The change amounted to acceptance of the report of the subcommittee by the president over the recommendations of his secretary of defense. The committee had concluded in its report that:

> For policy reasons, we have employed military aviation in a carefully controlled restricted, and graduated buildup of bombing pressure which discounted the professional judgment of our best military experts and substituted civilian judgment in the details of target selection and the timing of strikes. We shackled the true potential of air power. . . .
>
> It is high time, we believe, to allow the military voice to be heard in connection with the tactical details of military operations.[110]

The charges of those in Congress and in certain segments of the media that the military were being undermined by the civilian administration could not be weathered without concessions. From Lyndon Johnson's vantage point the parallels to President Truman's experience with military dissent over the conduct of his war must have been salient. Such concerns were important throughout the three-year period, though the threat of a defection of the military supported by a block of congressmen and senators became most real in 1967. In surveying the president's situation in August of that year, a British magazine characterized his policy choice succintly: "Mr. Johnson's decision to strike new targets has very little to do with any calculation about the course of the war in Viet-Nam itself. The President's real target is in Washington."[111]

Conclusion

It is inadequate, though accurate, to describe the decisions of the air war as presidential because the source of policy was considerably more complex. An explanation of the policy of bombing North Viet-Nam best procedes at several levels. In terms of the stated objectives, the policy was a failure, and this is where analysis should begin. The intelligence community did not immediately characterize the effectiveness of the programs in any consistent fashion for decision makers, and what is more significant, the divergent interpretations appear to have resulted from something other than just "honest differences." The performance of the intelligence function for the air war, in fact, involved some gross distortions attributable to various kinds of unfortunate organizational arrangements. Intelligence estimates and evaluations were not so much the basis upon which policy choices could be made as rationale for decisions already taken and resources to be used in support of a position in debates with bureaucratic opponents. Analysis was made to fit the consumer's need. Although the intelligence picture was, for some time unclear and distorted, it did eventually come into focus for many civilians, and the image was not one of success. Civilians who would then have curbed the air war instead of escalating it, confronted its military advocates in continual debates and often in ritual-like proceedings. The air force and the navy had significant interests at stake in the bombing from individual careers at one level to aircraft carriers at another, from incremental budget allocations in the next fiscal year in the short run to the valued roles and missions of their particular service over the long term. Ironically, civilians in OSD who sought to control the military actually provided incentives, along with congressional budgetary committees, for dysfunctional competition in the field and service advocacy of an even more aggressive air campaign.

The debate over the bombing, however, ultimately centered on the JCS, the secretary of defense and those in his office, and the president. The leverage of the military turned in large part upon certain political facts and assumptions held most important by the president. It was because of such presidential perceptions that elements in Congress sympathetic to the military's position were so important in shaping policy and temporarily resolving the debate in 1967. The president certainly perceived the conflict over the continuation and escalation of the air war from the special vantage point of his office, and it could not have been otherwise. At the same time, however, his administration was becoming increasingly inhospitable to those within who sought to provide advice from other vantage points, a response that might well have been avoided. The president himself was clearly setting the tone and choosing isolation.

So at the operational level the specific decisions of the air war depended upon the continuous resolution of a sequence of civil-military conflicts. At a higher level the air war was part of a military policy in Viet-Nam and a national foreign policy which can be accounted for only by including other calculations. These were the calculations that followed from the political vulnerability of the office of the presidency on the one hand and the basic policy premises of the president and his structuring of policy advice on the other.

V. EXPLAINING THE GROUND STRATEGY: 1965–67

The military strategy of the United States in South Viet-Nam from the spring of 1965 through the spring of 1968 was the strategy of "search and destroy." It did not become the American strategy as a result of a joint decision by civilians and military leaders; some of the latter and many of the former thought that it was a costly failure. And yet it prevailed. An explanation of the ground strategy requires an examination of the process by which it was made—it will not do to characterize it as simply the best perceived means to a commonly agreed upon end. In that, it is like the other half of the military policy, the air war over North Viet-Nam—its content and persistence could only be accounted for by looking into the workings of the decision-making process.

As early as 1964, well before the appearance of any regular American ground combat units, the American military in Viet-Nam sought to standardize the expressions used to describe various kinds of combat operations. In a section of the official *Report on the War in Vietnam*, General William C. Westmoreland, the former commander of the United States forces in Viet-Nam, notes that:

> The first operational term was "search and destroy." Operations of this type were designed to find, fix in place, fight and destroy (or neutralize) enemy forces and their base areas and supply caches. This was essentially the traditional attack mission of the infantry.[1]

After a discussion of other kinds of operations, Westmoreland goes on to say that the term "search and destroy" ultimately had to be abandoned because it had become "distorted": "Somehow, it was equated in the public mind with aimless searches in the jungle and the destruction of property."[2]

The commander's sensitivity to the misunderstanding of search and destroy operations is itself understandable. Such operations were the main component of the United States Army's ground combat strategy in South Viet-Nam from 1965 through 1968;

they were much criticized, and General Westmoreland was the chief advocate, architect, and defender of the strategy during that period. At the same time it is easy to see how the general's desire to change terminology falls short of meeting the criticisms of the strategy. It would be more appropriate to see how the strategy came to be adopted, examine the criticisms and alternatives that emerged, and try to explain why it persisted in the face of considerable opposition.

Adopting a Strategy

In the spring of 1965 the first regular United States ground combat units were introduced into Viet-Nam. Marines arrived in March and soldiers, the 173d Airborne Brigade, arrived in May. Prior to their arrival there were Army Special Forces Units, usually operating on a small scale in remote areas, and a military advisory mission of considerable size in Viet-Nam. Although these American military personnel numbered well over 20,000, the introduction of regular combat units signaled a dramatic change in the nature of American involvement and completely redefined the American commitment. The series of critical decisions during the first half of 1965 leading to the ground combat role has properly been the subject of much attention. Together they are the closest thing to a decision to go to war in Viet-Nam that we have. Our purpose here, however, is not to look at the decision and its impact in broad terms, but to focus upon the relatively narrow question of the strategic concept under which the troops would be used. Since the principals involved differed over the most appropriate strategy, the choice in the spring of 1965 had immediate significance and long range political importance to later attempts at change.

The marines arrived in March after a February marked by repeated requests from the military for their deployment. On February 11 a JCS memorandum to the secretary of defense called for the deployment of a Marine Expeditionary Brigade (MEB) to Da Nang, as well as other action in Southeast Asia. The JCS rationale at that point was the same as the one used in their first request for such a deployment in November 1964; to provide security for the American air base at Da Nang and deter retaliation on it that might be expected after the initiation of air strikes against the north.[3] On February 22, General Westmoreland requested two Marine Battalion Landing Teams (BLTs) for Da Nang, and four days later the commander in chief in the Pacific, Admiral Sharp, seconded the request and added F-4 aircraft for troop support. Maxwell Taylor, ambassador to South Viet-Nam, and former chairman of the Joint Chiefs of Staff, also supported the request of the commander of the United States Military Assistant Command in Viet-Nam. He did so, however, only after presenting a long argument as to why it should not be supported. In a February 22 cable to the State Department, Taylor noted that security was a legitimate concern, but doubted that, even if a whole brigade were deployed, the base could be secured against a mortar attack. Most important, this former military man went on record early as reluctantly supporting even a minimal security role for United States troops, and went on to warn of the dangers ahead:

> As I analyze the pros and cons of placing any considerable number of Marines in Da Nang area beyond those presently assigned, I develop grave reservations as to wisdom and necessity of so doing. Such action would be a step in reversing long standing policy of avoiding commitment of ground combat forces in SVN. Once this policy is breached, it will be very difficult to hold the line.[4]

A message to Taylor on Febrary 26 announced Washington's decision to send the two battalions of marines.[5]

On March 5, three days before the marines actually arrived in Viet-Nam, CINCPAC sent an "Eyes Only" message to the chairman of the Joint Chiefs, General Earle Wheeler.[6] The message called for the immediate deployment of the 9th Marine Expeditionary Brigade to provide still more security for Da Nang. The military situation was declining steadily, if unevenly, and would continue to do so over the next several months. Admiral Sharp's request would ultimately be superseded, however, by the recommendations of the army chief of staff, General Johnson. On March 14, after seven days in South Viet-Nam, Johnson returned to advocate deployment of a full American division to one of two alternative sets of locations—either primarily to the Saigon areas at Bien Hoa/Ton Son Nhut, and the coastal cities of Qui Nhon and Nha Trang, and the inland position at Pleiku, or primarily in the highland provinces of Pleiku, Kontum, and Darlac (see figure 2). Johnson and Wheeler both favored the second deployment.[7] After he saw the ratio of the number of South Vietnamese troops freed for other activity to the number of United States troops introduced, the secretary of defense also favored the highlands location.

What is interesting here is that in a recommendation that ostensibly introduced the alternative of a conservative enclave

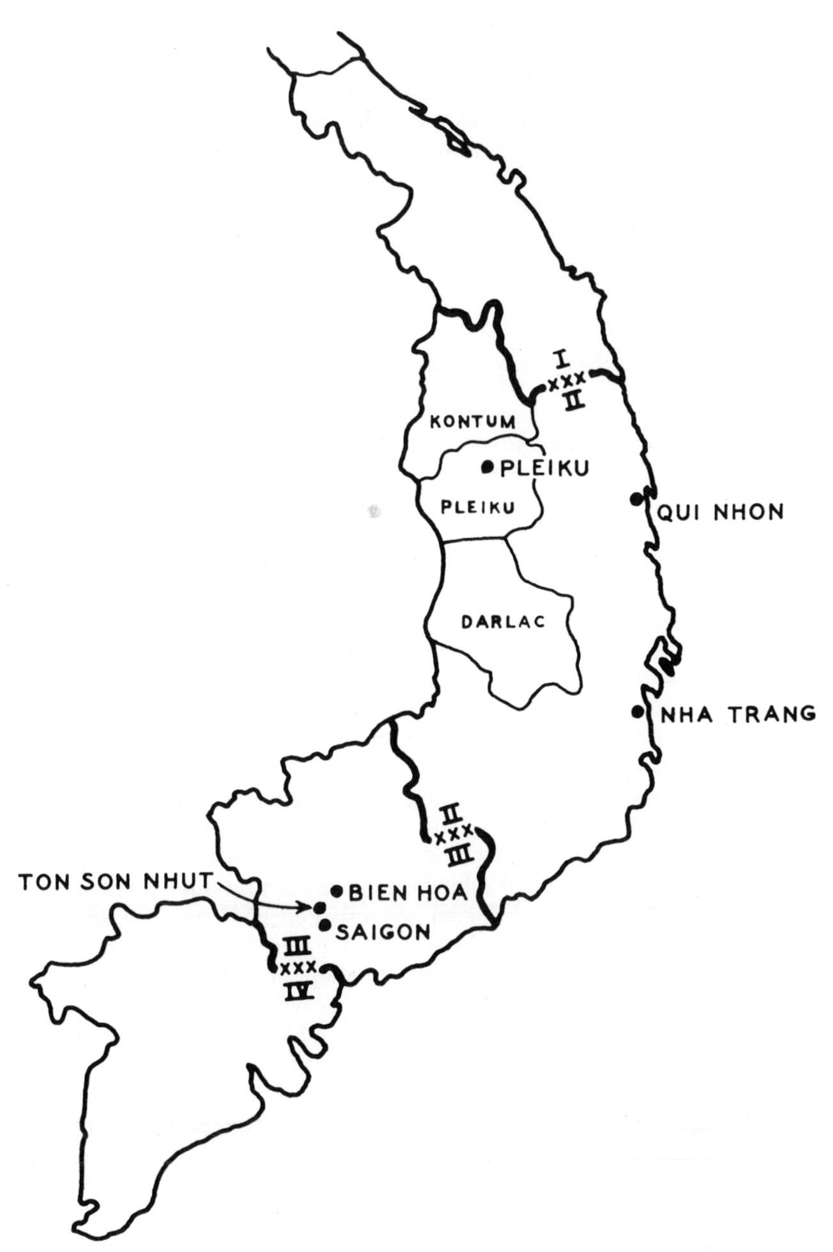

SOUTH VIET-NAM

strategy for the United States in a coastal deployment of forces, what was actually advocated was an aggressive search and destroy strategy. There were two alternatives to be sure, but one was favored by the two senior military actors and had a special appeal to McNamara. That appeal was based on the figures that may have indicated the second alternative deployment was "efficient" in freeing ARVN, but it is unlikely that the figures showed very clearly the strategic concept entailed in such a deployment. An American division based largely at Saigon and two other coastal locations could remain in a defensive-security role or could move more aggressively to the adjacent countryside, but it would essentially be in the rear with the population, leaving the ARVN to engage the enemy in force in the sparsely populated highlands. If it were deployed to the three highland provinces as Johnson and Wheeler advocated, however, United States troops would have little to defend and much freedom to pursue the enemy. The ARVN would be left with the security role on the coast. Just as the deployments suggested alternative strategies of shield and sword for American troops, the strategies suggested alternative goals: denying the enemy access to the population and winning victory by stalemate on the one hand, and seeking victory by defeating enemy forces in the field on the other. What had to be extracted from Johnson's early recommendation emerged more clearly as the spring wore on.

Taylor was the first to try to push to the fore the question of the appropriate mission for future American troops sent to Viet-Nam. His March 18 State Department cable contrasted the risks and benefits of a highland versus a coastal strategy, but it did not produce a prescription.[8] Only after his cable also failed to produce any reaction from Washington did the ambassador follow it nine days later with a call for an "offensive enclave" strategy, and thus deny support for the nascent army position. The army's position was, at the same time, taking shape in a JCS memorandum and in a separate report by General Westmoreland entitled "Commander's Estimate of the Situation in SVN." The March 20 JCSM proposed sending two American divisions to Viet-Nam—a marine division going to their existing Tactical Area of Responsibility (TAOR) in the northernmost military region, and an army division going to Pleiku in the central highlands.[9] Westmoreland's half-inch thick report to Washington had been weeks in the making and, on the subject of deployment, was consistent with the JCS position. It recommended the commitment of two American divisions, embraced the highlands mission, and specifically rejected any kind of enclave strategy. It was likely, therefore, that the field commander had planned to pursue the aggressive strategy involving sizeable American units operating in the countryside in place of South Vietnamese troops even before the first marines arrived, reportedly to provide security for an American coastal base. Putting aside the issue of deception or complicity among senior military, it is undeniable that Westmoreland was considerably more advanced in his thinking about the American role in Viet-Nam than Ambassador Taylor or, it would turn out, than several principal Washington decision makers.

Both Taylor's and the military's input were considered in the National Security Council meetings of April 1 and 2. On April 6 National Security Action Memorandum 328 was issued and included presidential approval for an

> 18–20,000 man increase in U.S. military support forces . . . two additional Marine Battalions and one Marine Air Squadron . . . [and] a change of mission for all Marine Battalions deployed to Vietnam to permit their more active use under conditions to be established and approved by the Secretary of Defense in consultation with the Secretary of State.[10]

The decision was as characteristically incremental as it was ambiguous on the key points. Although the two battalions were clearly not the two divisions requested, the large size of the support package led the JCS to believe that the intent was to unofficially endorse the deployment of more troops, and they proceeded to plan as if approval had been won. Their interpretation was not disingenuous since Ambassador Taylor drew the same conclusion after seeing the NSAM.[11] One month later Assistant Secretary of Defense for International Security Affairs John McNaughton had to inform the deputy secretary that the JCS had assumed more than was intended.[12]

As for the change in the marine mission, the *Pentagon Papers* analyst thought it meant the end of the security role for American troops and "signalled the beginning of the relatively more ambitious enclave strategy."[13] Although the mission of simple base defense was set aside, it is not clear to whom NSAM 328 could have signalled the adoption of the enclave concept. Certainly not to the commander in the field, for five days after the NSAM, Westmoreland cabled CINCPAC that in spite of Washington's reluctance he still wanted an American division for the highlands. His position had not changed; a highland deployment implied search and destroy, while only the coastal location permitted enclaves. It is possible that civilian decision makers believed an enclave strategy would lead to victory by causing a stalemate in the south, and it is also possible that they believed they could prevail upon the military to pursue such a strategy. Indeed, the Honolulu conference held on April 20 brought the principals together and seemed to endorse the coastal strategy. McNamara, McNaughton, and Assistant Secretary of State William Bundy met with Taylor, Westmoreland, Wheeler, and Admiral Sharp and agreed on recommending a total of 82,000 American troops for Viet-Nam, all to be assigned to coastal, populated positions. But ambiguity about the military's acceptance of enclaves should have been dispelled by a JCS memorandum ten days after the conference which offered as part of the rationale for new troop requests the preparation "for the later introduction of an airmobile division to the central plateau. . . ."[14] In short, the Joint Chiefs were stating their intention of introducing their newest division-size combat unit to the highlands and characterizing coastal deployment up to that point, not as a combat strategy itself, but as a preliminary support step in the direction of beginning the strategy of search and destroy.

Still, there is the question of whether the civilians understood this, or whether they were genuine believers in the potential success of an enclave strategy. One answer is that although civilian principals differed in their expectations about the utility of stalemate on the ground and the impact of the bombing of the north on the situation in the south, they were not at that point prepared to embrace a plan of action involving several hundred thousand American troops in costly large-unit battle engagements. This would be less interesting if it were not for the fact that the army was so prepared. The language of NSAM 328 and the exchanges at Honolulu indicate that the president and his principal civilian advisors saw the enclaves not only as possibly the first step toward larger involvement but also as a step more easily reversible than others that might have been taken. Some thought air power plus enclaves would work, and others opposed doing more, even if they did not work. There was, then, a gap between the civilian and military positions, and the chairman of the Joint Chiefs and the commander in the field were attempting to close it by bringing the civilians over to their position.

During the months of May and June the course for the next three years was set. In a May 8 message to CINCPAC, Westmoreland set out his "concept of operations" for South Viet-Nam; there were three "Stages" and four "Phases." Advancing through the Stages, United States and Allied forces would move from secured bases to "deep patrolling" beyond initial tactical areas of responsibility, to long-range search and destroy operations. The parallel Phases would bring troops from defense of secure coastal enclaves to offensive operations launched from them, followed by defense of inland enclaves and more offense from those bases.[15] Discussion in May over South Vietnamese concurrence with these American plans and coordination with American troops gave way to near panic in early June. On June 5 the Saigon Mission Intelligence Committee reported a series of ARVN defeats and said United States troops would probably be needed.[16] Two days later Westmoreland forwarded more depressing news and an explicit recommendation to CINCPAC: "In order to cope with the situation outlined above, I see no course of action open to us except to reinforce our efforts in SVN with additional U.S. or Third Country forces as rapidly as is practical during the critical weeks ahead."[17]

Admiral Sharp's response to Westmoreland's request went to Washington the same day and supported the general in his request for troops but not in the critical matter of the location of the most important unit, the Airmobile Division. Sharp wanted it to be based at Qui Nhon and operate in the coastal province of Binh Dinh rather than the highlands. Although his concern was probably limited to logistics—he explained his preference in terms of the risks of supporting an inland division under the current conditions—the result was to provide support for Ambassador Taylor's more broadly-based opposition to highlands deployment. The JCS, who on June 9 had accepted Westmoreland's recommendation, reversed themselves two days later in a memorandum to the secretary and favored the Qui Nhon coastal location. At the same time they informed MACV, through CINCPAC, that more troops were about to be approved for Viet-Nam, and that they wanted to know where Westmoreland intended to put them. Decisions about the location and use of troops had become an issue. Since the JCS inquiry concerned only the single brigade that was due for approval and not as yet the division which was originally requested, the precedent for a rather thorough control of troop movement by Washington might have been set with this message. But this was not to be. In a June 13 response, General Westmoreland first noted the seriousness of the situation in the south, pointing out that the ARVN had already lost five battalions, and then made a series of eight recommendations including the following: "Deploy the U.S. Army Air

Mobile Division (and logistic increment 3) through Qui Nhon to An Khe, Pleiku and Kontum (approximately 21,000 personnel)."[18] After reemphasizing his desire to use new troops in the central plateau region, Westmoreland, in the words of the *Pentagon Papers* analyst, "made a big pitch . . . for a free hand to maneuver the troops around inside the country."[19] On June 26 he was granted that freedom, presumably by the president, and he never relinquished it. William Bundy informed Ambassador Taylor of Westmoreland's authority to put American troops into combat "in any situation in which the use of such troops is required by an appropriate GVN commander and when, in COMUSMACV's judgment, their use is necessary to strengthen the relative position of GVN forces."[20]

The next major troop authorization decision did not come until the middle of July when thirty-four battalions, including the Airmobile Division, were approved. The last attempts at preventing that decision and the commitment that went with it were made by Under Secretary of State George Ball and, with less enthusiasm, by William Bundy. In a June 28 draft memorandum Ball correctly pointed out that Westmoreland, by his own strategic plan, was jumping to Phase III with the deployment of new units for inland operations. Ball argued that if American troops already approved were kept on the coast in a defensive posture, a holding action could be fought with minimal losses while a political settlement was negotiated. His July 1 memorandum for the president essentially recommended cutting losses and withdrawing under whatever cover could be provided by negotiated arrangements. The under secretary was therefore explicitly linking the strategic concept of coastal deployment with the political goal of disengagement. Assistant Secretary of State Bundy, in another memorandum for the president on the same day, recommended keeping United States troops in coastal enclaves while a diplomatic solution to the war was sought. Unlike Ball, Bundy did not take the position that losses should be accepted if necessary to achieve an exit and, in fact, recommended holding the Airmobile Division and an infantry division ready for deployment. Neither view prevailed.

From the start, the question of the strategic concept was intertwined with the question of where troops were to be based. By insisting on his right to place troops where he thought best, Westmoreland was asserting his prerogative on how to use the troops. There is ample evidence that the military understood this and did not slip by incremental choices into large-scale ground engagement; but that instead they, and especially the field commander, pursued a course designed to involve as many American units as possible, quickly and actively, in combat. Westmoreland was not, as one deputy assistant secretary of defense characterized him, a "boy scout," blindly accepting the mission in Viet-Nam because he was told to without any conception of what he was about.[21] The MACV commander may have been mistaken in his perception of the task in South Viet-Nam, but he had the closest thing to a classic plan of engagement one could have for Viet-Nam, and he thought he understood the problem. Certainly he was much more of an aggressive initiator than he has been given credit for. Search and destroy was the "traditional attack mission of the infantry," and General Westmoreland maneuvered, in the beginning of 1965, to get into a position that would enable him to pursue that mission.

The implications for future changes in the strategy had to do not only with the field commander's early preeminence but also with the association of the coastal strategy with withdrawal. Although a variety of operations and tactics might have been conducted by troops deployed along the populated coast, the distinctions between operations could hardly be the salient part of future recommendations after the concept of enclaves had become a part of a conservative stalemate strategy and, in the end, the suggested means to a hasty retreat. In short, the method by which the strategy of search and destroy was adopted in 1965 provides the beginning of an explanation for its persistence.

Some Criticisms of the Ground Strategy

For the purpose of military operations, the Americans divided South Viet-Nam into four regions (see figure 2), also known as "Corps" or "Tactical Zones." The northern military region (I Corps or ICTZ) was, until mid-April of 1967, the exclusive preserve of the marines. Although they operated under the general direction of Westmoreland, they were free for some time to conduct their own operations in their own way, quite separate from the army and its operations in the other three Corps. Criticism of the search and destroy strategy is usually directed at the army in South Viet-Nam, and not at the marines, who conducted themselves differently and were the subject of different kinds of criticism.

The object of the search and destroy strategy was attrition—to kill as many of the enemy as possible. The object was not to hold ground. The tactics of search and destroy were intended to bring large units of United States troops in contact with large units of the enemy under conditions favorable to the Americans. This meant that either small American units would move into the countryside to seek the enemy and draw upon support if needed, or large units would undertake search operations. In both cases the idea was to make use of the greater mobility of American troops and their truly massive firepower. Helicopters provided the mobility, and an abundant supply of close air support and artillery provided the firepower.

Critics of search and destroy have argued that it was both strategically and tactically ill-conceived. Strategically the war was being fought in the wrong place for the wrong objective. The object should have been to hold ground, the ground occupied by the population. The people of South Viet-Nam are concentrated along the coast around Saigon and in the Mekong delta, not in the central highlands. The strategy, it is argued, should have subordinated military objectives to the basic political goal of winning the support of the population by clearing the enemy from, and holding, populated areas. The specific nature of the operations recommended as part of a population-oriented strategy varied with the critic, but the essential difference was in the location of troops, which always entailed a mode of operations and set of goals easily distinguishable from the large unit search and destroy strategy of the army.[22] The roots of this rather fundamental criticism extended back to 1962 when State and Defense debated the question of whether the conflict in South Viet-Nam should be treated as essentially political or military in character. The army prevailed, but the debate continued.

The second kind of critique of Westmoreland's strategy was directed at the specifics of combat operations; it was said that the tactics employed did not serve the stated objectives of taking the offensive militarily while at the same time supporting political efforts. There are several points here, the most common one being the failure of typical army operations to successfully "fix" the enemy. The standard procedure in large unit operations involved sweeping an area, using helicopters to move troops and air and artillery strikes to "prep" landing zones for the helicopters. The initial warning fire and the failure to "close the back door" or set up a "hammer and anvil" in the process of a sweep would routinely lead to the escape of those enemy units that might have actually been in front of the sweep—except for those that chose to engage. It would perhaps be a minor technical point if this were not the form of the classic search and destroy operation, if it did not imply that the enemy was the one who really had the initiative, and if it were not such a pervasive criticism, uttered to no avail.[23]

The availability of helicopters allowed for the impressive mobility of these operations and, to some degree, required them. Sir Robert Thompson wrote that "It is probable that without the helicopters 'search and destroy' would not have been possible and, in this sense, the helicopter was one of the major contributions to the failure of strategy."[24] While Sir Robert is no doubt correct, the reverse is probably also true and explains as much; without search and destroy the helicopter would not have been possible—at least not in such large numbers.

Other tactical level criticisms focus upon the use of the "body count" as a measure of success and the extensive use of air and artillery strikes. Since there was no attempt to hold ground and the objective was to defeat the enemy by attrition, the principal basis for evaluating progress was the "body count," the number of enemy reported killed in a particular period or action. Given this quantitative measure of success, army personnel responded as individuals in organizations usually do:

> The incentives for field commanders clearly lay in the direction of claiming a high body count. Padded claims kept everybody happy. . . . Off-the-record interviews with officers who had been a part of the process revealed a consistent, almost universal pattern: in a representative case, battalions raised the figures coming from the companies, and brigades raised the figures coming in from the battalions.[25]

The resulting distortion in whatever evaluation of operations would have been possible from counting enemy dead is obvious. Only slightly less obvious is the incentive for distortion in the behavior of troop commanders who forsook some missions, such as population protection, for others which provided the opportunity to excell in that activity which was being monitored. The emphasis on producing a good "body count" undercut the incentives to conduct "stability operations" and thus made search and destroy even less likely to complement efforts aimed at the population.[26]

The danger inherent in the use of air power in counterinsurgency activity was stated plainly some time ago:

> Now the first rule in the employment of the Air Force in punitive police work is to be absolutely sure of the guilt of the people against whom you propose to take action. . . . Bombing the wrong people,

even once, would ruin the Government's reputation, and would take years to live down.[27]

This particular warning was issued in 1937 by a British air commodore lecturing on the tactics of "policing the Empire." But the problem of being certain of the guilt of those subjected to bombing, or distinguishing Viet Cong from villager, was still a critical one in Viet-Nam in 1967. The problem became even more serious when "punishment" was meted out by indiscriminate fires from fast-flying jet aircraft or artillery located miles from the scene. This eventually became a significant issue in the use of force in South Viet-Nam. One Defense Department study of air and artillery use revealed the following:

> In 1966, some 65 percent of the total tonnage of bombs and artillery rounds used in Vietnam was expended against places where the enemy *might* be, but without reliable information that he *was* there. The purpose of these unobserved strikes was to harass, discourage, and drive off the enemy if he happened to be around. (Emphasis in the original.)[28]

The conclusion reached by many critics was that air-strikes and "harassment and interdiction" by artillery cause more alienation of the population than could ever be justified on military grounds. Examples of tragedies from reported mistakes in every year of the war provided support for the criticism of the use of massive firepower, and if they were not enough the certainty that there were many times more unreported errors was persuasive. Ready availability of large scale destructive weapons was, therefore, essential to large unit search and destroy operations. Like large numbers of helicopters, these weapons made the strategy possible if not inevitable.[29]

Alternatives

There was broad criticism of the strategy conducted by the army in the lower three Corps south of the northern military region. The strategy, however, did not change until the summer of 1968 when General Creighton Abrams replaced Westmoreland as field commander. During the three years of search and destroy, American casualties mounted and enemy pressure increased. The Tet holiday offensive in 1968 demonstrated to anyone who might have doubted it that the entire country, including cities and other populated areas, was vulnerable to the enemy. Why, then, did a strategy that was widely criticized persist so long? Were alternatives not clear to the army? Did the civilians in Washington not recognize that the war they had decided to fight might have been better fought at less cost?

First, it is clear that the army actively rejected alternatives. This is demonstrated by Westmoreland's advocacy of search and destroy not only during the spring of 1965 but also before and after that time. Since 1961 the army had tolerated, but never embraced, the counterinsurgency fad among civilians in the administration. The politically-oriented pacification advocates clashed repeatedly with the military advisory mission in Viet-Nam and the JCS in Washington. Even the army's own Special Forces, whose mission was redefined in the early sixties to that of a small elite counterinsurgency unit designed to operate in co-operation with indigenous troops, was shunned by the army establishment. As Alain C. Enthoven and K. Wayne Smith note, "a Service tends bureaucratically to neglect or undervalue . . . new or unconventional missions that the Service feels will draw funds away from traditional missions."[30] Although the Green Berets might have become inadequate for the task after the scale of operations changed in 1965, the army establishment's hostility to them had much to do with their unorthodox style and independence—the latter partly resulting from their CIA support. In essence, the army rejected the proposition that there was anything really special about the special warfare of counterinsurgency, even when the conflict was indisputably an insurgency. By 1967 the army field manual, entitled "Counterguerrilla Operations", devoted a single paragraph to the Special Forces and wedged it between longer ones on communications and military dogs.[31]

Between 1965 and 1968 an alternative to the army's strategy was evident in the operations of the Marines in I Corps.[32] Although they were ill-suited to Viet-Nam in terms of their traditional mission and equipment, the marines adapted quickly in ways the army did not for years. Essentially an assault unit with a high "front end surge capability," the marines were put into South Viet-Nam for an extended period without anything to assault. For almost two years they responded by staying primarily on the coast, operating out of enclave positions. Their operations included a program in which specially selected units were placed in hamlet complexes where they lived with and protected the population. Much has been made of these Combined Action Companies and Platoons (CAP), and in many ways they demonstrated an exceptional sophistication. Although the presence of an American CAP unit may have done little more than decrease the likelihood that a hamlet would be the victim of misguided American artillery or air strikes, the marines' involvement in population-directed activity at the cost of more traditional combat roles provided a striking contrast to the army's standard military response.

Since the marines lacked much of the equipment of the army, especially the helicopters, they made good use of long range patrolling and stressed small unit action. Until 1967 they were conducting the kind of tactical operations many had been advocating for all of Viet-Nam and doing it within a strategic concept of fortified coastal enclaves.[33] In 1967 the marines began to take up static inland positions along an east-west line south of the Demilitarized Zone and increasingly engaged in search and destroy style operations. Some have attributed the change in tactics to increased pressure from General Giap and others to pressure from General Westmoreland. In any case, the marines found themselves, as Giap noted, "being stretched as taut as a bowstring over hundreds of kilometers," eventually to be trapped at Khe Sanh.[34] Although they probably will be remembered for that blunder, the argument here is that when they had the flexibility, the marines responded to the conditions of the conflict in Viet-Nam significantly better than their army counterparts fighting the same war in adjacent Corps. MACV was, of course, aware of their operations.

There are still the questions of whether the civilians recognized the weakness of the army strategy and whether they attempted to change it. In the beginning, during the spring 1965 build-up, there is no doubt that the secretary of defense supported the aggressive strategy of Westmoreland. His July 20 memorandum for the president recommended doubling the number of American maneuver battalions in Viet-Nam and authorizing a new mission in which the troops were "by aggressive exploitation of superior military forces . . . to gain and hold the initiative . . . pressing the fight against VC/DRV main force units in South Vietnam to run them to [the] ground and destroy them."[35] Although McNamara ultimately was no more satisfied with the ground strategy than he was with the bombing campaign, there is no evidence of his efforts to change the former, as he had attempted to change the latter.[36]

There were other civilians, however, who did try to influence the combat operations in South Viet-Nam. In January 1967 Walt Rostow circulated a draft NSAM at the request of the president on future strategy in Viet-Nam. Of the several responses it prompted, the one from the Office of the Under Secretary of State (Nicholas deB. Katzenbach) was the most interesting. The thrust of the State paper was at the failure of the strategic concept of operations in the south. After pointing out that while the language of counterinsurgency survived, "the Vietnamese Army (ARVN) has never escaped from its conventional warfare mold," the report went on to say that "on balance . . . U.S. combat forces remain essentially oriented toward conventional warfare." This was true in spite of the marine CAP effort in I Corps and some "ingenious adjustments" elsewhere. The argument of the paper proceeded from the observation that "U.S. combat forces have been increasingly committed in search and destroy operations even outside the highlands area," to assert that

> The claims of top US and GVN military officials notwithstanding, the waging of a conventional war has overriding priority, perhaps as much as 9 to 1 [as compared to pacification], according to personal judgments of some US advisors. Saturation bombing by artillery and airstrikes, for example, is an accepted tactic, and there is probably no province where this tactic has not been widely employed. . . .[37]

The State paper did not change policy nor could it have. Its analysis was far from thorough and it did not present a clear prescription. Nevertheless it did raise the issue of the dual objectives in South Viet-Nam—political and military—and suggested that strategy aimed exclusively at the second would surely sacrifice the first.

Two months later MACV provided the stimulus for another attack upon the ground strategy, this time from the Office of Systems Analysis located within the Office of the Secretary of Defense. Alain Enthoven, the assistant secretary for Systems Analysis, took the opportunity of an unexpected MACV troop request to send McNamara two memoranda in early May one entitled "Force Levels and Enemy Attrition," and the other, a longer one, dealing with the general question of "Increase of SEA FORCES." Drawing upon some studies done in his office, Enthoven made the point that while MACV based its troop requests on the need to increase the attrition rate of the enemy, there was no evidence that the two were related: "These results imply that the size of the force we deploy has little effect on the rate of attrition of enemy forces."[38] This was a natural conclusion based on an analysis of engagements during 1966 that showed it was the enemy who had chosen to engage United States forces in 80 percent of the cases. It was also a startling conclusion—the enemy had the initiative on the ground. The second, more sweeping, conclusion of the assistant secretary was that, in the end, all American military efforts would be wasted if we did not "match the nationalism we see in the North with an equally strong and patient one in the South." It did not seem that Enthoven extracted this from any staff study, but from his astute observation that the North Vietnamese were motivated by more than "just Marxism." There was nationalism in the north, welding the people together, "just as it does so many other peoples today." Enthoven recognized that nothing would be won if stability was lost and was convinced that sending more troops would only increase Hanoi's ability to manipulate the American casualty rate; therefore, he opposed the troop increase and recommended that Westmoreland be told "to start making good analyses of his operations."[39]

As 1967 wore on, criticisms of the ground strategy from Systems Analysis no longer had to be stimulated from the outside—they poured forth. Writing about the output four years later, Assistant Secretary Enthoven appears modest, but he was correct:

> We carried on an unofficial, unsolicited, and small-scale effort consisting mainly of (1) making a number of pilot studies on various aspects of the war and (2) publishing the *Southeast Asia Analysis Reports.* With one or two possible exceptions, neither the *Reports* nor the studies had a significant impact on major Vietnam decisions.[40]

According to a staff member who helped produce the studies, the case against the strategy of attrition was well developed by the fall of 1967, even if clear alternatives, beyond recommending small unit action, were not suggested. It was not until the critical days of March 1968 that civilians in OSD took the final step and proposed a detailed new strategy for Viet-Nam to replace Westmoreland's.

On January 18, 1968, the under secretary of the air force and the former assistant secretary for ISA, Townsend Hoopes, sent a memorandum to the outgoing secretary of defense, Robert McNamara. Hoopes was interested in stopping the bombing so that negotiations might begin. His message discussed the linkage between the bombing of North Viet-Nam and American casualties in South Viet-Nam. The link was not "militarily real," he said, but it was "politically real," since Americans had come to believe that bombing in the north saved American lives in the south. This being so, Hoopes concluded:

> A decision to halt the bombing would accordingly seem to require a corollary decision to alter the ground force strategy—away from hyper-aggressive "search and destroy" operations . . . toward what have been called "seize and hold" operations in the populated areas, where the people of South Vietnam actually live.[41]

On February 13, two weeks before Clark Clifford officially took office, Hoopes sent the new secretary a letter in which he pursued his argument that "an aggressive ground strategy that generates high casualties may prove to be an insurmountable obstacle to a bombing halt, even if such is judged by U.S. officials to be in the national interest."[42] Hoopes's criticism of the strategy of attrition drew upon the evidence of its weakness produced by Systems Analysis; two weeks later the major attack from ISA did the same.

On February 27, after his return from a trip to Viet-Nam, General Wheeler presented a report with recommendations to the president. Among the more significant requests from MACV which Wheeler seemed to be conveying was Westmoreland's requirement of 206,756 more troops, or a new ceiling of 731,756 men by the end of the calendar year. The president responded by ordering a review of Viet-Nam policy and directed Clifford to conduct it. The new secretary of defense rapidly translated the task into a series of nine critical questions to be answered about the policy and assigned each question to specific segments of the bureaucracy. It was then the job of a staff group in ISA to prepare a single paper, drawn from all but two of the papers produced by the other agencies, for presentation to the president by the secretary.[43] On February 29 the ISA group, headed by Leslie Gelb, produced the first draft of the memorandum. The first section was devoted to an evaluation of the current situation in South Viet-Nam and possible alternatives to it.

Discussion of the part dealing with the ground strategy began on March 1 and lasted two days. The paper began with a bleak assessment of ARVN capabilities and went on to characterize the outlook for the government of South Viet-Nam in terms that were bleaker still. The argument then proceeded to Westmoreland's strategy of attrition and dismissed the likelihood of its achieving success given the enemy's ability to continue to supply fresh troops—an ability that could not be sufficiently damaged no matter what the size of the American troop increase and no matter how many American bombs were dropped. If South Viet-Nam were still to be "saved," the next step was a logical one:

> Our military presence in South Viet Nam should be designed to buy the time during which ARVN and the GVN can develop effective capability. In order to do this, we must deny the enemy access to the populated areas of the country and prevent him from achieving his objectives of controlling the population and destroying the GVN.[44]

But the draft for the president did not stop at recommending that MACV's mission be redefined to population protection, though it did that explicitly. The ISA group went on to describe in the fullest detail a "demographic strategy of population security," complete with a Corps by Corps description of appropriate activities and battalion locations, eight advantages of adopting the plan, and six recommendations on how to implement it.[45] An alternative to search and destroy had emerged from civilian councils.

This "demographic strategy," to no one's surprise, was immediately attacked by the chairman of the Joint Chiefs who, the *Pentagon Papers* analyst says, was "appalled at the apparent repudiation of American military policy." Wheeler found "two fatal flaws," one, that the population would suffer if the battlefield were moved to the coast, and two, that a static defense would leave the enemy free to mass near population centers. Paul Warnke, the assistant secretary of defense for ISA, responded the following day and observed that the Tet Offensive had already demonstrated the vulnerability of the cities which could now only be lessened by the new strategy. He added that if troops were removed from the hinterland, it would become more difficult for the enemy to mass troops near cities—especially if United States units remained capable of mobile operations. General Wheeler's reply drew upon a back channel message from Westmoreland of the same day explaining how new forces would be used and what they could achieve and a study produced by the staff of the Joint Staff explaining why the enemy had to be engaged in the highlands. Neither military nor civilians were persuaded by the other's arguments, so Warnke and Phil Goulding, the assistant secretary of defense for Public Affairs, were assigned to write a second draft of the memorandum. On March 3 a draft was produced that was essentially the same as the final one sent to the president the next day. The reformers had been routed. The debate over the ground strategy was finally settled by the elimination of the civilian recommendations. Even the few sentences that suggested giving "intensive study to the development of a new strategic guidance to General Westmoreland," were followed by the assurance that "the exact nature of the strategic guidance which should be adopted cannot now be predicted." ISA's powers of prediction had apparently lapsed at a most critical moment.

The Ground Strategy: Controlling the Civilians

The search and destroy strategy of General Westmoreland prevailed for three years even though it appears to have been weak on several levels, and alternative comceptions were available from Special Forces and marine operations. It prevailed also in spite of mounting criticism from civilian leaders. To explain why the ground strategy persisted, we will want to account for the army's failure to perceive the need for change, and the civilians' failure to act upon the need once they did perceive it.

The senior military initially embraced search and destroy undoubtedly because they thought it was a strategy with which they could win the war. Since wars are won by killing, or posing the prospect of killing, enough of the enemy to make him want to stop fighting, the military response to an enemy who would not sit still and fight was to pursue him. Otherwise he could not be killed and the war could not be won. From this purely military point of view, search and destroy is not unreasonable. Since the army did have such a perspective, and the conflict in Viet-Nam was defined as a clash of armies, the Vietnamese population was, at most, something to be avoided. MACV, the chief of staff of the army, and the chairman of the Joint Chiefs, all schooled in the classical tactics of ground combat, responded to the task by defining it as nearly as possible in familiar terms, so that it could be performed with available capabilities and according to established patterns. In short, we can begin to explain the strategies of search and destroy and attrition as a response of an organization and organization men to a problem which happened not to fit very well into preestablished categories. General Wheeler's reply to an interviewer who asked him about adopting an alternative strategy, such as enclaves or coastal population defense, revealed his commitment to the most traditional military formulation of the conflict in Southeast Asia:

> Unless you match or overmatch the action taken by the enemy . . . predictably you're going to lose . . . the side with the initiative comes out on top. If you lose the initiative, you'll lose the military success you are seeking. . . . Field commanders throughout history have

broken their backs to achieve the initiative. You must carry the fight to the enemy. . . . No one ever won a battle sitting on his ass.[46]

Although the ground strategy was partly, and perhaps initially, an organizational response, there were other reasons for the military to embrace it. "One great appeal of this strategy," as Sir Robert Thompson put it "was that it did not involve the South Vietnamese."[47] The ARVN, who had become known for conducting a variation of the American strategy, called "search and avoid" were not thought of as reliable by American officers. Relations with local South Vietnamese political-military leaders were strained, and Westmoreland was hostile from the start to command relations or combat operations involving dependence on them. Moving away from the free wheeling operations in the highlands to the activity of population defense would have required a degree of coordination with Vietnamese, if not dependence upon them, which the army preferred to avoid.

Another appeal of the strategy of attrition was that it allowed the American officers to do what they most wanted to do. While in subtle ways the training and organizational patterns of the army tended to produce a particular definition of the task in Viet-Nam, the reward structure of the organization was also providing incentives in not so subtle ways for officers to reach the same definition. Officers were usually in Viet-Nam for a one-year tour, and that tour usually included more than one assignment. Since the successful officer is one who has succeeded at a series of different posts, the desire for promotion leads the officer to try to do well quickly in successive roles as he "gets his ticket punched" or "make the stations-of-the-cross." Ward Just describes a typical route:

An ambitious infantry captain would want, first, to command a company in combat and, second to go to staff as assistant G-3 (operations). In Viet-Nam, despite the homage paid to "Vietnamization" no career-oriented officer wants to spend his time as an advisor; he wants to command *American* troops in a highly visible role, (emphasis in the original).[48]

As a result every career-minded officer wanted not only combat experience but also combat success during that part of his tour spent "with the troops." Search and destroy gave officers the opportunity to perform well in ways that would not be guaranteed under a more conservative strategy of population defense. There was also the potential for the distortion of behavior in this arrangement since the criteria for evaluating an officer could not be any clearer than the criteria for evaluating the strategy—and no one ever was sure of how we knew we were winning. Officers who needed or wanted to score quick success while briefly in command were known to have engaged in unnecessarily aggressive tactics in order to increase enemy body counts, or in order to capture an objective such as a hill that did not need capturing and would soon be abondoned.[49]

The same pattern of short tours with multiple assignments helps to explain the persistence of the ground strategy in another way. Part of the reason the army did not learn more, and adjust as it gained more experience in Viet-Nam, was that rotation kept limiting the amount of experience individuals could gain and kept removing men who had managed to achieve a higher level of competence and understanding of their task. In other words, the structure tended to insure that a variation of the "Peter Principle" would operate.[50] At the same time the workload made it unlikely that many army officers in Southeast Asia would be in a position to focus upon comparative tactics, much less to contemplate the strategy as a whole within any larger political context. There was always a tremendous amount of pressure to do the everyday tasks, to run to keep up. The atmosphere of a combat field staff, furthermore, was not supportive of internal criticism even if some had been generated.[51] The crisis atmosphere increased an already strong tendency to conform and to support, and to interpret the confusing signals coming from the Viet-Nam environment as optimistically as possible.

Even the institutionalized arrangements for learning and adaptation that did exist had little chance of success. The monthly MACV meetings of division commanders designed to pool information in order to improve tactics and strategy produced a multitude of contradictory tactics—all successful.[52] There was apparently no attempt to sort out the differences and reconcile them because there was no need to; the strategic concept valued attrition, and by the only available indicators of success, everyone was succeeding in his part of the war. The failure by the army to compare and contrast the efficiency of different kinds of operations within the army corps makes the failure to evaluate army operations against those of the marines a good deal less surprising. Westmoreland and his staff were not likely to learn from the marines for the same reason, so little was drawn from the experience of his own commanders. In the absence of a better strategy, except for the production of kill-ratio's and body counts, the situation remained essentially noncompetitive within the army and between the army and the marines. Unfortunately, those quantitative indicators of success in Viet-Nam proved to be more manipulable and less reflective of success as defined by civilian leaders than traditional indicators, such as the locations of battle lines, had been in wars past.

Some people in Washington, in Systems Analysis especially, thought their evaluations and critiques should have influenced operations even though internal military critiques had not. They were perhaps right, but it is understandable that they were also not influential. Relations between Systems Analysis and the military had always been marked by mistrust and hostility, so the army naturally looked at the civilian studies with suspicion. They were skeptical of the motives, skeptical of statistical analysis with its potential for manipulation, and skeptical of the validity of the data base—which of course they had supplied. Just as important was MACV's fear that the adoption of any civilian recommendations would destroy the last preserve of military prerogative—the actual conduct of combat operations.[53] It was not likely that Defense Department civilians would affect a change in strategy or tactics by force of argument alone.

Within the terms of this discussion, we can adequately account for General Westmoreland's early enthusiastic advocacy of a search and destroy strategy and for the tenacity with which the army held to it. It remains to look at the Washington decision makers and explain why they allowed the military to prevail.

One former senior civilian policy maker from ISA saw the reluctance of ISA to interfere with the ground strategy as "the product of a long-standing unquestioned tradition of autonomy of the field commander." He added that even the Chiefs wouldn't argue with Westmoreland.[54] The tradition was critically important and it did extend to the military chain of command. Enthoven points out that the JCS attempted no systematic evaluation of strategy until late in 1967, and restricted the mandate of the evaluating group even then.[55] With Westmoreland's early insistence on autonomy and the Chiefs' respect and support for it (in spite of their own occasional misgivings), civilian reforms faced not only the force of tradition, but powerful actors committed to preserving it as well. For the secretary of defense this did not mean that the military were beyond control in South Viet-Nam, but that the cost of exercising control would be very high.

In a 1967 interview with Henry Brandon, McNamara explained his failure to intervene in the ground strategy in terms of his lack of military expertise and the need to depend on the men actually in the field. When Brandon pressed him, citing Winston Churchill as one who differed, McNamara observed that he was not Churchill and insisted that in this case he preferred to respect the military's competence.[56] This apparently was the secretary's position in the beginning and for some time after. He was satisfied to provide Westmoreland with what he said he needed. His view changed however, as it had changed with respect to the bombing; except that his behavior was different in the two cases. The evidence indicates that McNamara became extremely disenchanted with search and destroy but did not see himself as having the resources to do anything about it. Townsend Hoopes writes that McNamara "complained privately of the error and waste inherent in search-and-destroy operations," but he felt he needed explicit presidential support to act.[57] Another senior bureaucrat in OSD said that McNamara had refused to support those in his office who had sought reform in 1967 "because he didn't think the military would let him get away with it."[58] What had become of the doctrine of civilian control and the image of McNamara running the Pentagon?

To the extent that the doctrine and image convey simple hierarchical relations, they are obviously in error. The structurally defined superior-subordinate relations in the Pentagon, as in any organization, were conditioned by many factors besides hierarchy. To put it another way, compliance is always more than a matter of communicating, and sometimes it is a matter of bargaining. McNamara had prevailed over the military in several areas, especially weapons acquisition decisions, in the early years of his tenure. Those were years of relative peace, and they were decisions on hardware. Operating in these issue areas, the secretary had substantial resources in his reorganized OSD and a bargaining position enhanced by broad presidential support. In 1965 the years of war began and McNamara chose to involve himself in the decisions of war, especially in the air war. The secretary's bargaining position *vis a vis* the military in time of war is not nearly as good as in time of peace, partially because the latter's political potency rises and partially because the military also control the instruments necessary to the execution of policy. On relatively weaker ground than before, McNamara found himself engaging the military on the bombing strategy, bargaining every other week over the targets to be released. He recognized that he was stretching himself thinly and operating at a disadvantage, so that when he bargained with the military over the size of the periodic troop requests the process was really one more of form than substance, more "give" than "give and take."[59] He could not hope to deny MACV their troops at the same time that he was attempting to deny CINCPAC and the JCS their targets. As a result, the military were frequently heard complaining about restrictions on the air war and the rationing of targets, but never about restraints on the conduct of the ground war or the refusal to supply troops.

The secretary of defense had chosen not to interfere with the field commander in South Viet-Nam. If he had attempted to keep a close rein on troop deployments as they were requested by Westmoreland, he might have been able to indirectly influence the strategy without overtly violating the rule of military autonomy in the field.[60] But McNamara was not even in a position to do that before the devastating Tet Offensive had occurred, and before the climate of advice around Lyndon Johnson had changed. The secretary could not oppose the military on both the war issues without the support of the president.[61] And the president, no matter what his propensities, was always aware that he risked political catastrophe whenever he pushed the JCS too far. It is unclear when McNamara would have acted had he been able; the record is not nearly as complete on the ground strategy as it is on the air war. Certainly he would have acted by the middle of 1967, but by then his grip was already slipping. By August the president had completely undercut him, first in the unrelated decision on the antiballistic missile system, and then by the release of virtually all remaining targets in North Viet-Nam.

The Role of the President

There is a temptation to see the issue of civilian control of strategy reduced to a matter of presidential prerogative. A British observer who followed the course of the war closely suggests just such a conclusion: "Unless, therefore, the President himself feels confident enough to change military strategy, there is no one who dares to interfere with the military's own judgment, and no machinery through which control can be exercised."[62] It would almost seem that the complicated bureaucratic struggles and compromises some would focus upon are largely a distraction from what was essentially a presidential system.

But, one asks, what makes a president feel "confident enough to change military strategy?" The answer is complex but it turns in part upon the amount of support the chief executive has from senior bureaucrats and other actors—"men who dare to interfere with military judgment." So while the president is less likely to engage the military on their own ground unless he is supported by advisors, his advisors will not venture to interfere unless they are supported by the president. The point is that the matter is not simply one of presidential prerogatives, but one of politics as well. That is not to say that all senior actors, including the president, are somehow roughly equal, or that some specific level of consensus must always precede decisions. Rather, it is to say that beneath the undeniable reality of the president as final arbiter is the more subtle reality of the constraints on presidential choice; that as obvious as it is that senior actors depend heavily on the confidence of the president to maintain their own influence, only slightly less obviously does the president need to avoid open defections over war policy if he is to maintain his standing with Congress and the electorate. The president did make the broad decisions about how the war was to be conducted, but understanding those decisions requires an appreciation for the vulnerabilities of the office of the presidency—for the political costs attached to some policy choices for the president.

It became more and more difficult for the secretary of defense *and* for the president to control the military strategy in Southeast Asia as the American commitment became larger and policy came to depend more heavily on military means. The cost to everyone in opposing the military increased as their autonomy became legitimized by war. Changing the strategy, however, was not simply a matter of deciding to pay the costs, as some have suggested. It was also a matter of manipulating the situation so that the costs of interfering would be reduced.[63] For the ground strategy, that process began seriously in 1967 in the Office of Systems Analysis. By early March 1968, much more had become possible as we have seen, but still the costs were too high. In the following month the standing of the military had begun to slip; there was wider recognition of the situation in South Viet-Nam, the positions of advisors changed, a new coalition of sorts was formed, and the political climate for undertaking the reversal of the military policy was improved. Although the political risks of resisting JCS and MACV pressure were diminished, the extent to which this was a product of the president's decision not to run for reelection cannot be determined. Perhaps the cost and risks seemed so much lower after March 31 because the price had already been paid.

VI. VIET-NAM AND THE POLICY PROCESS

The sources of American policy in Viet-Nam were complex. The deepest roots of policy were, in the first instance, imbedded in the culture, character, and ideals of the American people. Less removed from the policy, but still fundamental to it, were the post-World War II values, fears, and images of the rest of the world shared by the people and their leaders. The central focus of this study is upon those factors that were a good deal more proximate to the actual policy choices for Viet-Nam. The character of the policy-making process cannot stand alone as an explanation of America's venture in Southeast Asia, but it can and ought to be part of any broadly conceived explanation of events, especially if that explanation attempts to provide a base for prescription for future policy. Since the policy-making process does have the potential for some degree of manipulation, and since we have focused upon it as a significant, independent variable in this case, we would do well to address it directly in conclusion. After some restatement of the link between Viet-Nam policy and the policy making, we will do just that. The more general discussion of the policy process will deal with the propositions of "bureaucratic politics," because it was from this perspective that the analysis of Viet-Nam policy was conducted.

The Persistence of Policy

The assumptions of principal decision makers about the international arena and domestic political forces were as Gelb, Ellsberg, and others have stated them. The Kennedy and Johnson men did share, to varying degrees, critical perceptions about the national and international impact of Viet-Nam decisions—they came to the problem "carrying similar intellectual baggage." But as true and significant as this was, when one looks closer at the important periods, it is possible to discern differences in analysis and calculations among participants. In the period from 1961 to 1963, the State Department provided markedly different interpretations of the conflict in Viet-Nam, and the policy of that period reflects State's influence.[1] Beginning with the Johnson presidency in 1964 the locus of decision making shifted almost entirely to the White House staff and to ISA in the Defense Department. During that year, and especially during the "policy review" in the fall, the range of analysis was narrowed and the choices that emerged were limited. The only remaining source of genuinely divergent evaluations was George Ball, who was to become a sort of dove-in-residence. His dissent, as James C. Thomson put it, was "institutionalized," while other less important persons who dissented were "domesticated."[2]

The policy-making process was less open in 1964 and 1965 than it had been in earlier years, and it would close still further in 1966 and 1967. Critical decisions about the war, including the bombing of the north, were made at the regular Tuesday lunch meeting of a few top actors, operating without agenda, minutes, or staff. The Office of the Secretary of Defense, like the State Department, was eventually excluded from the center of decisions as the president sought counsel with even fewer advisors.[3] The premises and perceptions of the president and those close to him could be held and were reenforced over the years in large part because of the ever increasing centralization of the decision-making process.

The point is that whether policy making is an open or closed process has consequences for the content of policy. In terms of an evaluation of the means to our involvement in Viet-Nam, the fact that the process became closed permits us to account for the persistence of the initial premises about the nature of the conflict held by principal actors. The description of Viet-Nam decision making in this study is of increasing exclusiveness. Many who might have offered threatening or competing interpretations and analyses were subtly put aside or rudely made unwelcome—some leaving the administration. To the list of such notables as Hilsman, Harriman, Ball, Bundy, Moyers, McNamara (even Humphrey), and eventually Clifford, who suffered exclusion of one kind or another, many others should be added who must have been deterred by the example of the fate of their superiors.[4]

In recognizing that policy is rooted in the process by which it is made, the extent to which the nature of the process is in turn determined by the chief executive should not be missed. The president, after all, can manipulate process by setting the informal tone of tolerence or intolerence of dissent by formally delegating authority to some actors and limiting access to others and by structuring the procedures for collective decisions so as to maximize the pressure for consensus or to encourage diversity. Some observers have characterized the way this executive prerogative is exercised as "style," and have correctly noted that Johnson's style was unlike Kennedy's. But that puts it too simply. The point is that a president's propensities for organizing senior level decision making for national security policy, his procedural premises, should not be lumped together with other idiosyncratic traits of presidential style. It would seem that proposals to limit this kind of manipulation would be strengthened if analysts could suggest the ways in which policy process and policy content are linked. The better a president understands the effect of isolating himself from critics, the way policies gather momentum within the bureaucracy, and the dangers of certain structures for collective decision making, the less likely are such factors to distort his intent and weaken the responsiveness of policy to the external environment.

In practise, of course, restraining a president with propensities for dysfunctional arrangements of the upper level policy-making process would not be easy. Presidents may not be quick to recognize that dissent from policy, whether manifest in the population at large or among senior advisors, should be tolerated and sometimes cultivated in order that their flexibility be preserved. Nevertheless, part of the virtue in dissent is the wider choice of options that may be presented to a president who allows divergent views to flourish within his administration. In a political sense, the president who confronts a united bureaucratic alliance is likely to have less maneuverability than one who can take a position that, although at odds with one faction, has already been advocated and legitamized by another. Francis Rourke's observation is to the point:

> Bureaucratic advice is most compelling in its impact on policy decisions when it approaches unanimity in viewpoint. Hence, the traditional safeguard against the aggrandizement of bureaucratc power through advisory channels has been the assumption that administrative officials and organizations will disagree on foreign policy questions and that this disagreement will give the public and its elected officials an opportunity to choose among alternative lines of advice from the executive apparatus.[5]

Unfortunately presidents may not only fail to appreciate this at times but also are least likely to appreciate it when it is most essential that they do. When decisions are most difficult because the consequences are so grave, it is human for the man who has the ultimate responsibility to seek as much unified support as he can gather, rather than to cultivate views that can sound like heresy before a decision and become a political liability after it. So, common sense may make us less optimistic about the possibilities of preventing the isolation of future presidents, but the Viet-Nam experience should convince us that even partial success would make the effort worth while.

The Conduct of Policy

We have up to now been discussing the broad outline of policy—the continuous decision to stay in Viet-Nam and to "save" it. But from the analysis of the Kennedy policy, the consensus to begin bombing, and the conduct of the air war and the ground strategy, it is clear that the range of choice was considerably broader in Viet-Nam, the possibilities much greater than "in" or "out." There was conflict and compromise over the best course during the period of 1961 to 1963, and only a superficial consensus to bomb prevailed in 1965 beneath which actors held to diverse goals and expectations; there was continuous bargaining over the targets and other specifics of the bombing of North Viet-Nam, and muted, ineffective dissent was heard from some over the pursuit of search and destroy in South Viet-Nam. In each case the marks of compromise among principal participants are evident in the shape of the decisions. The ground strategy was an example of one-half of the compromise over the war policy, that is, a concession by civilians seeking to maintain a handle on the other half which was the air war. Beyond the initial premises of the policy makers, high level bureaucratic compromise and interaction were a vital part of the process by which the real content of policy was determined. It was another part of the way in which "the system" worked, and it does not appear that this part always worked well, that the compromises were always for the best.

The effects of organizations as units performing in a way consistent with their traditional roles and identities also had an impact on policy, as did the operating procedures and reward structures internal to the organizations. The military services had large stakes in the way the war was conducted, and their recommendations and activity reflected an interest in protecting their investment. Distorted behavior was evidenced within the military intelligence agency and by those executing policy in the field—in the air force, the navy and the army. The source of distortion could be traced to the incentive structure internal to the organization, parts of which were provided by civilian overseers. As a result, a policy which was in varying degrees a product of compromise among senior actors also bore the imprint of organizations that acted to shape it as they proceeded to execute it. The effects of organizational phenomena on policy were also part of the system, part of the way the system worked—or failed to work.

The kind of explanation for America's involvement in Viet-Nam put forth by Leslie Gelb and Daniel Ellsberg and discussed in the first chapter is not so much inaccurate as it is inadequate. By relying upon the shared cold war images of the principal policy makers and focusing on presidential prerogatives, their analysis reduces the decision process to the level at which a lone actor calculated how best to achieve his objective—calculated what had to be done to save South Viet-Nam and the next election. But the president is not the only actor even when he is the one who finally chooses. His calculations will turn out the way they do, as will his choice, in large part because of the way the bureaucratic-political apparatus has defined the situation and his options, and because interests, besides his own and the nations, will have advocates that he will not want to ignore. The president, partial creator of the system that serves him, is also constrained by it and may become to some degree the victim of it. In the case of Viet-Nam policy, we have argued that the bureaucratic-political system was not working well and that an adequate explanation of policy would have to take account of that; it would have to go beyond the president's choice to the way the choice came to be structured and even to how decisions were interpreted in the process of their execution.

The thrust of analysis in this study has been at the foreign policy-making process and the link between that process and the substance of policy. We will now move from the Viet-Nam case to the broader issue of how we may best explain American foreign policy and most usefully conceive of the policy-making process.

The Bureaucratic Perspective

Politics involves the exercise of power and the restraint of power. It involves compromise. American politics, it is well known, is marked by compromise, bargaining, and mutual accommodation at all levels of government. Political analysts have produced an abundance of studies of policy making and analytical descriptions of the policy-making process, most of which point to the decentralized, diffuse, competitive, pluralistic character of public policy decision making. Until relatively recently, however, most of these studies had to do with domestic policy and issues. Only lately, have analysts of American foreign policy begun to see decision making for these issues in terms similar to those of domestic policy.[6]

In 1959 Roger Hilsman described the foreign policy-making process as one of consensus building, in which "the issue or problem confronted requires the reconciliation both of a diversity of values and goals and of alternative means and policies." He concluded that "the relative power of . . . participating groups is as relevant to the final decision as the cogency and wisdom of the arguments used in support of the policy adopted."[7] This sort of description of the way America chooses her weapon systems and her wars is a significant departure from conventional explanations that turned upon the dictates of the national interest and the necessities of international politics. In 1969 Graham Allison characterized the traditional mode of analysis and explanation of foreign policy in formal terms, calling it the "Rational Policy Model," and contrasted it with two other formal paradigms of explanation.[8] Under his "Bureaucratic Politics" and "Organization Process" rubrics, Allison grouped assumptions and arguments about policy making that were taken for granted in domestic policy and drew out their implications for foreign policy. Many others had focused upon the interactions of bureaucratic elite to account for specific policy outcomes, and some had made use of insights from organizational theory in explaining seemingly inexplicable behavior in the lower levels of organizations, but it was Allison, using the Cuban missile crisis as an illustrative case, who made everyone conscious of the potential benefits of consistently viewing events in foreign and security policy from the vantage point of competing, domestic governmental elites.

In the preceding chapters United States policy in Viet-Nam was analyzed from a perspective that relies heavily upon Allison's work. This perspective forsakes the more traditional analysis in which the assumption is made that a nation-state is a unitary actor seeking, in a rational manner, to maximize its utility with respect to some set of national goals. By adopting the bureaucratic perspective, we move to a lower level of analysis where, for example, the policy of the United States in Southeast Asia is accounted for in terms other than the pursuit of the national interest or the protection of national security. It is a perspective that leads, instead, to explanations for policy in terms of the politics internal to large organizations, politics among senior governmental actors, and at times, the politics of national elections. Those who occupy the uppermost positions in the foreign policy bureaucracy are assumed to share many critical perceptions about the nature of the international and domestic arenas, as well as a broad understanding of what is meant by the national interest. Although these shared images do set limits within which policy may range, limits that may be relatively narrow, they cannot account for the content of policy nor can they alone explain why some policies persist over time. Resort to the processes by which policy is made becomes necessary. The president, his assistants in the White House, the secretaries and assistant secretaries, and the senior military bring different experience and perspectives to foreign policy issues. Of central importance to those actors associated with the large bureaucracies of the military services, the Departments of State and Defense, and the intelligence agencies is the maintenance of the stature, role, and budgets of their organizations or organizational subunits. Their perspective on matters of foreign policy is strongly influenced by their bureaucratic affiliation. Although some senior actors who help make policy are without such association, they have often already made an investment in a policy by virtue of their previous stands and therefore proceed with a personal interest, if not also a bureaucratic one, to protect.

The senior actors try to shape foreign policy outcomes so that they will be consistent with what they see as the national interest. They will do this by bargaining and compromising, by forming coalitions, and by using whatever leverage is available to them. The president is one of these actors, but a very special one. He has an exceptional amount of formal authority, and he is a source of power for many other actors who make use of their association with him. Yet the president cannot do everything he wants, since he often wants things that will cost him more than he is willing to pay. The president is vulnerable in Congress and in the electoral arena, and governmental actors may use this vulnerability to move the president on an issue or to restrain him from moving.

The president, it has been pointed out, creates much of the bureaucratic environment in which he operates.[9] Although this is certainly true, it does not free the chief executive from dependence upon the individuals around him and the structure he creates. The intelligence agencies will still be needed to provide information, and the military will still have an independent base of support which will expand with the start of hostilities. The president may manipulate the Office of the Secretary of Defense, his White House National Security staff, and even the State Department, but he will not escape the cross pressures from multiple actors, the constraints of routinized bureaucratic responses, and the threats of actors who would raise the legislative or electoral costs of action. The president is more than just "first among equals" since important decisions are ultimately his to make. But beneath what is obviously true about the enormous power of the presidency, is the subtle truth of the constraints on the office that help explain so much about policy.

The senior actors head large organizations that are in actual contact with the international environment. These organizations gather information, process and package it, and provide this information to decision makers. They also execute the decisions made by the decision makers. Organizations, subunits, and individual members of organizations often do not perform the tasks that they are supposed to, so that information flows are distorted, policy options are unnecessarily limited, and policy itself is carried out with waste, and not in the manner intended by those who made it. In short, the fact that large organizations are involved in making and executing foreign policy also has implications for the content of policy.

Some Essential Questions

The information required to produce explanations of foreign policy events in terms of the bureaucratic perspective is quite different from that required for more traditional analyses. Given an action taken on the part of a nation that can be linked to the conscious authorization of some related action by senior governmental actors, the following kinds of information should be sought: Who are the relevant senior actors? What are their positions in government? What position have they taken in the past on the same issue? What kinds of salient images or premises about the world do they operate from? What are the interests of the organization or subunit of organization to which they belong? How much influence does each actor have in this action area and how much will each exert? How do actors attempt to gain desired outcomes, and how, ultimately, are their conflicting efforts resolved into an outcome? How much of a gap develops between the outcome of the "decision process" and the outcome of the "implementation process?"[10]

These obviously are not the only questions that need to be asked and, indeed, just trying to answer them would lead one to ask a good many more. In fact, these research questions should lead the would-be bureaucratic-political analyst to inquire in a more general way about the essential links in this kind of explanation of events. If he is properly led, four new questions would seem to emerge: first, to what extent do "shared images," the perceptions of basic political reality of principal decision makers, condition or even determine the actors' positions on an issue?; second, how and why do organizations matter to policy if decisions on important matters are made at the top by the president and those close to him?; third, how reliable is the inference that where an actor stands on an issue will depend upon where he sits in the government?; fourth, what can be said about the way conflict among senior actors is ultimately resolved in the form of agreed-upon policies? These questions and the issues involved in each case will be dealt with below.

Shared Images

Even those who argue that American foreign policy is made by men who bargain on issues from stands consistent with their own parochial concerns in government do not hesitate to admit to the importance of "a set of values and images of the world that are taken for granted by most of those in the bureaucracy, and a second (largely overlapping) set which they see the public as holding."[11] To think that there were not some such common ground between foreign policy elites would seem to be unreasonable. The issue for the observer of bureaucratic politics, however, is whether these shared images are a constraint on the bureaucratic process or the principal determinant of its outcome, whether they simply condition policy debate or, when it matters most, preclude debate.

From a study of the 1967 ABM decision, the impression is left that commonly held perceptions of the international situation served only to set boundaries within which the arguments could permissibly range:

> The debate within the executive branch about whether or not to deploy ABM, and if so of what kind, was carried out within a context of a set of widely shared images about the role of the United States in the world and the nature of the threats to its security.[12]

By contrast, in the case of the continuous decision to stay in Viet-Nam, there is some agreement that the shared perceptions of principle decision makers had a more active influence on policy. James C. Thomson, for example, points to the significance of the "legacy of the 1950's" and Daniel Ellsberg posits the "1950 thesis" to help explain the shared sensitivity of actors to the "loss" of another Asian state to Communism.[13] Ellsberg sees the Viet-Nam decision makers so bound to action by the imperative of avoiding a McCarthy-style purge that only the specific character of the American response is left to be explained by other factors. Bureaucratic actors, then, may perceive some issues within an identical framework, the effect of which will be to narrow the range of acceptable positions and policy choices. In terms of the bureaucratic perspective, the shared images at least serve to define the point at which a policy game begins and limit the bounds of play. Whether they carry a heavier weight in explanation will have to be determined from the evidence in each case. At the same time, the undesirable effects of bounding the rationality of choice in the actual policy process are obvious enough since viable options may be excluded from consideration by commonly held but utterly inappropriate assumptions of decision makers.

The analyst who takes the perspective of bureaucratic politics must, therefore, take account of limits imposed by the shared imagery of the actors. Some have argued that those limits are most confining in a crisis or in a near crisis atmosphere. In critical periods common perception may seem to extend right down to agreement on what the national security requires. Is it possible, then, to escape the conclusion that the bargaining and compromise of bureaucratic politics are put aside and that the limitations of organizational processes become irrelevant as soon as the vital interests of the nation are at stake?

Several points may be made by way of an answer: first, the presumed effects of crisis upon the policy process are based more on "common sense" than empirical evidence; second, to talk of putting aside "parochial norms" in a crisis is to oversimplify actor motivation; and third, although crisis decision making may be removed from organizations, the effects of organizations may not be removed from the decisions.

Looking back on foreign policy crises, there can be little doubt that "top" decision makers disagreed over the character of the appropriate American response. When the "chips were down" in 1954 in Viet-Nam, in 1961 in Cuba, in 1963 in the nuclear test-ban negotiations, in 1968 in Viet-Nam again, and in 1972 in the strategic arms limitations talks, the "national security" did not provide unambiguous cues. Perhaps the best evidence is contained in Graham Allison's own study of the Cuban missile crisis of 1962—a crisis against which others pale and in which bureaucratic politics and organizational phenomena were critical.

The reason some analysts jump to the conclusion that the complex processes of bureaucratic politics suddenly become reduced to simple rational model calculations in the face of real danger may have to do with an assumption about how actors reach positions on an issue. It is, however, neither a tenet of the bureaucratic perspective nor a real-world truth, that political actors consciously choose to maximize their perceived organizational and personal interests at the expense of what they perceive to be the national interest. Actors tend to take stands on issues that are consistent with their "seats" in the bureaucracy because they really see the world from the vantage point of their position. Listen once to the chief of naval operations speak passionately of the critical needs of the navy and you will not doubt his sincere belief that what is best for his service is best for the national security, indeed, for the broader national interest. There is no evidence that as the stakes rise actors remove the tinted glasses through which they view everyday matters and begin to see issues with new objectivity. Crisis decisions, like noncrisis decisions, are made by men with different opinions about what is the best course of action for the nation.

A bureaucratic perspective must allow for the impact of images and assumptions shared by the policy-making elite, but it is far from clear even in extreme cases, that the policy process is transformed by this sort of consensus into the kind of endeavor envisioned by those holding to a more traditional view of the sources of foreign policy.

The Influence of Organizations

Although an analyst taking the perspective of bureaucratic politics may be largely occupied with the behavior of senior government actors, he should also look eslewhere. He should be careful that his perspective does not exclude the role of organizational processes in formulating and executing policy. Appreciation is acquired, not by thinking of organizations as collections of individuals working to reach common objectives, but as groups of people, restricted by patterns of acceptable behavior, striving toward separate and often conflicting goals. From this conception, one is led to Michel Crozier's position that power relations are of prime importance and should be the subject of study at every level of organization: "Subordinates can be considered as free agents who can discuss their own problems and bargain about them, who do not only submit to a power structure but also participate in that structure."[14] If power is diffused throughout the organization of government, then execution of decisions is not only a matter of skill but also of will; an organization may be hierarchically arranged, but winning subordinate compliance involves more than the communication of commands. To study the making of policy at the top of bureaucracy and the execution at the bottom can be as misleading in foreign policy as in any other field. The point is made forcefully by Norton Long:

> The separation of policy formation from policy execution in any hard-and-fast way is probably as untenable as the old politics-administration dichotomy itself. . . . There is scarcely any significant policy execution step that does not present discretionary activity. Such activity always has a policy aspect. If one equates policy formation with a political process, then every significant area of discretion is open to and needs political analysis.[15]

Organizational theorists have made considerable efforts to explain why it is that decisions are being made by people who are only supposed to be carrying them out, with outcomes antithetical to ends they are supposed to be serving. It seems that the irony to be found in the behavior of large organizations can be traced to the division of labor that is invariably required. Organizations have mandates to pursue rather broad goals. Therefore, they must first factor the broad goals into more operationally manageable subgoals and then factor the organization into operating units, subunits, and so on down. The result is that subunits have goals that are really subgoals, or they have ends that are really means. The potential for difficulties, which may have already suggested itself, is heightened by the realization that the factoring process can continue right down to the level of the individual who performs his task according to a routine, a "performance program," or a "standard operating procedure."

Members of organizations have various kinds of supports and incentives to make decisions that sacrifice goals for subgoals, that reverse ends and means. The priorities of subunit members are influenced by a selective exposure to information, an unconscious, conflict-reducing selective perception of information, and continuing support for a limited frame of reference from in-group communication.[16]

A specific incentive to goal distortion can be traced to the original purpose of factoring, that is, to permit coordination and control. Superiors seeking to control subordinates find that evaluation of output is difficult or impossible. The result is that the superior seeks the security of whatever tangible indicators of performance there may be, and the subordinate consequently emphasizes behavior in that activity, with neither member concerned with its broader significance. The resulting "drift to quantitative compliance" is as common as it is undesirable: "Only the observable and measurable aspect of behavior can be controlled. These are often the most trivial and unimportant from the standpoint of the long-range success of the organization."[17]

Members of an organization will act contrary to the stated goals of the larger organization not only because of the supports of cognitive mechanisms and the incentives provided by insecure superiors but also because they will generally act to protect and improve their own positions. When they are presented with a situation in which they must choose between furthering the long-run interests of the organization or the short-run interests of themselves, the more abstract entity is likely to take second place. It is from the perspective of an organizational actor constantly confronted with such choices that Gordon Tullock develops many of the suggestive propositions in his study of bureaucracy.[18] The member is a "politician" seeking to win "allies" and please his "sovereigns" whether it be in choosing to which group he owes his temporary loyalty or in deciding how much and what kind of information to pass upward. In other words, not only do information flows in an organization suffer from the distortion and selection of cognitive mechanisms but also from the conscious choice of members who shrink from forwarding information that might cause a superior to feel displeasure by contradicting his beliefs, or cause confusion by offering too complex an argument or too sophisticated an analysis. This leads Tullock to conclude that when things are really bad in a bureaucracy, information flows *downward* as subordinates try to learn what superiors want to hear.

Although organizations usually do what they are supposed to do, their operations are marked by these pathologies frequently enough so that their effects become important to an understanding of the content of policy and to a statement of the bureaucratic perspective. Senior actors will understand issues and issue environments in terms of information that has filtered up through the various levels of organizations; they will make policy decisions only to have them remade in the process of "execution." Distortion of information moving up through an organization will have an impact on choice at the upper levels, and distortion of authoritative communication in the process of transmission down through an organization will extend the prerogatives of choice to those charged with executing policy. Recognizing this, the analyst must be prepared to look at the motivation of specific organizational units and subunits, where necessary, for an adequate explanation. The character traits of specific organizations and the behavior patterns of organizations in general must be recognized by analysts if only because bureaucrats themselves account for them in their actions. For example, the resistance to change in most organizations, is well known, and the special "curator mentality" of State Department desks is notorious.[19] Even when the choice of policy by an organization appears to all a mistake, rationalization rather than alteration is likely to follow. It is difficult to avoid applying Harold Wilensky's observation to the various bureaucracies involved in the Viet-Nam war:

> Organizational theory often assumes that where an existing policy satisfies organizational goals, there is little search for alternatives but that when policy fails search is intensified. This assumption underestimates man's capacity for clinging to prophecies already proven wrong.[20]

We should be especially careful to avoid the conclusion that the mark of lower level organizational processes is removed when at some point a matter becomes an issue to be bumped upward and put in new hands. Before a crisis is recognized, organizations have dealt with the issue, transmitted information about it, and structured the situation to which there will be a response. Even after a crisis is full blown, the set of policy options from which actors can choose may be limited to those that organizations already have in their repertoire, and the tasks they are called upon to perform will be subject to, and shaped by, standard operating procedures. When there is a crisis, the president and his advisors may actually have even *less* opportunity to design a tailored response simply because of the pressures of time.[21]

It is not enough to say that senior players act to further the interests of their organization (when they are members of organizations), because organizational interests can be specified beyond organizational "maintenance." Morton Halperin has suggested categorizing interests to be protected as autonomy, morale, essence, roles, missions, and budgets.[22] Whatever the merits of this particular typology and from the evidence of Viet-Nam it would appear to have considerable merit, it is clear that some specification of organizational concerns will aid in explaining the positions and arguments of senior actors. In sum, recognizing organizational phenomena and drives to sustain organizational identity can add significantly to an analysis that takes into account shared perceptions among principal actors, but which focuses upon the diversity in perspective of those same actors, who see individual issues from their particular vantage point in the bureaucracy.

Bureaucratic Interest and Issue Position

One proposition that has become central to the style of analysis being proposed here is that where an actor stands on a particular issue depends upon where he sits in the bureaucracy. Expressing the link between bureaucratic interest and issue position just that way neatly conveys an essential inference pattern that is useful in explanation. Unfortunately when stated so simply it can also be a distortion. Any number of observers have pointed out that you cannot always tell what an actor's position is going to be, nor explain why it was what it was, by reference to his location in the government.[23] This is certainly true, and because it is, analysis is sometimes more difficult; but only if it is true for one reason is the bureaucratic perspective undercut.

Consider the following circumstances under which an actor might not be "cued" to take a particular position on an issue by his bureaucratic position: He is not a member of the government, but a temporary consultant called upon in a crisis—an "ad hoc actor;" he is a special advisor to the president without any organization to protect; he is seated within a large organization, but the issue before him impacts upon several of his organizational interests and no preference scale is immediately obvious, or he cannot discern *how* outcomes will impact upon various interests; he is an actor whose organization happens not to be affected by the outcomes of the issue before him. These are common situations in which either an actor lacks a seat in an organization or has a seat that is simply not relevant to any one stand on some particular issue or set of issues. When this is the case an analyst must look elsewhere to predict or explain the way senior actors behave. The past experience of an actor, for example, may be cited to account for a particular perspective—Dean Rusk's fear of China and George Ball's European orientation come to mind in the case of Viet-Nam. Even more useful for explanation and prediction is evidence that an actor has "invested" in a position on an issue by his past stands, since actors will tend to protect

their investment and guard their influence in future recommendations. This is not to say that men do not change their minds, even in advising the president, but that they recognize a cost in doing so and therefore will respond only reluctantly to evidence that they were wrong. They do not protect an organization's interests, but their own.

In many cases, then, an analyst can offer reasonable explanations for the different positions taken by senior actors even when those positions appear to be unrelated to the simple protection of any organization's or organizational subunit's identity, mission, or budget. We acknowledge that many actors do not make decisions constrained by the need to protect such interests, but we do claim that policy is made by actors who are likely to have different positions and seek different outcomes—in most cases for reasons that are understandable at this level of analysis. What is essential to the bureaucratic perspective, however, and the point at which it is vulnerable, is that when an actor does see his position on an issue as unambiguously affecting the future influence of his organization, its morale, or the size of its budget, he does take a stand to protect those interests. This is a central assumption, and if it were to be proven inaccurate often enough or at critical points, then the analysis would be damaged. In fact, in the explanation of Viet-Nam policy, organizational stakes and bureaucratic-political orientation are extremely useful, and consistently so, in accounting for the positions of principal actors.

The above should not be taken as a cynical exclusion of concern for the "national interest" because, as noted earlier, people tend to interpret the nation's interest in the light of their more immediate concerns. Issues that clearly seem to involve national security will be viewed in parochial terms, but terms that are nonetheless thought to be consistent with the national security:

> Troops in Europe is a budget issue for the Army and for the Budget Bureau; it is an issue of relations with allies for State; of the President's prestige and influence on Capitol Hill for the White House Congressional Staff; of balance of payments for the Treasury.[24]

Finally, it is intuitively pleasing to argue that where someone stands tends to be related to where he sits. It is not surprising that bureaucratic actors perceive other bureaucratic actors as taking their organizational unit's position, which in turn can be characterized and often projected for any particular issue. Regrettably perhaps, actors often will assume the most parochial motives for, and be extremely critical of, whatever substantive position is advanced by those in another bureaucracy dealing with the same issue. In one study that dealt in part with bargaining relations among different parts of a bureaucracy on the issue of the Military Assistance Program, the author concluded: "Perhaps the most surprising result of this study is that stereotyped policy positions for the various agencies involved in the Military Assistance Program are seen to be: independent of personality; predictive; reliable; independent of the issue. . . ."[25]

The Use of Bargaining

For all the virtue there may be in evaluating policy from the perspective of competing bureaucratic actors, in the end, the simple truth emerges that it can be very difficult to pick the winners of the competition. It may be useful to begin with a willingness to believe that the idea of presidential decision making is a "cloak to shield the elaborate process of executive legislation and bargaining through which the policies are eventually hammered out."[26] It is suggestive to talk of the process of "aggregation," a confrontation of power by which successful actors become the "winning coalition." It is certainly useful to try to avoid circularity by specifying not only that those with power win but also that they do so because of their bargaining advantages, skill, and the perceptions of others.[27] Nevertheless, it is unsatisfying and not productive of explanation or prediction to have analysis stop short of the outcomes of the bargaining process, to point to the dynamics of accommodation but only hint at their nature. More should be said.

Some important foreign policy decisions may be made with what appears to be unanimity, with very few exchanges between actors that seem designed to produce concessions. This is likely to happen less because all perceive the situation the same way than because policies are often complex and, even before any bargaining, can have "something for everybody." An argument was made in chapter III, for example, that the multifaceted appeal of the policy of bombing North Viet-Nam accounts for its wide embrace, rather than any genuine policy consensus.

More often, however, the situation is one of conflict, with actors seeking to express the intensity of their feeling in a variety of ways. The trades they are willing to make across issues is one such way. The secretary of defense may deal with the military over several procurement matters, support for an arms control measure, the conduct of an air war and the pursuit of a ground war, all at the same time. Such a situation leads not only to simple compromises on a particular issue but also more complex understandings across issues. The bargaining that does occur across or within issue areas need not be explicit, with a concluding contract. The foreign policy decision-making milieu provides adequate political order for implicit "deals": "Bargaining requires the capability to signal and communicate, to discern one's interests and derive means for achieving them, to interact, to predict the behavior of the other party, and possibly to sanction that behavior."[28] It is not unusual for these conditions to prevail in the foreign policy bureaucracy.

It is likely that many important bargains will be implicit and never see the light of public exposure. This is true not only because the political order exists to allow it to occur but also because deals between actors which affect foreign and military policy may lack legitimacy. Where there is public debate, whether on ABM deployment or the deployment of the marines in Viet-Nam, the terms of the argument may reflect not the real stakes as perceived by the actors, but a more acceptable disagreement over the proper means to reach mutually desired and legitimate ends. The compromise struck over the air war in North Viet-Nam followed debate centering on effectiveness, when in fact the participants differed on the more basic issues of the conflict; the military had a considerable investment in budgets and missions tied to acceptance of its position, and though their senior actors sought to protect that investment, their arguments were framed in other terms. The analyst who has correctly assessed organizational and actor interests will be more likely to uncover the true nature of implicit arrangements when they do become manifest in policies. Unfortunately, he will also be more likely to see policies in terms of arrangements and motives which were never intended.

When foreign policy making is seen as a process of collective decision making, the participants may be expected to benefit from situations that produce advantage in other collective, semi-hierarchical decision arenas. An actor who can influence the outcomes in more than one issue area, for example, especially if the areas are of importance to other participants, can be expected to benefit from his broader scope. Those who were senior actors in the Office of International Security Affairs in the Defense Department during the Kennedy and Johnson years were very likely aided by the breadth of their domain in the course of operating in each particular policy area. The benefits of being able to influence outcomes on several issues rather than on one are perhaps clearer in a body like Congress. The legislature obviously functions by trading and compromise, and committee assignment as well as rank are important to an actor's power. Although understandings are likely to be more subtle when reached within the foreign policy-making bureaucracy, the same sort of advantage can be won by holding power in several areas at one time.[29] Perhaps the best example is the immense power of the president, which is in part a function of the scope of his influence.

It would be useful to a discussion of this sort if formal power and personal, or informal power, could be distinguished. That unfortunately proves to be a difficult task. But if we take the position that all power is "liquid," that it is fungible to some degree like currency, then making the distinction becomes less critical.[30] In other words, actors may be thought of as receiving a certain amount of authority when they enter the policy process by virtue of their bureaucratic position. In a very broad way they are limited in the power they may have over outcomes and the issue-games they can play by the vertical and horizontal elements of their location. From this perspective it is accurate to talk not only of negotiation involving trades in the exercise of power in different issue areas, but of actors accumulating power by collecting credits in bargaining or even changing the structure which initially provided them with the formal authority of their position. Similarly, power may be reduced if, in using it, negotiation was required and debts were incurred. Power may be expended because several actors have influence over the outcome of an issue-game and getting the necessary consensus involves costs. The result is that senior actors may understandably not wish to "spread themselves too thinly" on many issues and will only reluctantly enter major battles in which the prices of victory, even if assured by constitutional structure, will come very high.

One of the interesting facts of American policy making is that few actors ever expend all their power and make the ultimate effort to buy their desired outcome. Almost no one resigns in protest.[31] In spite of all the battles that were clearly fought over Viet-Nam policy, and all those that some say they fought, there were no significant casualties in Washington, only "retirements from public service." The cost to the president and the impact on his policy, had some of those who left done so by resigning publicly over the war issue, would have been tremendous. If half of the secretaries, assistant secretaries and presidential advisors who later said they left because of the war had said they were doing so at the time they left, the thin fiction of a united administration could not have persisted. If half of those who stayed on "to restrain those who would have escalated the war even more" had taken all their formal and personal power and spent it in a noisy "exit" from the administration, they might have accomplished more quickly what they say they ultimately won in 1968. It seems that this type of expenditure is not considered a legitimate move, at least not for civilians, even when the stakes are as high as they were in Viet-Nam. That is in a way unfortunate, because if resignation were more common, its threat would be as viable for an assistant secretary as for a member of the Joint Chiefs, and as a result, policy would either be moderated or disaffection would become public.

By treating power as currency and issues as commodities, it is possible to focus on the costs of outcomes to actors in the bargaining process. Such a focus may help explain the selective zeal of a secretary of defense in overseeing the military in time of peace but not in time of war, the incredible momentum of policies once investment in them is made, the seeming autonomy of actors who are supposed to be subordinates but whose forced compliance would involve high costs, and the interdependence of policy outcomes across issues and over time. The bargaining process should be a focal point for investigation if the bureaucratic perspective is to be a fruitful one.

This view of the way American foreign policy is made, what has here been called the bureaucratic perspective, has led some to despair—and worse. One observer has criticized the bureaucratic focus and called it "dangerous" in part "because it undermines the assumptions of democratic politics by relieving high officials of responsibility"—the argument that if bureaucratic structures and organizational processes are responsible for policy, then policy makers cannot be responsible and trying to hold them accountable is purposeless.[32] Another observer has attacked the "bureaucratic-political studies" on the grounds that, although they have descriptive power, they also legitimize the status quo "as a fundamentally 'natural,' and unalterable condition," and present "an uncritical acceptance of things-as-they-are, a set of psychological premises that pull toward cynicism."[33]

About the first criticism, one might argue that the supposed political irresponsibility is not a necessary corollary of a bureaucratic analysis, though at the same time, one wonders what should be done if it were entailed as the critic claims. If the bureaucratic perspective does force us to see things in ways we had not seen before, and if some of what is revealed is unsettling, should we conclude that it will be best to close our eyes? Fortunately the analysis that is advocated does not destroy governmental responsibility but sharpens it by defining more clearly the stakes and options for all involved.

The second criticism, that focusing on bureaucratic politics ennobles the status quo, is also off the mark. It is quite possible to formulate prescriptions to improve the policy process, even if that process is thought to be a complex, decentralized one. Understanding bureaucratic relations, and shifting power and advantage to change the way power is distributed is one way of manipulating the process to change outcomes. This is done almost routinely in a new administration, often with mixed results. Although bureaucratic politics persists, the nature of the politics and the outcomes change. It is likely that one objective of an analyst who focuses upon White House-State-Defense-military relations is to help those who would restructure relations—not to disparage the attempt to do so.

The same sort of argument can be made about changing organizational procedures. After discovering that distortions occur in performing tasks and explaining some of the reasons why they occur, it becomes possible to manipulate incentives within, and improve responses from, the organizations that make and execute foreign policy. Dysfunctional behavior at the lower levels of large bureaucracies, like the protection of parochial interests by senior actors at the top of large bureaucracies, will continue, but the bureaucratic perspective can aid in reducing the impact in some cases and by anticipating it in others.

Another point to be made follows from the first, and it is that elected decision makers can and should be held responsible for policy. They are certainly no more immune from public accountability in foreign affairs because of their limited knowledge, because of the intractability of bureaucracies with which they must deal, and because of the multiple centers of power that they must satisfy, than they are in domestic affairs where they may have even less control over outcomes. They, and expecially the president, are far from being at the mercy of a system that is to a significant degree malleable and manipulatable by them, and in which they ultimately do have the opportunity to choose—if often only between alternatives involving very high personal costs, instead of among the many options an outside observer may perceive. As for the deeper sense in which some would like to hold all senior policy makers responsible, it does seem that it is more difficult to do so if the bureaucratic perspective is adopted than if a simpler conception of the way policy is made and executed is accepted. All that will be said here, however, is that although circumstances varied with individual actors, in the case of Viet-Nam policy in the 1960s, one would look in vain among the principal participants for one who was so much a creature of the foreign affairs apparatus that he should not receive credit for policy if it is deemed a happy success or blame if it is seen as a miserable failure. After arguing the importance of the structure of the system in determining the content of the policy, it still seems that accurate perception and opportunity for choice existed in sufficient amounts to permit such a statement.

Three final observations about the application of the bureaucratic perspective should be added. The first, alluded to earlier, is that taking this perspective in analysis entails a potential error parallel to the "intellectualist fallacy" of the traditional state-as-actor explanation.[34] For just as the traditional analyst is likely to attribute motivations to nations and accept calculations which were in fact never made in the councils of government, the analyst atuned to bureaucratic politics is likely to attribute motivation and calculations to individual governmental actors that were never present or made either—a Machiavellian fallacy.

The second observation is simply a recognition of scale. Although accepting the assumptions of the approach of bureaucratic politics does have implications for understanding a nation's behavior toward other nations—for international relations—the approach does not provide a framework for understanding the gross, collective behavior of nations over time. Bureaucratic politics proceeds within an international context described by students of the relations between states: "Today, the structure of alliances, power, and domination in the world sets limits upon the actions of states and policy-makers, no matter what their ideological persuasion, the state of domestic opinion, or individual ideals."[35] Nor, we would add, no matter what the distribution of internal power among competing bureaucracies.

The final point is that traditional analysis, with its emphasis on national interest and security, cannot be abandoned if policy is to be evaluated. A wretched policy for the United States may be perfectly understandable as a superb compromise among competing interests, but it must ultimately be evaluated as undesirable by some criteria of what is in fact good for the nation. Debates over what is or is not in the national interest should not be suspended while we try to better understand the complex sources of policies that will inevitably be rationalized in terms of the national interest.

Conclusion

It is risky to draw morals from the Viet-Nam experience, but there is certainly adequate justification to prescribe change at two general levels. The first involves restructuring of the decision-making process at the top, around the president. This is not only a matter of manipulating the way the NSC is used or not used but also a matter of defining the role of principals like the special assistant for national security affairs, the secretaries of state and defense, the chairman of the joint chiefs, and the director of the CIA. Obviously the nature of the inputs expected from the organizations below the principals, especially the State Department, is also critical. In discussing the sources of inputs to Viet-Nam decisions, we have referred to the system as "open" or "closed" and noted the ways in which insulation took place; describing policy compromise, we have seen the strengths and weaknesses of the various bargaining positions of bureaucratic actors and the results. The Viet-Nam experience suggests that the foreign policy-making apparatus should be structured so as to guarantee the opportunity for greater access to the highest councils and insure that there is a diversity of inputs—ideally provided by some permanent mechanism.[36]

This, it should be made clear, is not the same as arguing simply for the presentation of multiple policy options without concern for who makes the presentation. If it were, then the highly centralized NSC system that was created and run by Henry Kissinger in the Nixon administration might be the answer; it is not. An "open system," where diverse inputs from the foreign affairs bureaucracy are presented and advocated, free from manipulation and screening by a presidential advisor, even an exceptionally capable one, is what is needed. Rourke has called this "organizational pluralism" and finds it to be preferable to, and quite distinct from, the centralized Nixon-Kissinger arrangement:

> Without a multitude of conflicting organizational interests and centers of power, it is difficult to see how the vigor and variety of dialogue and dissent at lower echelons can be sustained. Inevitably, the centering of so much authority in the office of the special assistant for national security affairs will have a depressing effect upon independence of thought and initiative at other levels of the system.

What is clearly required is organizational strength at the bottom as well as the top, if executive deliberations are to retain any vitality.[37]

Special emphasis should probably also be given the role of the State Department. The proper role of State has been the subject of considerable debate and the issue is not about to be settled here. The evidence from the Viet-Nam case, however, is that exclusion of its experts and its perspective is extremely unhealthy.[38] The question of the most desirable civil-military relationship is closely related to the issue of a vital Department of State. Much of what has been said here about the air war and ground strategy had to do with the bargaining position of the military *vis-á-vis* the civilians, and the clear implication is that that position must be weakened if civilian control in time of war is to be realized. Such control may depend upon involving State more, rather than less, when military force is being used or contemplated.

The second area of difficulty involves the internal arrangements, incentives, and procedures of organizations. Although there are built-in incentives to dysfunctional activity in every organization, those in the foreign policy and military bureaucracies can be particularly costly. Evaluating how well tasks are performed by individuals or subunits by measuring some activity taken to be indicative of successful task completion will invariably maximize behavior that "measures well"—whether or not it is consistent with the performance of the assigned task. Too often OSD and the military sought to insure compliance with the aid of quantitative indicators only to finally provide incentives to do that which was inconsistent with what everyone understood to be the objectives of the organization.

Some of the other ills of organizational operations are of the same variety and generally call for the same kind of prescription. The difficulty in the Defense Intelligency Agency, for example, was essentially one of reward structure: too many of its members were subject to rewards only if they did not provide the information for which the DIA was created to provide. The military services have similar problems throughout their organizations and, in this, they are not alone. The solution to these kinds of problems must begin with a sensitivity to the incentives and reward structure that exists within the organization. These final comments are supposed to suggest the range of prescriptions that flow directly from the Viet-Nam experience, and no more. Many observers have tried to devise specific ways of "fixing the system," and no doubt others will continue to do so.[39] It is good, furthermore, that that is happening, since the way we make and carry out our foreign policy appears to have a lot to do with the quality of the policy that is produced and the chances of its succeeding. Of the many lessons that might be learned from Viet-Nam, this ought to be among the least debatable.

NOTES

CHAPTER I

1. Arthur Schlesinger, Jr., *The Bitter Heritage: Vietnam & American Democracy, 1941–1966*, rev. ed. (New York: Fawcett World, 1968).

2. See Leslie H. Gelb, "Vietnam: Some Hypothesis about Why and How." (Paper prepared for the annual meeting of the American Political Science Association, September 1970.); idem, "Vietnam: The System Worker," *Foreign Policy*, no. 3 (Summer 1971), pp. 140–67; Daniel Ellsberg, "Escalating in a Quagmire." (Paper presented at the annual meeting of the American Political Science Association, September 1970.); and idem, "The Quagmire Myth and the Stalemate Machine," *Public Policy*, no. 2 (Spring 1971), pp. 217–74.

Although it is convenient to refer to a Gelb-Ellsberg thesis for the purpose of this discussion, it is unlikely that either author would appreciate the designation and, in fact, their analyses do differ on particular points and in overall evaluations.

3. Gelb, "Vietnam: The System Worked," p. 165.

4. Taking it as more than a set of very suggestive propositions does not seem defensible to this analyst, so the phrase "bureaucratic perspective" is preferred to "model" or "paradigm."

5. Alexander L. George, David K. Hall, and William E. Simons, *The Limits of Coercive Diplomacy* (Boston: Little, Brown, 1971), p. 14.

CHAPTER II

1. See Leslie H. Gelb, "Vietnam: The System Worked," *Foreign Policy*, no. 3 (Summer 1971).

2. Townsend Hoopes, *The Limits of Intervention* (New York: David McKay, 1969), p. 14. George Ball did not recall that the requirement was limited to posts in developing nations: "There was a time when every Ambassador about to go abroad . . . even if he were to go to the Court of St. James's . . . was supposed to spend three months going to Counter-insurgency school—just in case some activity began to develop in Green Park" (quoted in Jean Stein, *American Journey: The Times of Robert F. Kennedy* [New York: Harcourt Brace Jovanovich, 1970], p. 208).

3. Arthur M. Schlesinger, Jr., *The Bitter Heritage*, rev. ed. (New York: Fawcett World, 1968), p. 20.

4. Ward Just, *Military Men* (New York: Alfred A. Knopf, 1970), p. 200.

5. *Department of State Newsletter*, no. 61 (May 1960), p. 2.

6. Marvin Kalb and Elie Abel, *Roots of Involvement* (New York: W. W. Norton, 1971), p. 122.

7. Ibid., p. 124. They add, "McNamara, Taylor, and Rostow became early converts, and their White House standing soared. Rusk never converted."

8. One State Department critic unkindly suggests that because of bureaucratic time lag COIN is now catching on at State—ten years too late. John Franklin Campbell, *The Foreign Affairs Fudge Factory* (New York: Basic Books, 1971), p. 76.

9. The total aid package was for $42 million, most of it going for equipment and supplies for a 20,000-man increase in the South Vietnamese Army. A partial text of the CIP appears in *The Pentagon Papers: The Senator Gravel Edition*, 4 vols. (Boston: Beacon Press, 1971), 2:24–25.

10. Ibid., pp. 34–35. The full text of the memorandum is included. This section and this chapter generally depend heavily on the documents of vol. 2 of the Gravel edition of the Pentagon study.

11. Ibid., p. 31.

12. The introductory section of the report, entitled "A Program of Action to Prevent Communist Domination of South Vietnam," is included in ibid., p.. 35–36.

13. Ibid., p. 443.

14. Ibid., p. 44. The narrative treats the differences between the May 1, 3, and 6 drafts.

15. Ibid., p. 53. This is from the May 6 final version, but the excerpt is essentially the same as the State Department's May 3 draft.

16. Ibid., pp. 44, 53.

17. The texts of the entire JCS memorandum and NSAM 52 are included in ibid., pp. 44–45 and pp. 642–43 respectively.

18. A partial text of the vice-president's report is included in ibid., pp. 56–58.

19. Portions of the texts of the NIE, MAAG, White, Nolting, and State Department reports are reproduced in ibid., pp. 69–72. Differences between Nolting's interpretations and those of his superiors in the State Department would become increasingly more pronounced until the ambassador's replacement. Nolting's friendship for Diem would prove to be an obstacle not only in getting objective information from the field (the upward flow of communication) but in gaining his compliance with directives from Washington (the downward flow and execution of policy). This was a classic case of a subunit in a bureaucracy pursuing secondary goals at the expense of the primary mission of the organization. An actor, in this case a field representative, came to identify with and invest in an instrumental goal, the maintenance of the Diem regime, and could only perceive the stated mission of the organization in terms of the instrumental goal; i.e., the interest of American foreign policy appeared to depend upon supporting Diem. Under such circumstances Washington could expect an ambassador to try to commit policy in the direction the ambassador desired by exaggerating the negative consequences of acts other than the ones he recommended, and also by altering the tone and even the content of messages relayed to the host country.

20. Minutes of the NSC meeting are not included, but parts of a Gilpatric memorandum on it are quoted in ibid., pp. 79–80.

21. Ibid., p. 79. A rare difference in opinion in such a matter between the JCS and the Commander of the Pacific Command (CINCPAC), Admiral Felt, was registered when the latter sent an evaluation to Washington which said that it appeared to him to "add up in favor of our not introducing U.S. combat troops until we have exhausted other means for helping Diem," p. 84.

22. Complete texts of cables are included in ibid., pp. 88–91.
23. Ibid., p. 94; a partial text of the Taylor report is included.
24. Ibid., p. 96.
25. Ibid., p. 105. In November 1961, John Kenneth Galbraith sent a long cable to President Kennedy on this point. He gave voice early to the soon to be popular refrain, "Diem must go."
26. Ibid., pp. 108–9.
27. Ibid, pp. 110–16. The conditions to be met by Diem were specified more fully in the memorandum itself, and were further detailed more forcefully in a November 14 communication to Nolting.
28. Daniel Ellsberg, "Escalating in a Quagmire." (Paper presented at the annual meeting of the American Political Science Association, September 1970.), p. 13. The Pentagon narrator was less certain in putting forth this explanation, *Pentagon Papers* 2:116–17.
29. *Pentagon Papers* 2:651. The full text of Lemnitzer's memorandum for General Taylor, "Counterinsurgency Operations in South Vietnam," is included.
30. Ibid., p. 681. The full text of the Hilsman research memorandum, "Progress Report on South Vietnam," is included.
31. Ibid., p. 687.
32. Ibid., p. 725. See the partial text of NIE, pp. 53–63, for the intelligence community's assessment in April 1963. Like many such estimates its tone is cautiously optimistic—so cautious, in fact, that it could not be faulted even if catastrophe were to follow.
33. Jean Lacouture, *Vietnam: Between Two Truces* (New York: Vintage Books, 1966), p. 49; and Sir Robert Thompson, *No Exit from Vietnam* (New York: David McKay, 1970), p. 171. Lacouture nicely describes a fully assembled "Strategic Hamlet Kit" as "model barberd-wire enclosures . . . so gaily white washed that even the most nearsighted of the guerrillas could be sure not to get entangled in them. Even the mines had to be indicated with [nationalist] flags. . . .," p. 151.
34. *Pentagon Papers* 2:691. The full text of Hilsman's research memorandum, "The Situation and Short-Term Prospects in South Vietnam," is included.
35. Ibid., p. 670. The full text of Galbraith's memorandum, "Viet-Nam," is included. Indicative of the State-Defense breach were reports that, during a briefing at the White House, Hilsman pressed General Lemnitzer to the point that McNamara had to intervene to permit Lemnitzer to finish.
36. Ibid., p. 729.
37. Ibid., p. 233.
38. Accounts of the August 24 message may be found in ibid., pp. 234–35; Chester L. Cooper, *The Lost Crusade* (New York: Dodd, Mead, 1970), pp. 212–13; and Roger Hilsman, *To Move a Nation* (New York: Dell Publishing, 1967, reprinted by Doubleday, 1967), pp. 487–90.
39. Ibid., p. 283.
40. Ibid., p. 742.
41. Quoted in U.S. Congress, Senate Committee on Foreign Relations, *Background Information Relating to South Asia and Vietnam* (Washington, D.C.: Government Printing Office, 1969), p. 145. The secretary's prediction can be attributed simply to bad judgment or, as one observer claims, to McNamara's concern over the military's reaction to his report. The hypothesis is that McNamara asked Kennedy to be allowed to say the

battlefield situation was good as an offering to the military. He would have needed an offering because, as a civilian, his call for a change in the military's tactics from "terrain sweeps which have little permanent value" to "clear and hold operations" was very unusual and because his advocacy of a policy of pressure on Diem was contrary to what SACSA Krulak recommended. See Charles Bartlett and Edward Weintal, *Facing the Brink* (New York: Charles Scribner's Sons, 1967), p. 89. It is noteworthy that the ground strategy did not change, however, and that in the future McNamara refrained from similar recommendations. See chapter 5 for a more complete discussion of the ground strategy and civilian efforts at influencing it.

42. Patrick Anderson, *The President's Men* (Garden City, N.Y.: Doubleday, 1968), p. 384.

43. Hilsman discusses the degrees of dovishness of decision makers in Stein, *American Journey*, p. 204, and does not hesitate to apply labels. Of the military, the Pentagon, Rostow, and McNamara he says: "They were extreme hawks, and Rusk was a mild hawk, though much more of a hawk than he ever permitted to be known." He puts John Kennedy, his brother Robert, Harriman, Forrestal, and himself in the opposing faction and adds: "Lyndon Johnson was out of it, he was not involved at all." In retrospect it is easy to see how the line-up could be rearranged by, for example, lumping Hilsman and Rostow together and contrasting them with an actor such as George Ball, whose political solutions were much less demanding of American resources.

44. Kalb and Abel, *Roots of Involvement*, p. 111.

45. *Pentagon Papers* 2:189. Text of Hughes research memorandum, "Statistics on the War Effort in South Vietnam Show Unfavorable Trends," ibid., p. 770.

46. Cooper, *Lost Crusade*, p. 256.

47. The Kennedy writers (Schlesinger, Sorenson, Hilsman) are not the only ones to take this position. An Institute for Defense Analysis group concluded: "Had the State Department pulled together the threads of the responsibility intended for it, the national security staff [McGeorge Bundy's] might not have developed as it did. When the State Department did not appear to be as responsive, the staff moved in—not in a deliberate effort to acquire power but, in their view, in order to do the President's work." See Keith C. Clark and Laurence J. Legere, *The President and the Management of National Security* (New York: Frederick A. Praeger, 1969), p. 81.

48. Campbell, *Foreign Affairs Fudge Factory*, p. 54. In an article already cited, James C. Thomson makes a similar observation: "The kind of expertise accumulated by diplomats tends to make them more sensitive than any other institutional group to the complexity and diversity of foreign relations, and more inclined to be "anti-evangelist" in their approach to meeting foreign problems"; quoted in ibid., p. 69.

49. Clark and Legere, *President and National Security*, p. 96.

50. Bartlett and Weintal, *Facing the Brink*, p. 173.

Chapter III

1. *The Pentagon Papers: The Senator Gravel Edition*, 4 vols. (Boston: Beacon Press, 1971) 3:498.

2. Ibid., p. 150.

3. Ibid., p. 154. The statement was made at a February 20 meeting involving the secretaries of defense and state, the director of the CIA, and the chairman of the JCS.

4. Ibid., pp. 499–500.

5. Ibid., p. 56.

6. Ibid., p. 44.

7. The unity of the JCS on Viet-Nam was confirmed in an unpublished interview with the former chairman of the JCS on May 19, 1971. General Wheeler dated the start of the period of agreement at November 1964. In my own confidential interview with an officer who served on the Joint Staff of the JCS from 1965 through 1968, he said that there was no evidence of serious divisions of any kind over Vietnam from 1964 on. He pointed to General Green, commandant of the Marine Corps, as the most enthusiastic advocate of involvement. (All interviews cited in this study were conducted in the spring or summer of 1971 in Washington, D.C., unless otherwise noted.) The *Pentagon Papers* also include evidence of varying degrees of enthusiasm. See, for example, the memo from General Wheeler to McNamara of September 9, 1964, indicating the position of Generals LeMay and Green, ibid., p. 564.

8. Quoted in Henry Brandon, *Anatomy of Error: The Inside Story of the Asian War on the Potomac, 1954–1969* (Boston: Gambit Press, 1969), p. 28.

9. *Pentagon Papers* 3:173.

10. There is a section in the *Pentagon Papers* entitled "Military Pressures against North Vietnam, February 1964–January 1965." It is the conclusion of the narrator that the Tonkin attacks were legitimate and not purposely provoked. For the alternative view see Joseph C. Goulden, *Truth Is the First Casualty* (New York: Rand McNally, 1969); and Colonel James A. Donovan, *Militarism, USA* (New York: Charles Scribner's Sons, 1970).

11. From a speech at Akron University on October 21, 1964, quoted in Tom Wicker, *JFK and LBJ* (New York: William Morrow, 1968), p. 232.

12. *Pentagon Papers* 3:190.

13. Ibid., pp. 533–37.

14. See the *Pentagon Papers*' chapter on military pressures and the related documents on the Rules of Engagement for details of these activities.

15. See for example the accounts in Charles Roberts, *LBJ's Inner Circle* (New York: Delacorte Press, 1965); and Arthur M. Schlesinger, Jr., *The Bitter Heritage: Vietnam & American Democracy, 1941–1966*, rev. ed. (New York: Fawcett World, 1968).

16. *Pentagon Papers* 3:210. A detailed account of the policy review is included in the narrative, pp. 206–51. The documents alone on this period take up another ninety-six pages of the volume.

17. Ibid., p. 212.

18. Ibid., p. 214.

19. The options are described in memoranda dated November 7, by William Bundy and John McNaughton in ibid., pp. 601–6.

20. Ball's memorandum has recently been published in its original form entitled "A Light That Failed" in *The Atlantic Monthly* 230, no. 1 (July 1972), pp. 35–49. The four options were to continue the present policy, take over the war in South Viet-Nam, launch an air offensive against the north, and pursue a political settlement. Ball apparently discussed it with

McNamara, Rusk, and McGeorge Bundy but did not try to get it before the president until January when Bill Moyers read it and passed it to Johnson.

21. Wicker, *JFK and LBJ*, p. 244.

22. For a discussion of the place of "shared images" within a general bureaucratic perspective, see chapter 6 of this study.

23. Roger Fisher, *International Conflict for Beginners* (New York: Harper & Row, 1969), p. 47, discusses the question of continuing commitments; and Robert Jervis, *The Logic of Images in International Relations* (Princeton: Princeton University Press, 1970), p. 89, considers the problem of influence. There is an exchange in Graham Green's novel *The Quiet American* (New York: Modern Library, 1957) which gets to the third point. The character Pyle, supposedly based on Edward M. Lansdale, begins to explain why South Viet-Nam should be saved from the Communists by saying, "If Indochina goes . . . ," but he is cut off by Fowler, the English journalist: "I know that record. Siam goes. Malay goes. Indochina goes. What does 'go' mean?" It was a good question in the fifties and it would have been a good one to put to the Chiefs when they used almost the same words in the November policy debate. Does "go" imply a communist regime under the control of North Viet-Nam? or China? or the Soviet Union? or international communism? What does it mean for the condition of the people compared to their condition in a war or under a Western-oriented authoritarian regime?

24. No NASAM was issued, the White House files are unavailable, and the narrator of the *Pentagon Papers* can only conjecture.

25. In a confidential interview, an air intelligence officer who served aboard the USS Coral Sea in 1964 and 1965 described the operations.

26. Philip L. Geyelin, *Lyndon B. Johnson and the World* (New York: Frederick A. Praeger, 1966), p. 216.

27. Confidential interview with an air intelligence officer.

28. Townsend Hoopes, *The Limits of Intervention* (New York: David McKay, 1969), p. 30.

29. *Pentagon Papers* 3:321. A concise summary of the targets in the ROLLING THUNDER program until June 1965 (RT 14) is included also, pp. 284–86.

30. Authorization for strikes would come in one week packages with field commanders determining the timing; strikes would no longer be given special publicity nor would they be continually justified by reference to events in South Viet-Nam; coordination with the Vietnamese Air Force was not required.

31. Alain C. Enthoven and K. Wayne Smith, *How Much Is Enough?* (New York: Harper & Row, 1971), p. 95.

32. Both incidents are recorded in the excellent work by Vincent Davis, *The Admirals Lobby* (Chapel Hill: University of North Carolina Press, 1967), p. 219. For a fascinating study of the air force drive for autonomy see Perry McCoy Smith, *The Air Force Plans for Peace 1943–1945* (Baltimore: The Johns Hopkins University Press, 1970).

33. Much has been made of applying the lessons of the USSBS to Viet-Nam, perhaps because several of those involved in the survey were also involved in Viet-Nam policy, including John K. Galbraith, Paul Nitze, George Ball, and Walt Rostow. Most comments are either like that of General Gavin's in a 1966 Senate hearing. "I think the results of the Stra-

tegic Bombing Survey will show that as our bombing was increased, German production went up until we overran facilities. I don't think you can hold them [in Viet-Nam] by bombing it nor really win by bombing," or they resemble remarks by Senator Stuart Symington during a 1967 appropriation hearing: "As the strategic bombing survey of World War II showed the reason the North Vietnamese don't negotiate for peace is because of the light bombing being done over there." Looking through the literature on air power one finds a similar use of the USSBS by proponents and opponents alike. This is because the survey, even if read carefully, offers support at one place or another in its 316 volumes for either position. The following is offered as an illustration:

"On the first impression it would appear that the air attacks which laid waste to these cities must have substantially eliminated the industrial capacity of Germany. Yet this was not the case. The attacks did not so reduce the German war production as to have a decisive effect on the outcome of the war" (vol. 31, p. 2).

"Allied air power was decisive in the war in Western Europe" (overall report, p. 107).

"The mental reaction of the German people to air attack is significant. . . . Their morale, their belief in ultimate victory or satisfactory compromise and in their leaders declined, but they continued to work efficiently as long as the physical means of production remained" (overall report, p. 108).

"Bombing appreciably affected the German will to resist. Its main psychological effects were defeatism, fear, hopelessness, fatalism, and apathy. . . . War weariness, willingness to surrender, loss of hope in a German victory, distrust of leaders, feelings of disunity, and demoralizing fear were all more common among bombed than among unbombed" (overall report, p. 95). *United States Strategic Bombing Survey*, 316 vols. (Washington, D.C.: Government Printing Office, 1945–47).

34. Frederick C. Thayer, "Professionalism: The Hard Choice," *U.S. Naval Institute Proceedings* 97 (June 1971): 38.

35. *St. Louis Post-Dispatch*, February 7, 1971.

36. *Pentagon Papers* 3:230. Also see Charles J. Hitch's August 24 memorandum to McNamara taking issue with an air force study that said, "The evidence supports the conclusion that tactical air with nonnuclear munitions can prevent the takeover of Southeast Asia by CHICOM ground forces opposed by minimal friendly ground forces," ibid., pp. 549–50.

37. Suggested in a confidential interview with a military officer serving in OSD (Systems Analysis) in the Division of Forces and Manpower.

38. In March 1965 General McConnell was alone in advocating the destruction of all 94 JCS targets in 28 days. The JCS ultimately recommended a program similar to that put forth by CINCPAC, concentrating on interdiction. *Pentagon Papers* 3:341–43.

39. Ibid., p. 316. Taylor was of the same opinion two years later. See his *Responsibility and Response* (New York: Harper & Row, 1967), pp. 26–27.

40. Ibid., p. 689. Bundy also took the same position later when interviewed by Henry F. Graff: "The bombing," he said, "was chiefly important for maintaining South Vietnamese morale." *The Tuesday Cabinet* (Englewood Cliffs, N.J.: Prentice-Hall, 1970), p. 147.

41. Ibid., p. 201 includes excerpts from the critique. Also see Rostow's "Victory Thesis" of May 1965, ibid., pp. 381–82.

42. See Henry Brandon's discussion of Ball's position, *Anatomy of Error*, p. 50. Obviously the danger is that of the "effectiveness trap"—everyone goes along to preserve their effectiveness, and dissent never surfaces.

43. An interviewee who was a White House consultant at the time and who has reviewed the relevant material asserted, in a confidential interview in May 1970, that this was Ball's motivation.

44. Several of those interviewed familiar with the events at the time referred to the effect the Cuban missile crisis experience seemed to have on thinking about coercing the North Vietnamese. On the same point David Halberstam observes, "They forgot that in the Cuban missile crisis it was the Russians, not the Cubans, who had backed down, that the Cubans had been perfectly willing, if imperfectly prepared, to fight." "The Programming of Robert McNamara," *Harper's Magazine* (February 1971), p. 68.

45. Harry Howe Ransom, "The Politics of Air Power—A Comparative Analysis." In Carl J. Frederich and Seymour E. Harris, eds., *Public Policy*, (A Yearbook of the Graduate School of Public Administration, Harvard University, 1958) 8:92.

46. Quoted in Graff, *Tuesday Cabinet*, p. 56.

47. Quoted in *Pentagon Papers* 3:163.

48. Interview with James T. Kendall, chief counsel for the Senate Armed Services Committee, who asked and supplied questions for witnesses in August 1967 hearings on the bombing. McNamara shared a penchant for action common to several actors (e.g., McNaughton, the Bundys and Rostow) which would have predisposed him to the more activist course of pressuring the north. He is quoted as saying, "To take no action is to take undecided action." Graff, *Tuesday Cabinet*, p. 35.

49. Quoted in the *Washington Post*, June 25, 1971. The material was first published in the *Baltimore Sun* in a story by Washington Bureau Chief Phillip Porter. There is no mention of the message in the *Pentagon Papers* and Porter's use of it was intended to show that the president could not have decided to bomb as early as critics claim. But since skepticism over effectiveness did not preclude taking the action, it need not have precluded the decision to act which therefore could have been made at any time before the message.

50. Rowland Evans and Robert Novak refer to the President's impeachment remark in *LBJ: The Exercise of Power* (New York: New American Library, 1966), p. 546.

51. Daniel Ellsberg, "Escalating in a Quagmire." (Paper presented at the annual meeting of the American Political Science Association, September 1970.)

52. Noting a similiar argument, Richard Dudman writes that "Another defense of the bombing raids, provided privately by policy-makers in Washington, was that while they were not successful in themselves, they served to refute those who had been saying that a few taps at the North would be enough to bring the war to an end." "Military Policy in Vietnam," *Current History* 50 (February 1966):93. Moreover, one of the highest ranking participant-analysts in the Defense Department asserted, in a confidential interview, that this was the single most important reason for the bombing.

53. In looking at the same period William R. Simons also finds conflict-

ing objectives and a policy that reflected the conflict and compromise. Simons, however, considered only the overtly expressed objectives (negotiations, coercive diplomacy, infiltration, etc.) and not the underlying motivation for various positions, and he was certain not only of compromise but of dysfunctional compromise. In retrospect, however, the sources of conflict seem rather important, and it is not at all clear that an unambiguously pursued policy of coercive diplomacy would have been more desirable than the "irrational" one followed. See Alexander L. George, David K. Hall, and William E. Simons, *The Limits of Coercive Diplomacy* (Boston: Little, Brown, 1971), pp. 144–252.

54. Ibid., p. 214. In an interview with Benjamin Read, special assistant to the secretary of state, he stated that he thought the bombing decisions were made incrementally, largely the result of compromise forced by George Ball, together with the fears, shared by several others, of larger political costs.

55. State's Office of Asian Communist Affairs and INR saw special significance in the visit. See the *Pentagon Papers* 3:301–2. Chester Cooper claims that the premier took the attack as a personal insult. *The Lost Crusade* (New York: Dodd, Mead, 1970), p. 261.

56. *Pentagon Papers* 3:374.

57. George, *Limits of Coercive Diplomacy*, p. 199. Robert Jervis observes that ". . . when people spend a great deal of time drawing up a plan or making a decision, they tend to think that the message about it they wish to convey will be clear to the receiver," *Logic of Images*, p. 216. This has no doubt been relevant to communications throughout our Viet-Nam experience.

58. *Pentagon Papers* 3:333.

59. Quoted in U.S., Congress, Senate Committee on Foreign Relations, *Background Information Relating to Southeast Asia and Vietnam*, 89th Cong., 2d sess., March 1966, p. 218.

60. David Braybrooke and Charles E. Lindblom observe that, "Although there is a fundamental sense in which ends govern means, there is an equally fundamental sense in which proximate ends of public policy are governed by means." *A Strategy of Decision: Policy Evaluation As a Social Process* (New York: Free Press, 1963), p. 93.

61. Roger Hilsman, "Foreign Policy Consensus: An Interim Report." *Journal of Conflict Resolution* 3 (December 1959):363–64.

Chapter IV

1. *The Pentagon Papers: The Senator Gravel Edition*, 4 vols. (Boston: Beacon Press, 1971) 4:136. A sortie is the flight of one aircraft on one mission.

2. U.S., Congress, Senate Committee on Foreign Relations, *Background Information Relating to Southeast Asia and Vietnam* (3d rev. ed.). 90th Cong., 1st sess., July 1967, p. 255.

3. *Pentagon Papers* 4:56. The segments quoted are from an unspecified report included in the narrative.

4. Ibid., p. 137.

5. Ibid., p. 168.

6. Ibid., p. 184. Essentially, the proposals were either to focus strikes on the "Panhandle" or southern portion of North Viet-Nam, or to concen-

trate on logistics targets in the populated northeast section of the country.

7. The barrier is discussed in ibid., pp. 112–30.

8. *Pentagon Papers* 4:116. Some of the specifics of North Vietnamese countermeasures were described by a Russian observer in 1967: "Road transport in North Vietnam uses the so-called segmented system: motor vehicles move from place to place by short rushes at night time. For damaged bridges the North Vietnamese use removable installations for night. In the morning they are removed. Completely demolished bridges are replaced by ferries and floating bridges. There are bridges hidden near the riverside; they are thrown over at night time and removed in the morning. There are also light bamboo bridges which can be hidden under water in the event of an air raid. In addition there are ordinary pontoon bridges used by night and dismantled before dawn." B. Teplinsky, "The Air War over Indochina," *International Affairs* (Moscow, February 1967), p. 45.

9. *Pentagon Papers* 4:116–19.

10. Ibid., pp. 223–24.

11. One RAND study which was made public concluded that Hanoi benefited in several ways from the bombings. Not only did they receive an increase in aid from the Soviet Union and China, but the external threat also served to bolster popular morale and facilitate government control. As long as Russian and Chinese aid continued, the coercive strategy was doomed to failure. See Oleg Hoeffding, *Bombing North Vietnam: An Appraisal of Economic and Political Effects*, Memorandum RM-5213-1-ISA, (Santa Monica: The RAND Corp., December 1966).

12. Quoted in the *New York Times*, June 28, 1972, p. 18, from previously unreleased portions of the official government version of the *Pentagon Papers*.

13. *Pentagon Papers* 4:64–65.

14. Ibid., p. 66.

15. Ibid., p. 72.

16. Ibid., p. 111. The problem of North Vietnamese replacement of POL nearly as quickly as it could be destroyed is alluded to in James C. Thomson's witty parody, "Minutes of a White House Meeting, Summer 1967": "Colonel Black explained the previous night's raids on North Vietnam. We had knocked out 78 percent of North Vietnam's petroleum reserves; since we had knocked out 86 percent three days ago, and 92 percent last week, we were doing exceptionally well." Robert Manning and Michael Janeway, eds., *Who We Are: An Atlantic Chronicle of the United States & Vietnam 1966–1969*. (Boston: Little, Brown, 1969), p. 43.

17. During a confidential interview a highly placed civilian in ISA referred to this split in the CIA, and one of the principal leaders of the more pessimistic faction within the Agency confirmed it in another interview. It was not unusual for alternate briefings of the secretary of defense by the CIA to reflect the division since, in Carver's absence, someone with the opposite slant was likely to replace him. The RAND group was also divided for a time on the question of the effectiveness of the bombing.

18. Not only did the CIA and the DIA rely on the same sources for bombing data (i.e., the Navy, 7th Air Force, and MACV) but they even met and pooled data. The difference according to a senior CIA analyst who was interviewed, was in evaluation where there was no joint effort.

19. Much has been written in the literature of organizational theory on

the distortion of information flows, but for a discussion directed specifically at the problem it presents in the area of intelligence see Harold L. Wilensky, *Organizational Intelligence* (New York: Basic Books, 1967). At one point, Wilensky describes deliberate distortions by American and British advocates of precision and area bombing respectively during World War II: "To justify their own preconceptions, military experts committed to one or the other strategy used faulty intelligence predictions or manipulated intelligence estimates or downgraded or rejected intelligence that supported the rival strategy," p. 30. Similar kinds of distortion occurred during the Viet-Nam war.

20. Frederick C. Thayer, "Professionalism: The Hard Choice," *U.S. Naval Institute Proceedings* 97 (June 1971):38.

21. Patrick J. McGarvey, "The Culture of Bureaucracy: DIA, Intelligence to Please," *The Washington Monthly* (July 1970), p. 72. McGarvey spent fourteen years in intelligence work serving with Air Force Intelligence, the DIA, and the CIA.

22. Ibid.

23. Patrick J. McGarvey, *CIA: The Myth and the Madness* (New York: Saturday Review Press, 1972), pp. 150–51.

24. McGarvey recounts a specific case: "In one instance the Air Force Chief of Intelligence called my boss at DIA about a nearly completed estimate on U.S. bombing in Laos. He told him that he was sending a team down to change the wording of the estimate and that my boss had better remember what color his uniform was. Of course it was the same as the General's blue. The team arrived, and, over the protests of the DIA analysts, a compromise was reached." McGarvey, "Culture of Bureaucracy," p. 73.

25. A former Air Force Intelligence analyst writes, "To criticize the bombing meant, therefore, to hurt your own organization and to benefit its rivals. Stopping the bombing could be seen as a failure for the Air Force." He also claims that it was not unknown for the Air Force to withhold bombing reports from the Navy. Morris J. Blackman, "The Stupidity of Intelligence," *The Washington Monthly* 1 no. 8 (September 1969):26. (This article was first published by the author under the pseudonym Ariel.)

26. Ibid., p. 24.

27. Colonel Jack Broughton, USAF (Ret.), *Thud Ridge* (New York: J. B. Lippincott, 1969), p. 97. "Fragged," as used by Col. Broughton, does not meant to blow-up a superior officer with a fragmentation grenade as it did in South Viet-Nam. Rather, it refers to the fragmentation of a set of strike orders from headquarters into individual wing assignments.

28. Benjamin Wells, "H–L–S of the C.I.A.," *New York Times Magazine* (March 18, 1971), p. 52.

29. For a discussion of the "stakes" or roles, missions, capabilities, organizational essence, etc. see Morton H. Halperin, "Why Bureaucrats Play Games," *Foreign Policy* no. 2 (Spring 1971) pp. 74–88.

30. One could argue that even though naval air capability was heavily engaged, its primary function as protector of the fleet was not at issue: "Today's Navy fighters have but *one* basic mission—to destroy enemy aerodynamic vehicles (manned and unmanned) which may be used by the enemy to interfere with our offensive operations, or to attack the Fleet."

Captain Carl O. Holinquist, USN, "Developments and Problems in Carrier-Based Fighter Aircraft," *Proceedings: Naval Review Issue*, U.S. Naval Institute (May 1970), p. 226.

31. The marines had reason not to become involved in Viet-Nam in the first place. Some senior officers apparently thought that the character of the corps as an elite, mobile assault group would be sacrificed by taking on a mission of extended, stable presence in which essentially defensive operations would have to be conducted. Others did not believe the marines could afford the luxury of choice, and that survival as an independent service required that they involve themselves in any ground engagements in which regular Army units were committed.

32. The "essence" of each service as expressed in the priority of certain missions is well known among the military. There is always competition among principal subunits having their special missions (e.g., surface vs. submarine navy, armored vs. air mobile army, tactical vs. strategic air force), but there is little doubt as to which are the primary missions competing for dominance and which are peripheral. Budget allocations and promotion rates reflect the distinctions. See Halperin's "Why Bureaucrats Play Games" and *Bureaucratic Politics and Foreign Policy* (Washington, D.C.: The Brookings Institution, 1974) for a general discussion of priorities among missions, and the quantitative analysis now in progress by Arnold Kanter of the University of Michigan for evidence of the reflection of priorities in promotions among staff officers.

33. Phil G. Goulding, *Confirm or Deny: Informing the People on National Security* (New York: Harper & Row, 1970), p. 179.

34. U.S., Congress, Senate Committee on Armed Services and Committee on Appropriations, *Military Procurement Authorization for FY 1968:* Hearings before Committee on Armed Services and Defense Appropriations Subcommittee of Committee on Appropriations on S.666, 90th Cong., 1st sess., 1967, p. 887.

35. For a discussion of definitional distinctions between tactical and strategic air interdiction, see Raphael Littauer and Norman Uphoff, eds., *The Air War in Indochina*, rev. ed. (Boston: Beacon Press, 1972), pp. 17–26; and Edmund Dews, *A Note on Tactical vs. Strategic Air Interdiction*, RM-6239-PR (Santa Monica: RAND Corp., April 1970).

36. Perry McCoy Smith, *The Air Force Plans for Peace: 1943–1945* (Baltimore: The Johns Hopkins University Press, 1970), p. 97.

37. See Eugene Emme, ed., *The Impact of Air Power* (Princeton: D. Van Nostrand, 1959), p. 190.

38. Smith, *The Air Force Plans for Peace,* p. 97.

39. *Pentagon Papers* 4:4.

40. See Wilensky, *Organizational Intelligence*, p. 28.

41. The Sigma II study of the Joint War Games Agency, Cold War Division of the Joint Chiefs of Staff is referred to in a document entitled "A Light That Failed," written by George Ball on October 5, 1964 and published in *The Atlantic Monthly* 230, no 1 (July 1972), p. 39.

42. *Pentagon Papers* 4:201.

43. It as been noted in congressional testimony that the Russians have chosen not to pay for such a capability in their MIG 21 and 23 aircrafts: "The Soviet design philosophy for tactical fighters has emphasized maneuverability, speed, and altitude, rather than range/payload capability." U.S., Congress, Senate Committee on Armed Services, *U.S. Tactical Air*

Power Program: Hearings before Preparatory Investigating Subcommittee, 90th Cong., 2d sess., 1968, p. 15. This is not to say, however, that if Viet-Nam action did not provide the justification for such a capability, other rationales would not have emerged. The advantage in not having to maintain overseas bases might be one such rationale.

44. General Otto P. Weyland, "The Air Campaign in Korea," *Air University Quarterly Review*, no. 3 (Fall 1953), quoted in Eugene Emme, *The Impact of Air Power*, p. 395. For a thorough but one-sided review of the role of air power in Korea see Colonel James T. Stewart, USAF, ed., *Air Power: The Decisive Force in Korea* (Princeton: D. Van Nostrand, 1957).

45. Quoted in Richard N. Goodwin, *Triumph or Tragedy: Reflections on Vietnam* (New York: Random House, 1966), p. 57.

46. George A. Carter, *Some Historical Notes on Air Interdiction in Korea*, P-3452 (Santa Monica: RAND Corporation, September 1966). Robert McNamara drew upon Carter's study during his ordeal before the Stennis subcommittee in 1967 and had it inserted in the record.

47. Ibid., p. 12. Consider Carter's description of enemy countermeasures in Korea and then compare them with the descriptions of North Vietnamese tactics such as the one provided in footnote 8, chapter 4: "When air power forced them off the roads and rails during the day, they traveled by night. They built multiple parallel bridges to decrease the effectiveness of bridge-busting; the usual number of by-passes was four or five, but for one key bridge, they built no less than eight by-passes. They built 'underwater bridges' to escape detection from the air. They built bypasses around critical points in the supply routes. They used removable bridge spans to prevent reconnaissance flights from detecting repaired bridges. They broke truck convoys up into small units (4 or 5 trucks) to avoid detection. . . . They used shuttle trains on very short stretches of track to carry supplies between break points; the supplies were then moved by truck, oxcart, or coolie to a waiting train and hauled to the next obstacle."

48. Enthoven writes that "the Air Force was dominated by the advocates of strategic air power, who had little interest in tactical air power. In fact, the Tactical Air Command was a poor cousin, and it tried to emulate the Strategic Air Command (SAC) by developing an overseas theater-based nuclear delivery capability, a kind of 'junior SAC,' rather than taking seriously the task of preparing to provide air support for the Army in a conventional war. To change Air Force thinking and build up tactical air power would require strong outside pressure. Indeed, in the early 1960's the Air Force resisted increases in tactical air forces decided upon by the Secretary of Defense for fear that they would come out of SAC's budget." Alain C. Enthoven and K. Wayne Smith, *How Much is Enough?* (New York: Harper & Row, 1971), p. 9. Until the navy introduced the A-6 "Intruder" there had been no all-weather attack aircraft capable of flying at night. Specially converted C-130 and C-119 cargo planes filled in over the trail system for lack of any other slow-moving attack craft to perform the mission.

49. Relations between the two could also have become cooperative if a compromise position would have been found, or if they agreed to limit the scope of competition for resources in some way. If the allocator of resources seeks the benefits of free competition, this becomes a coalition against him. The services often operated in this way vis-a-vis the secretary of defense.

50. Interestingly, the section on Systems Analysis in an Institute for Defense Analysis study begins with the question, "Precisely why did military men regard Systems Analysis as the prime enemy?" Part of the answer has to do with the matter of expertise and the resistance to accepting "non-line" input and knowledge as legitimate. In an organizational study of the Forest Service concerned with flood control, Ashley Schiff found a similar tendency among those in uniform to believe that they had a monopoly on expertise no matter what evidence might be presented by civilians: "Exalting expertise, the Service believed it alone could master the requisite knowledge." See Ashley L. Schiff, *Fire and Water* (Cambridge: Harvard University Press, 1962), p. 166.

51. Enthoven and Smith, *How Much Is Enough?*, p. 99.

52. Enthoven makes an effort to depreciate the role: "The Systems Analysis Office did not have a prominent, much less a crucial, role in the Viet-Nam War. Prior to June 1965 it had no role at all, and afterward it was never closely involved with the development of strategy or operations. Such matters were largely outside its charter." Enthoven and Smith, *How Much Is Enough?*, p. 270.

53. If the navy flew at less than .95 sorties and Systems Analysis maintained its estimate of the aircraft's capability to fly at 1.35 sorties, the civilians could claim that the navy could perform the same mission with less aircraft if they were used efficiently. Obviously the navy would not want to fly at more than the 1.35 rate either. The discussion of System Analysis's evaluation procedure depends heavily upon confidential interviews with those involved in the evaluation process.

54. Broughton, *Thud Ridge*, p. 62. In the words of another air force colonel who had served in Viet-Nam, "The calculation was that 'if you don't hit 'em today, you might not get 'em tomorrow.' "

55. Ibid., p. 96.

56. U.S., Congress, Senate Committee on Armed Services, *Air War Against North Viet-Nam:* Hearings before the Preparedness Investigating Subcommittee, 90th Cong., 1st sess., 1967, p. 479. For a good part of the war a ROLLING THUNDER package would specify fixed targets permitted for strike, sorties allowed per target, and the total sorties, including those for armed reconnaissance, allowed in the two-week period.

57. Joint Logistics Review Board, *Logistic Support in the Vietnam Era* 2:208. The JLRB was appointed by Deputy Secretary of Defense David Packard in February 1969 and was directed by General F. S. Besson, U.S.A. They worked with a staff of over a hundred and produced a comprehensive and mildly controversial review plus evaluation of the logistics of the Viet-Nam war. For a discussion of the bomb shortage see Claude Witze, "The Case for a Unified Command: CINSEA," *Air Force and Space Digest* (January 1967), p. 28.

58. Confidential interview.

59. Frank Harvey, *Air War—Vietnam* (New York: Bantam Books, 1967), p. 112. He refers specifically to the carrier "Constellation."

60. U.S., Congress, *Air War Against North Vietnam:* Hearings, p. 103.

61. Air Force enthusiasm for the submarine has dissipated since the emergence of the Polaris missile-firing submarine with its threat to the missions of manned bombers and land-based ICBM's—both are Air Force weapons.

62. U.S., Congress, Senate and House Committees on Armed Services,

CVAN-70 Aircraft Carrier: Hearings before the Joint Senate-House Armed Services Subcommittee, 91st Cong., 2d sess., 1970, p. 7.

63. The *Pentagon Papers,* vol. 4, part 1, provides a detailed account of the progress of the air war and Littauer, *Air War in Indochina* includes a nice analytical summary, pp. 39–43.

64. Arthur Schlesinger, Jr., "Eyeless in Indochina," *The New York Review of Books* (October 21, 1971), p. 30.

65. The North Vietnamese apparently believe that the slow process of escalation was critical to their successful response. The following is an excerpt from a 1967 North Vietnamese military analysis: "The might of the U.S. Air Force lies in the fact that it has many planes, modern technical means, bombs and bullets, and available airfields in Thailand and South Vietnam, and at sea. It can attack us from many directions, on many targets, under different weather conditions, by day and by night. However, given their political isolation and the present balance of international forces, the U.S. Air Force is compelled to escalate step by step, and cannot attack the North massively and swiftly in strategic, large-scale, surprise bombings. Our North Vietnam can gain the time and circumstances necessary to gradually transform the country to a war footing, to further develop its forces, and to gain experience in order to deal the U.S. Air Force heavier blows." Quoted in Patrick J. McGarvey, *Visions of Victory: Selected Vietnamese Military Writings, 1964–1968* (Stanford: Hoover Institution Press, 1969), p. 156.

66. Alexander L. George, David K. Hall, and William E. Simons, *The Limits of Coercive Diplomacy* (Boston: Little, Brown, 1971), pp. 4–5.

67. Samuel J. Huntington, "Strategy and the Policy Process," *Foreign Affairs* 38 (January 1960):291.

68. Ibid. An excellent example of a presidential display of military approval occurred in 1968 when the final cutback in the bombing was announced only after General Creighton Abrams had journeyed from Viet-Nam to Washington to emphasize his assent and endorsement.

69. See Witze, "The Case for a Unified Command," p. 25.

70. *Pentagon Papers* 4:24–25.

71. Ibid., p. 126.

72. Ibid., p. 129.

73. See David Halberstam, "The Programming of Robert McNamara," *Harper's Magazine* (February 1971), p. 71, and Townsend Hoopes, *The Limits of Intervention* (New York: David McKay, 1969), p. 90. The account of Henry L. Trewhitt from an interview with General Wheeler should also be noted on the related issue of McNamara's tenure as secretary of defense: "General Wheeler, who had maintained a careful liaison between military and civilian viewpoints, had a concise reply to reports that some of the Chiefs had threatened to quit unless McNamara left: 'Bullshit.'" *McNamara* (New York: Harper & Row, 1971), p. 245.

74. See Henry Brandon, *Anatomy of Error: The Inside Story of the Asian War on the Potomac, 1954–1969* (Boston: Gambit Press, 1969), p. 157.

75. Interview with James T. Kendall, chief counsel for the Senate Armed Services Committee. The effect of the coming hearings on target allocations was quite clear—the JCS list of 94 targets gradually grew to a total of 242 from 1965 to July 1967; during the month of July the JCS reconsidered its list and on the day before the hearings began, August 8, added 185

targets from CINCPAC's list to bring the JCS list up 427. See U.S., Congress, *Air War Against North Vietnam:* Hearings, p. 294.

76. Interview with Benjamin Read, special assistant to the secretary of state until 1968. The *New York Times* version of the *Pentagon Papers* includes the complete text of an orientation memo for Clark Clifford from Assistant Secretary Paul Warnke describing the target approval procedure. *The Pentagon Papers As Published by the New York Times* (New York: Bantam Books, 1971), p. 621.

77. U.S., Congress, *Air War Against North Vietnam:* Hearings, p. 320. This discussion is limited to fixed, numbered targets from the JCS list. As of August 22, 1967, there had been only five fixed, unnumbered, recommended targets not authorized for strike.

78. Ibid., p. 297.

79. Ibid., p. 358.

80. *Pentagon Papers* 4:43.

81. In an interview with one of the two persons in ISA having primary responsibility for reviewing target requests, it was said that avoidance of civilian casualties was a first order priority.

82. *Pentagon Papers* 4:105.

83. Ibid.

84. Ibid., p. 254.

85. Confidential interview.

86. See Patrick Anderson, *The President's Men* (Garden City: Doubleday, 1968), pp. 340–45 for an account of Moyers' activity in the December 1965 coalition favoring a pause.

87. *Pentagon Papers* 4:25–26.

88. In testimony given before a joint session of the Senate Armed Services and Appropriations Committee in January 1967, McNamara said of the previous year's strikes, "The bombing of the POL system was carried out with as much skill, effort, and attention as we could devote to it, starting on June 29, and we haven't been able to dry up those supplies. . . . I don't believe that bombing up to the present has significantly reduced, nor any bombing that you could contemplate in the future would significantly reduce, actual flow of men and materiel to the South." Quoted in *Pentagon Papers* 4:112.

89. Goulding, *Confirm or Deny*, p. 178.

90. Hoopes, *Limits of Intervention*, p. 85.

91. Quoted in Enthoven and Smith, *How Much Is Enough?*, p. 292.

92. A. J. P. Taylor, *English History, 1914–1945* (New York: Oxford University Press, 1965), p. 519.

93. Anderson, *The President's Men*, p. 384. Anderson also suggests that Johnson may have intended Rostow to serve as a sort of lightning rod for criticism.

94. Chester L. Cooper, *The Lost Crusade* (New York: Dodd, Mead, 1970), p. 391.

95. For an account of McGeorge Bundy's change of mind see David Halberstam's "The Very Expensive Education of McGeorge Bundy," *Harper's Magazine* (July 1969).

96. John P. Roche, "The Jigsaw Puzzle of History," *New York Times Magazine* (January 24, 1971), p. 15.

97. Ibid.

98. A president who puts a price on dissent breeds men who see them-

selves as caught in the "effectiveness trap"—men who perpetually forego dissent and its risks today in order to save themselves to fight another day. Although this can easily become part of a routine "going along to get along," it is nonetheless true that an actor's power and influence in the upper reaches of government has much to do with the status of his relations with the president. In an unusual statement Dean Rusk, the former secretary of state, observed: "The real organization of government at higher echelons is not what you find in textbooks or organizational charts. It is how confidence flows down from the President. That is never put on paper—people don't like it. Besides, it fluctuates. People go up—and people go down." Dean Rusk, *Life* January 17, 1969), p. 62B, quoted in Morton Halperin, "Sources of Power in the Foreign Affairs Bureaucracy." (Paper presented at the annual meeting of the American Political Science Association, 1972), p. 8.

99. See James C. Thomson's review of Marvin Kalb and Elie Abel's *Roots of Involvement* entitled "The Quandry of Vote-namization," *Washington Post* (April 10, 1971).

100. *Pentagon Papers* 4:54.

101. *Pentagon Papers* 4:39.

102. Ibid., p. 144.

103. Hoopes, *Limits of Intervention*, p. 131.

104. U.S., Congress, *Military Procurement Authorization for FY 1968:* Hearings, p. 697.

105. Hoopes, *Limits of Intervention*, p. 132.

106. Ibid., p. 151.

107. Rowland Evans and Robert Novak, *LBJ: The Exercise of Power* (New York: The New American Library, 1966), pp. 563–66.

108. In an interview, James T. Kendall, chief counsel for the Senate Armed Services Committee, said that he had visited Viet-Nam and talked with the miiltary prior to the hearings. At a stopover at CINCPAC headquarters in Hawaii he found that "Admiral Sharp was not bashful about expressing his views." There was also a briefing of the committee staff by the military in Washington exactly one month prior to the meetings.

109. U.S., Congress, *Air War Against North Vietnam:* Hearings, p. 10.

110. Quoted in the *Pentagon Papers* 4:204.

111. "The Impatient Ones," *The Economist* 224, no. 6469 (August 9, 1967):629.

CHAPTER V

1. Admiral U. S. G. Sharp, USN, and General W. C. Westmoreland, USA, *Report on the War in Vietnam* (Washington, D.C.: U.S. Government Printing Office, 1968), p. 91.

2. Ibid.

3. See references in *The Pentagon Papers: The Senator Gravel Edition*, 4 vols. (Boston: Beacon Press, 1971), 3:399 to JCSM 982-64 dated November 23, 1964 and JCSM 100-65 dated February 11, 1965, pp. 400 and 427. Much of the discussion here is based upon a well-written segment of the papers entitled "American Troops Enter the Ground War." Fundamentally, however, the interpretation of the Pentagon analyst is misleading in its representation of the strategic concept as evolving during the first four months of involvement. It is unlikely that any evolution went on in military

minds and more unlikely still that a concept other than the military's could have prevailed at that time.

4. *Pentagon Papers* 3:418. Although he was always an active supporter of American involvement in Viet-Nam, Taylor's position in 1961 contrasts with that in 1965 when he failed to join other policy makers in their enthusiasm for a wider commitment.

5. Just before the marine deployment Assistant Secretary of Defense John McNaughton attempted a rather unusual sleight of hand by cabling that the 173d Airborne Brigade was being substituted for the marines. By the following day MACV, CINCPAC, and Taylor made their objections known in unambiguous fashion and stopped the substitution. The *Pentagon Papers* analyst hypothesizes that McNaughton sought to limit the capability of the American unit to engage in combat. The Airborne travels considerably lighter than a Marine BLT, it would be less visible, incapable of sustaining itself for any length of time, and would have arrived without the marines' tradition of intervention.

6. *Pentagon Papers* 3:403.

7. Ibid., p. 453.

8. Ibid., p. 446.

9. See JCSM 204-65 in Ibid., p. 469.

10. Ibid., p. 703.

11. See the text of the ambassador's April 12 cable to the State Department in Ibid., p. 449.

12. JCSM 321-65 of April 30 listed part of the March JCS recommendation as approved, and on May 5, McNaughton sought to make the correction, Ibid., p. 411.

13. Ibid., p. 448.

14. See JCSM 321-65 in Ibid., p. 458.

15. Ibid., pp. 411–12.

16. Ibid., p. 413.

17. Ibid., p. 440.

18. Ibid., pp. 470–71. See also pp. 412–14, 438–41, and 468–73.

19. Ibid., p. 471.

20. Ibid., p. 415.

21. The same characterization was made by others in the Office of the Secretary of Defense who were closely involved in troop deployment assessments.

22. Sir Robert Thompson has written extensively about an alternative strategy for Viet-Nam emphasizing police action within secured areas and the use of small unit combat techniques outside such areas. See *No Exit From Vietnam* (New York: David McKay, 1970). In another treatment of strategy, Frank E. Ambruster suggested massive "clear and hold" operations expanding slowly to larger areas, but only after security was attained in the initial locations. See Ambruster et al., *Can We Win in Vietnam* (New York: Frederick A. Praeger, 1968).

Suggestions from those inside the government were along similar lines. Townsend Hoopes, former deputy assistant secretary of Defense for ISA called for a "hedgehog strategy" that would seek to "clear and pacify a respectable area within a chosen perimeter—and concentrate on governing this area." See his *Limits of Intervention* (New York: David McKay, 1969). A senior officer in the CIA, long concerned with the insurgency in

Viet-Nam, favored an enclave strategy over search and destroy, provided the enclaves were not allowed to become isolated (confidential interview). Generally, although the descriptive phrase and particulars varied, the thrust was at a strategy focusing upon the population. They were rejecting the army's sequential approach of destroying the enemy's combat units first and then turning back to "pacify."

23. This criticism was stressed in confidential interviews with a marine company commander and aide to General Westmoreland, and a former marine officer, RAND analyst, and special assistant to the deputy assistant secretary for Systems Analysis specializing in the tactics and strategy of the ground war. There is also a well-written, critical book about American military and pacification efforts in one area of South Viet-Nam which focuses on one "battle"—the battle of Easter Sunday—in which the operation's failure follows from the failure to "fix" the enemy. See Harvey Meyerson, *Vinh Long* (Boston: Houghton Mifflin, 1970).

24. Sir Robert Thompson, *No Exit from Vietnam*, p. 136.

25. Alain C. Enthoven and K. Wayne Smith, *How Much Is Enough?* (New York: Harper & Row, 1971), p. 295.

26. Sir Robert Thompson cites a case in which a marine officer explicitly stated that the need to produce a good body count deterred him from other operations. *No Exit from Vietnam*, pp. 136–37.

27. Air Commodore C. F. A. Portal in a lecture at the Royal United Services Institution in London, May 1937 entitled "Air Force Co-operation in Policing the Empire," in Eugene Emme, ed., *The Impact of Air Power* (Princeton: D Van Nostrand, 1959), p. 357.

28. Enthoven and Smith, *How Much Is Enough?*, p. 306. Even allowing for so-called free fire zones, the percentage is very high and there would seem to be enough other reports to support their conclusion that "the effects of such strikes on civilians in VC and friendly areas were often undesirable, probably creating more VC than they eliminated."

It should be noted that Systems Analysis is not free from responsibility here, as one of their former analysts has pointed out. It seems that they evaluated and supplied artillery units at least partly on the basis of munitions expended and thus provided added incentive for blind "H and I"—harassment and interdiction fire. It was only in 1970, in a *Washington Post* story out of Saigon (November 15) that it was reported that a formal policy directive was passed down "to stop using artillery for 'harassment and interdiction' and reduce sharply the number of tactical bombing strikes flown by U.S. jets."

29. A fine illustration of the way the sophisticated equipment of the war could determine operations is provided by Josiah Bunting, a former army officer who has written a bitter novel about combat in the delta of South Viet-Nam. One particular mission turned into a disaster after senior officers decided that the enemy must be approached by a water route. The decision was based, not on tactical considerations of the usual kind, but on the calculation that after all the publicity over the effectiveness of the "brown-water Navy" the visiting secretary of the navy would be disappointed by an operation that did not make use of the Riverine Force. See Bunting's *The Lionheads* (New York: George Braziller, 1972).

30. Enthoven and Smith, *How Much Is Enough?*, pp. 92–93.

31. U.S. Army FM31-16 (March 1967), p. 78 states that "As far as

counterinsurgency operations are concerned, special forces units have the capability to provide planning, training, advice, and operational assistance to selected host country forces."

32. For unrestrained praise as well as description of marine activity see William R. Corson, *The Betrayal* (New York: W. W. Norton, 1968) and Colonel James A. Donovan, USMC (Ret.), *Militarism, U.S.A.* (New York: Charles Scribner's Sons, 1970). Sir Robert Thompson also favorably contrasted marine activity with that of the army, see *No Exit from Vietnam*, p. 138–39.

33. In 1967 the marines' strike team concept was adopted in other Corps by some army commanders. For a discussion of the tactics and their slow dissemination, see F. J. West, Jr., *The Strike Teams: Tactical Performance and Strategic Potential*, P-3987 (Santa Monica: The RAND Corp., January 1969).

34. Patrick J. McGarvey, *Visions of Victory: Selected Vietnamese Military Writings, 1964–1968* (Stanford: Hoover Foundation Press, 1969), p. 224.

35. *Pentagon Papers*, 4:24. It has also been suggested that McNamara was surprised by Westmoreland's strategy, expecting him to move more slowly from secure coastal positions, see Henry L. Trewhitt, *McNamara* (New York: Harper & Row, 1971), p. 228.

36. McNamara did try to influence strategy some years earlier in 1963, but was noteably unsuccessful, see fn. 41, ch. 2.

37. *Pentagon Papers*, 4:396–99.

38. Ibid., p. 462.

39. Ibid., p. 463.

40. Enthoven and Smith, *How Much Is Enough?*, p. 292.

41. Hoopes, *Limits of Intervention*, p. 133.

42. Ibid., p. 153.

43. William Bundy and Philip Habib's paper on South Vietnamese domestic politics contributed by the State Department and General Taylor's paper on alternative strategies went directly to the White House. The others, from State, the CIA, the Treasury, and the Joint Staff went to ISA, see the *Pentagon Papers*, 4:550.

44. Ibid., p. 564.

45. Ibid., pp. 565–68.

46. Quoted in Henry F. Graff, *The Tuesday Cabinet* (Englewood Cliffs: Prentice-Hall, 1970), p. 128. As unfortunate as the general's answer was, McGeorge Bundy's should be regretted still more. He said, "All of South Vietnam is an enclave, the populated area is all accessible from the sea—that's what's wrong with the Gavin position," p. 95. Actually, the fact that the populated area was accessible from the sea was what was most *right* about the proposal. Since the United States controlled the sea, supply was guaranteed, the likelihood of isolated, untenable enclaves emerging was less, and what was generally a defensive posture was enhanced.

47. Sir Robert Thompson, *No Exit from Vietnam*, p. 135.

48. Ward Just, *Military Men* (New York: Alfred A. Knopf, 1970), p. 111.

49. See Donovan, *Militarism, U.S.A.*, p. 46.

50. "In a hierarchy every employee tends to rise to his level of incompetence." See Laurence J. Peter and Raymond Hull, *The Peter Principle* (New York: Bantam Books, 1970).

51. See Enthoven and Smith, *How Much Is Enough?*, p. 299. Sir Robert Thompson singles out the pressure of everyday workload to help explain the failure to evaluate, see *No Exit from Vietnam.*

52. F. J. West, Jr. has described a MACV meeting in which successive commanders stood up to advocate opposite tactics without any attempt to resolve the contradiction in a paper entitled "Problem Recognition and Organization Adaptation in a Counterinsurgent Environment," presented at a meeting of the Military Operations Research Society at West Point, June 1970.

53. F. J. West, Jr. discusses these points in his paper, "Problem Recognition."

54. Confidential interview. Alexander George has observed that "In contrast to the practice of some other armies, United States theatre commanders had always been given considerable freedom to decide on tactical operations in the field." Alexander L. George, David K. Hall, and William E. Simons, *The Limits of Coercive Diplomacy* (Boston: Little, Brown, 1971), p. 4.

55. Enthoven and Smith, *How Much Is Enough?*, p. 300.

56. Henry Brandon, *Anatomy of Error: The Inside Story of the Asian War on the Potomac, 1954–1969* (Boston: Gambit Press, 1969), p. 164.

57. Hoopes, *Limits of Intervention*, p. 147.

58. Confidential interview.

59. An Army colonel who served under the director of Plans and Policy of the JCS from 1965 to 1968 offered a description of the standard procedure followed after a troop request—Westmoreland would ask the JCS for a certain number of troops; the JCS would recommend that number to McNamara who would argue with Wheeler and the JCS to try to reduce the size of the request; if he failed, he would go to Viet-Nam and try to get Westmoreland to lower the number he requested; Westmoreland would reduce the number and MACV's request would then be endorsed by the JCS and recommended to the president by the secretary. News accounts at the time of McNamara's Viet-Nam trips also seemed to suggest that something like this was happening.

60. The ground strategy did change under the new field commander, General Creighton Abrams, concurrent with the withdrawal of American troops. The new president had made the reduction of American casualties a chief objective for the military, and the strategic concept under which U.S. troops were used was appropriately revised. The idea of making the reduction of American casualties, rather than the increase in the enemy's, a primary goal for the army was suggested internally in OSD under McNamara, but it was never adequately supported.

61. David Halberstam writes of McNamara: He had chosen above all else to control the Pentagon, and with the war he had lost control of the machinery. . . . Rather than being a Defense Secretary for seven years, a case could be made that he was really only in charge for four. He spent his time and his resources trying to hold the generals back. . . . See his article, "The Programming of Robert McNamara," *Harper's Magazine* (February 1971), p. 63.

Although similar characterizations were made by several of those who worked with the secretary, one, a deputy assistant secretary, reversed the "trade." In a confidential interview, he argued that McNamara avoided tampering with the war in order to save himself for battles with the military over resources and budget matters. But this does not seem consistent with the evidence of McNamara's efforts to influence the bombing of North Viet-Nam. Another point that might be added, which has not been discussed in this chapter, is that McNamara virtually forced the military to accept the idea of building a physical and electronic barrier along the DMZ. Although the ill-fated "McNamara Line" had more to do with the air war than the ground strategy, it was another war issue in which the secretary chose to expend time and political energy, see Trewhitt, *McNamara*, pp. 161–62.

62. Brandon, *Anatomy of Error*, p. 165.

63. In their book, *How Much Is Enough?*, p. 307, Enthoven and Smith write that "The President and his key advistors sought candid assessments of the war, but they would not pay the political costs in terms of friction with the military to get them." According to an analyst who worked under Enthoven in Systems Analysis in 1966 and 1967 producing those "candid assessments," Enthoven refused to push critical papers up to McNamara or on to the military until 1967 when the assistant secretary decided he was going to leave the government.

Chapter VI

1. This is the subject of chapter II.

2. The fall 1964 policy review is discussed in chapter III. See James C. Thomson's "How Could Vietnam Happen? An Autopsy," *The Atlantic Monthly* 221 (April 1968):47–63, for a description of the domestication process.

3. The isolation of the president and the fate of those in ISA and Systems Analysis who sought to change policy is discussed in chapters IV and V. For an excellent description of the way the State Department was excluded from decision making and communications about decisions already made see Chester L. Cooper's *The Lost Crusade* (New York: Dodd, Mead, 1970), especially pp. 413–15. For a critique of the Tuesday lunch decision-making procedure see Keith C. Clark and Laurence J. Legere, *The President and the Management of National Security* (New York: Frederick A. Praeger, 1969), p. 85, and Henry F. Graff, *The Tuesday Cabinet* (Englewood Cliffs: Prentice-Hall, 1970). Because he interviewed the participants in the meetings repeatedly over a period of time, Graff's observations are particularly interesting.

4. There is another aspect of the decision-making process that is relevant here. It is likely that the collegial style of decision making also contributed to sustaining the original consensus of Viet-Nam through the effects of group phenomena. Although the impact of group decision making on policy was not a theme developed in this study, it has been the focus of analysis for other observers. The propensity for risk-taking, stereotyping, conformity and false consensus, oversimplification, and moral self-righteousness mark the deliberations of groups that make evaluations and choices. One or more of these tendencies may bear upon the outcome in any particular case. Because of the distortions in perception and analysis that may result from "group-think," simply knowing the initial premises of individual actors is not enough to explain decision making over a period of time, or to prescribe in order to prevent similar errors in the future. For a general discussion see, for example, Robert Jervis, "Hypotheses on

Misperception," *World Politics* 20, no. 3 (April 1968):454–79, and Joseph H. de Rivera, *The Psychological Dimension of Foreign Policy* (Columbus: Charles E. Merrill, 1968). For particular application to Viet-Nam, James C. Thomson's article noted above is suggestive as is Irving L. Janis's chapter on the war in his *Victims of Groupthink* (Boston: Houghton Mifflin, 1972). Janis recognized that his thesis, like that of his study, was at odds with the Gelb-Ellsberg characterization of our Viet-Nam involvement, and so he made a special effort to refute it just as we have here. See pp. 111–13.

5. Francis E. Rourke, *Bureaucracy and Foreign Policy* (Baltimore: Johns Hopkins University Press, 1972), p. 23.

6. National security policy, taken as a subfield of foreign policy, has been studied from this perspective for some time. See for example, the studies of Warner Schilling, Paul Hammond, and Morton Halperin. A nice collection of articles is provided in a book edited by Halperin and Arnold Kanter entitled *Readings in American Foreign Policy: A Bureaucratic Perspective* (Boston: Little, Brown, 1973). A thorough treatment of the propositions of this style of analysis is provided in Halperin's book entitled *Bureaucratic Politics and Foreign Policy* (Washington, D.C.: The Brookings Institution, 1974).

7. Roger Hilsman, "Foreign Policy Consensus: An Interim Report," *Journal of Conflict Resolution* 3 December 1959):365.

8. Graham T. Allison, "Conceptual Models and the Cuban Missile Crisis," *American Political Science Review* 63 (September 1969):689–718. For a more extensive statement of Allison's contributions see his *Essence of Decision* (Boston: Little, Brown, 1971).

9. See Stephen Krasner, "Are Bureaucracies Important?" *Foreign Policy*, no. 7 (1972), p. 169.

10. These questions are not unlike those that Hilsman wanted to have answered: "The conflict-consensus model leads us to ask who the participants are in the policy-making process, what roles they play, what kinds of power they have available to influence policy and what techniques they use." "Foreign Policy Consensus," p. 373.

11. See the discussion in Graham T. Allison and Morton H. Halperin, "Bureaucratic Politics: Theory and Policy Implications," in Raymond Tanter and Richard Ullman, *Theory and Policy in International Relations* (Princeton: Princeton University Press, 1972), p. 56.

12. Morton H. Halperin, "The Decision to Deploy the ABM: Bureaucratic Politics in the Pentagon and in the White House in the Johnson Administration." (Paper presented at the annual meeting of the American Political Science Association, September 1970.)

13. Thomson, "How Could Vietnam Happen?" pp. 47–63; Daniel Ellsberg, "Escalating in a Quagmire." (Paper presented at the annual meeting of the American Political Science Association, September 1970.)

14. Michel Crozier, *The Bureaucratic Phenomenon* (Chicago: University of Chicago Press, 1964), p. 150. The author refers to power as "the new central problem of the theory of organization."

15. Norton E. Long, "The Administrative Organization as a Political System," in Sidney Mailick and Edward H. Van Ness, eds., *Concepts and Issues in Administrative Behavior* (Englewood Cliffs: Prentice-Hall, 1962), p. 118.

16. See James G. March and Herbert A. Simon, *Organizations* (New

York: John Wiley, 1958), p. 152 for a discussion of these cognitive mechanisms.

17. Victor A. Thompson, *Modern Organization* (New York: Alfred A. Knopf, 1961), p. 160. When there is an unsuccessful search for criteria by which to evaluate output, Laurence J. Peter and Raymond Hull conclude that "a superior who has reached his level of incompetence . . . will probably rate his subordinate in terms of institutional values. . . . In short, such an official evaluates input." The effect is to reinforce an already strong tendency of organizations to uniformity and conformity. *The Peter Principle* (New York: Bantam Books, 1970), p. 25.

18. Gordon Tullock, *The Politics of Bureaucracy* (Washington, D.C.: Public Affairs Press, 1965).

19. Thomson, "How Could Vietnam Happen?" p. 50.

20. Harold L. Wilensky, *Organizational Intelligence* (New York: Basic Books, 1967), p. 78. In a study of resistance to change in the Forest Service, Ashley L. Schiff attributes bureaucratic intransigence to the sunk costs of present policy: "Revision of information policy is likely to be deferred should alterations suggested by research findings appeal to undermine the organization's investment in ongoing programs. A normal bureaucratic proclivity to secrecy is exaggerated when the agency's previous stand has been cast in almost sacred terms." *Fire and Water* (Cambridge: Harvard University Press, 1962).

21. Stephen Krasner makes this point in an article which is otherwise critical of the bureaucratic perspective. See "Are Bureaucracies Important?" p. 176.

22. Morton H. Halperin, "Why Bureaucrats Play Games," *Foreign Policy*, no. 2 (Spring 1971), pp. 74–88.

23. See Robert J. Art's excellent article, "Bureaucratic Politics and American Foreign Policy: A Critique." *Policy Science* 4 (1973):467–90.

24. Halperin, "The Decision to Deploy the ABM."

25. Robert Axelrod, *Bureaucratic Decision-Making in the Military Assistance Program: Some Empirical Findings*, RM-5528-1-PR/ISA (Santa Monica: RAND Corp., October 1968), p. 16.

26. Samuel Huntington, "Strategy and the Political Process," *Foreign Affairs* 38 (January 1960):294.

27. See Allison and Halperin, "Bureaucratic Politics," p. 52.

28. Paul Y. Hammond, "Foreign Policy-Making and Administrative Politics," *World Politics* 17 (July 1965):662. William H. Riker's discussion of side payments suggests that the analyst must look for bargains across issues and across time as well: "Not only may a leader pay followers with promises about the content of the immediate decision for which the proto-coalition is formed, but also he may pay with promises about the content of future decisions. . . . By promises to seek or not to seek, to modify or not to some prospective decision (perhaps totally unrelated to the decision at hand), leaders can buy additional members of a proto-coalition, often without the necessity of modifying the current proposal." *The Theory of Political Coalitions* (New Haven: Yale University Press, 1962), p. 112.

29. See the discussion in James S. Coleman, "Foundations for a Theory of Collective Decisions," *American Journal of Sociology* 71 (May 1966): 621.

30. For an interesting discussion along these lines see James S. Cole-

man, "Political Money," *American Political Science Review* 64 (December 1970):1074–87.

31. Actors resigning from government service behave as though they had decided to stop using an unsatisfactory detergent, the effects of which they will not longer have to endure. If the logic of an argument put forth by Albert O. Hirschman is accepted, then the fact of an actor's continued association with the "product" makes a more resounding departure appropriate:

> "If I participate in the making of a foreign policy of which I have come to disapprove, I can resign my official policy-making position, but cannot stop being unhappy as a citizen of a country which carries on what seems to me an increasingly disastrous foreign policy. . . . The individual is at first both producer and consumer of such public goals as party policy and foreign policy; he can stop being producer but cannot stop being consumer." *Exit, Voice and Loyalty* (Cambridge: Harvard University Press, 1970), p. 102.

On this subject see also Warren G. Bennis, "When to Resign," *Esquire* (June 1972), pp. 143–90, and James C. Thomson, Jr., "Getting Out and Speaking Out," *Foreign Policy* (Winter 1973–74), pp. 49–69.

32. Krasner, "Are Bureaucracies Important?" pp. 160–63.

33. John Franklin Campbell, *The Foreign Affairs Fudge Factory* (New York: Basic Books, 1971), p. 38.

34. The phrase is used by Andrew W. Marshall in *Problems of Estimating Military Power*, P-3417 (Santa Monica: RAND Corp., August 1966), p. 19.

35. K. J. Holsti, *International Politics: A Framework for Analysis* (Englewood Cliffs: Prentice-Hall, 1967), p. 17. Harold and Margaret Sprout make much the same point, that the effects of "environmental factors" do not "derive from or depend upon the environed individual's perception." *The Ecological Perspective on Human Affairs with Special Reference to International Politics* (Princeton: Princeton University Press, 1965), p. 11.

36. A recent article by Alexander George calling for "multiple advocacy" in foreign policy-making is directed at accomplishing this among other objectives. See the "Case for Multiple Advocacy in Making Foreign Policy," *The American Political Science Review* 61 (September 1972): 751–85. Also see I. M. Destler's comment on the limits and costs of George's proposal and George's rejoinder—both in the issue cited above.

37. Rourke, *Bureaucracy and Foreign Policy*, p. 74.

38. There are several good sources for information about the State Department, its structure, and its role in the policy-making process, and a recent, readable, intelligent addition is John Franklin Campbell's *The Foreign Affairs Fudge Factory*. For an argument that the State Department should not be a principal actor in the making of policy, a position opposite to the one presented here, see William N. Turpin, "Foreign Relations, Yes; Foreign Policy, No," *Foreign Policy*, no. 8 (Fall 1972), pp. 50–61.

39. The Commission on the Organization of the Government for the Conduct of Foreign Policy is currently doing just that.

SELECTED BIBLIOGRAPHY

Books

Allison, Graham T. *Essence of Decision.* Boston: Little, Brown, 1971.

Anderson, Patrick. *The President's Men.* Garden City, N.Y.: Doubleday, 1968.

Brandon, Henry. *Anatomy of Error: The Inside Story of the Asian War on the Potomac, 1954–1969.* Boston: Gambit Press, 1969.

Broughton, Colonel Jack, USAF (Ret.). *Thud Ridge.* New York: J. B. Lippincott, 1969.

Campbell, John Franklin. *The Foreign Affairs Fudge Factory.* New York: Basic Books, 1971.

Clark, Keith C., and Legere, Laurence J. *The President and the Management of National Security.* New York: Frederick A. Praeger, 1969.

Cooper, Chester L. *The Lost Crusade.* New York: Dodd, Mead, 1970.

Corson, William R. *The Betrayal.* New York: W. W. Norton, 1968.

Crozier, Michel. *The Bureaucratic Phenomenon.* Chicago: University of Chicago Press, 1964.

Davis, Vincent. *The Admirals Lobby.* Chapel Hill: University of North Carolina Press, 1967.

de Rivera, Joseph H. *The Psychological Dimension of Foreign Policy.* Columbus: Charles E. Merrill, 1968.

Donovan, Colonel James A., USMC (Ret.). *Militarism, U.S.A.* New York: Charles Scribner's Sons, 1970.

Emme, Eugene, ed. *The Impact of Air Power.* Princeton: D. Van Nostrand, 1959.

Enthoven, Alain C., and Smith, K. Wayne. *How Much Is Enough?* New York: Harper & Row, 1971.

Evans, Rowland, and Novak, Robert. *LBJ: The Exercise of Power.* New York: The New American Library, 1966.

George, Alexander L., Hall, David K., and Simons, William E. *The Limits of Coercive Diplomacy.* Boston: Little, Brown, 1971.

Geyelin, Philip L. *Lyndon B. Johnson and the World.* New York: Frederick A. Praeger, 1966.

Goodwin, Richard N. *Triumph or Tragedy: Reflections on Vietnam.* New York: Random House, 1966.

Goulding, Phil G. *Confirm or Deny: Informing the People on National Security.* New York: Harper & Row, 1970.

Graff, Henry F. *The Tuesday Cabinet.* Englewood Cliffs: Prentice-Hall, 1970.

Halperin, Morton H. *Bureaucratic Politics and Foreign Policy,* Washington, D.C.: The Brookings Institution, 1974.

Harvey, Frank. *Air War—Vietnam.* New York: Bantam Books, 1967.

Hilsman, Roger. *To Move A Nation.* Garden City, N.Y.: Doubleday, 1967.

Hirschman, Albert O. *Exit, Voice and Loyalty.* Cambridge: Harvard University Press, 1970.

Hoopes, Townsend. *The Limits of Intervention.* New York: David McKay, 1969.

Jervis, Robert. *The Logic of Images in International Relations.* Princeton University Press, 1970.

Just, Ward. *Military Men.* New York: Alfred A. Knopf, 1970.

Kalb, Marvin, and Abel, Elie. *Roots of Involvement.* New York: W. W. Norton, 1971.

Lacouture, Jean. *Vietnam: Between Two Truces.* New York: Vintage Books, 1966.

Littauer, Raphael, and Uphoff, Norman, eds. *The Air War in Indochina.* rev. ed. Boston: Beacon Press, 1972.

McGarvey, Patrick J. *CIA: The Myth and the Madness.* New York: Saturday Review Press, 1972.

———. *Visions of Victory: Selected Vietnamese Military Writings, 1964–1968.* Stanford: Hoover Institution Press, 1969.

Mailick, Sidney, and Van Ness, Edward H., eds. *Concepts and Issues in Administrative Behavior.* Englewood Cliffs: Prentice-Hall, 1962.

Manning, Robert, and Janeway, Michael, eds. *Who We Are: An Atlantic Chronicle of the United States & Vietnam 1966–1969.* Boston: Little, Brown, 1969.

March, James G., and Simon, Herbert A. *Organizations.* New York: John Wiley, 1958.

Meyerson, Harvey. *Vinh Long.* Boston: Houghton Mifflin, 1970.

Riker, William H. *The Theory of Political Coalitions.* New Haven: Yale University Press, 1962.

Roberts, Charles. *LBJ's Inner Circle.* New York: Delacorte Press, 1965.

Rourke, Francis E. *Bureaucracy and Foreign Policy.* Baltimore: The Johns Hopkins University Press, 1972.

Schiff, Ashley L. *Fire and Water.* Cambridge: Harvard University Press, 1972.

Schlesinger, Arthur M., Jr. *The Bitter Heritage: Vietnam & American Democracy, 1941–1966,* rev. ed. New York: Fawcett World, 1968.

Smith, Perry McCoy. *The Air Force Plans for Peace, 1943–1945.* Baltimore: The Johns Hopkins University Press, 1970.

Tanter, Raymond, and Ullman, Richard, eds. *Theory and Policy in*

International Relations. Princeton: Princeton University Press, 1972.

Taylor, Maxwell D. *Responsibility and Response.* New York: Harper and Row, Publishers, 1967.

Thompson, Robert. *No Exit From Vietnam.* New York: David McKay, 1970.

Thompson, Victor A. *Modern Organization.* New York: Alfred A. Knopf, 1961.

Trewhitt, Henry L. *McNamara.* New York: Harper & Row, 1971.

Tullock, Gordon. *The Politics of Bureaucracy.* Washington, D.C.: Public Affairs Press, 1965.

Weital, Edward, and Bartlett, Charles. *Facing the Brink.* New York: Charles Scribner's Sons, 1967.

Wicker, Tom. *JFK and LBJ.* New York: William Morrow, 1968.

Wilensky, Harold L. *Organizational Intelligence.* New York: Basic Books, 1967.

Articles

Allison, Graham T. "Conceptual Models and the Cuban Missile Crisis." *American Political Science Review* 63 (September 1968): 689–718.

Art, Robert J. "Bureaucratic Politics and American Foreign Policy: A Critique." *Policy Sciences* 4 (1973): 467–90.

Coleman, James S. "Foundations for a Theory of Collective Decisions." *American Journal of Sociology* 71 (May 1966): 615–27.

———. "Political Money." *American Political Science Review* 64 (December 1970): 1074–87.

Dudman, Richard. "Military Policy in Vietnam." *Current History* 50 (February 196): 91–97.

Ellsberg, Daniel. "The Quagmire Myth and the Stalemate Machine." *Public Policy* (Spring 1971), 217–74.

Gelb, Leslie H. "Vietnam: The System Worked." *Foreign Policy,* no. 3 (Summer 1971), pp. 140–73.

Halberstam, David. "The Programming of Robert McNamara." *Harper's Magazine* (February 1971), pp. 37–71.

———. "The Very Expensive Education of McGeorge Bundy." *Harper's Magazine* (July 1969), pp. 21–41.

Halperin, Morton H. "Why Bureaucrats Play Games." *Foreign Policy,* no. 2 (Spring 1971), pp. 70–90.

Hammond, Paul Y. "Foreign Policy-Making and Administrative Politics." *World Politics* 17 (July 1965): 656–71.

Hilsman, Roger. "Foreign Policy Consensus: An Intermin Report." *Journal of Conflict Resolution* 3 (December 1959): 360–80.

Huntington, Samuel J. "Strategy and the Political Process." *Foreign Affairs* 38 (January 1960): 285–99.

Krasner, Stephen. "Are Bureaucracies Important?" *Foreign Policy,* no. 7 (1972), pp. 159–79.

McGarvey, Patrick J. "The Culture of Bureaucracy: *DIA, Intelligence to Please,*" *The Washington Monthly* (July 1970).

Roche, John P. "The Jigsaw Puzzle of History." *New York Times Magazine,* January 24, 1971, p. 15.

Schlesinger, Arthur M., Jr. "Eyeless in Indochina." *New York Review of Books,* October 21, 1971, pp. 23–32.

Teplinsky, B. "The Air War over Indochina." *International Affairs* (Moscow, February 1967), pp. 40–47.

Thayer, Frederick C. "Professionalism: the Hard Choice." *U.S. Naval Institute Proceedings* 97 (June 1971): 36–41.

Thomson, James C., Jr. "How Could Vietnam Happen?" The *Atlantic Monthly* 221 (April 1968): 47–63.

RAND Corporation Publications

Axelrod, Robert. *Bureaucratic Decision-Making in the Military Assistance Program: Some Empirical Findings.* RM-5528-1-PR/ISA (October 1968).

Carter, George A. *Some Historical Notes on Air Interdiction in Korea.* P-3452 (September 1966).

Dews, Edmund. *A Note on Tactical vs. Strategic Air Interdiction.* RM-6239-PR (April 1970).

Hoeffding, Oleg. *Bombing North Vietnam: An Appraisal of Economic and Political Effects.* RM-5213-1-ISA (December 1966).

Marshall, Andrew W. *Problems of Estimating Military Power.* P-3417 (August 1966).

West, F. J., Jr. *The Strike Teams: Tactical Performance and Strategic Potential.* P-3987 (January 1969).

Wiley, Marshall W. *A Proposal for Analyzing the Process of Decision-Making in Foreign Affars.* P-4100 (November 1969).

Public Documents

The Pentagon Papers: The Senator Gravel Edition. 4 vols. Boston: Beacon Press, 1971.

Sharp, Admiral U. S. G., USN, and Westmoreland, General W. C., USA. *Report on the War in Vietnam.* Washington, D.C.: U.S. Government Printing Office, 1968.

U.S. Congress. Senate. Committee on Armed Services. *Air War Against North Vietnam.* Hearings before the Preparedness Investigating Subcommittee, 90th Cong., 1st sess., 1967.

———. ———. Committee on Armed Services and Committee on Appropriations. *Military Procurement Authorizations for FY 1968.* Hearings before the Committee on Armed Services and the Defense Appropriations Subcommittee of the Committee on Appropriations, Senate, on S-666, 90th Cong., 1st sess., 1967.

———. ———. Committee on Foreign Relations. *Background Information Relating to Southeast Asia and Vietnam.* 3d rev. ed. 90th Cong., 1st sess., 1967.

———. Senate and House. Committees on Armed Services. *CVAN-70 Aircraft Carrier.* Hearings before the Joint Senate-House Armed Services Subcommittee, 91st Cong., 2d sess., 1970.

Library of Congress Cataloging in Publication Data
Gallucci, Robert L
Neither peace nor honor.
(Studies in international affairs, no. 24)
Based on the author's thesis, Brandeis University.
Bibliography: pp. 184–86
1. Vietnamese Conflict, 1961– —United States.
2. United States—Politics and government—1961–1963.
3. United States—Politics and government—1963–1969.
I. Title. II. Series: Washington Center of Foreign Policy Research. Studies in international affairs, no. 24.
DS558.G34 959.704'3373 74-24949
ISBN 0-8018-1682-3
ISBN 0-8018-1741-5 pbk.